SIMON & SCHUSTER

MARYSUE RUCCI
VICE PRESIDENT AND EDITOR-IN-CHIEF

SIMON & SCHUSTER, INC.
1230 AVENUE OF THE AMERICAS
NEW YORK, NY 10020
VOICE 212 698 1234 FAX 212 698 7453
marysue.rucci@simonandschuster.com

Dear Reader:

When *Other People's Children* by R.J. Hoffmann came across my desk, I opened it and did not close it until I finished the final page. This doesn't happen often; but it was a particularly wonderful experience because I'd been in a reading rut where nothing seemed to captivate me.

Enter *Other People's Children*, with the thorny ethical question at its heart, its three characters whose desires and intentions are seemingly at odds, and its plot that moves like a rocket—and I was cured.

Gail is a thirty-something married woman desperate to be a mom who has turned to domestic adoption. When teenaged Carli from a blue-collar town in Illinois finds out she's pregnant, she doesn't want to give up her dreams of college, so she decides to put her baby up for adoption. Marla, Carli's mom, works at the local factory and will relinquish her grandbaby to a stranger over her dead body.

I rooted for each character in turn. I couldn't figure out how I wanted it to turn out—who should "win" (but what is winning?)—and then I turned that final page for a pitch-perfect ending.

Propulsive, provocative, perfect for book clubs, and perfect to shake any reading blues, *Other People's Children* is a big-hearted and satisfying debut that I hope you love.

Warmly,

Marysue Rucci
Vice President & Editor-in-Chief, Simon & Schuster

Other People's Children

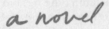

a novel

R.J. Hoffmann

SIMON & SCHUSTER
New York London Toronto Sydney New Delhi

Simon & Schuster
1230 Avenue of the Americas
New York, NY 10020

This book is a work of fiction. Any references to historical events, real people, or real places are used fictitiously. Other names, characters, places, and events are products of the author's imagination, and any resemblance to actual events or places or persons, living or dead, is entirely coincidental.

First Simon & Schuster hardcover edition April 2021

SIMON & SCHUSTER and colophon are registered trademarks of Simon & Schuster, Inc.

For information about special discounts for bulk purchases, please contact Simon & Schuster Special Sales at 1-866-506-1949 or business@simonandschuster.com.

The Simon & Schuster Speakers Bureau can bring authors to your live event. For more information or to book an event, contact the Simon & Schuster Speakers Bureau at 1-866-248-3049 or visit our website at www.simonspeakers.com.

Manufactured in the United States of America

1   3   5   7   9   10   8   6   4   2

Library of Congress Cataloging-in-Publication Data has been applied for.

ISBN 978-1-9821-5909-2
ISBN 978-1-9821-5911-5 (ebook)

For Sara, Roshan, and Grace—my forever family.

Gail

*

Gail didn't usually drink, but she stood on the patio and took a long sip from her third glass of pinot. It was disappearing quickly, evaporating, maybe. The first-birthday parties always cut especially deep, and this one proved no exception. There was a jump house, of course, and a section of the backyard had been fenced off for a petting zoo. Relatives had flown in from both coasts. A creepy clown was tying balloon animals that all looked like crickets. The birthday boy wouldn't stop crying, so he was sent upstairs with an aunt for a nap. But first-birthday parties were for the parents, not the babies, and certainly not for infertile women in their early thirties.

Gail searched in vain for someone she knew. A few faces seemed vaguely familiar from her husband's holiday party, but sorting the relatives from Jon's coworkers proved difficult. She spotted Jon standing by the jump house, the tallest in a cluster of men whose scruffy jeans and T-shirts marked them as programmers. Jon swiped his dark, shaggy bangs out of his eyes and laughed. They were probably talking sports or music or databases. Gail envied him—men floated upon the surface of their conversations, while women always insisted on diving so deep.

Days like today made Gail's lungs hurt. She had just fled the kitchen, where she was helping the baby's grandmother slice vegetables and heat up the chicken nuggets for dinner. The kitchen usually proved a safe haven at first-birthday parties—mindless tasks, no children. But the grandmother knew about Gail and Jon's situation and was asking all the wrong questions. *How long will it take? Is there a lot of paperwork? International or domestic? How much does it cost? Have you heard anything lately? How can you stand the waiting?* Stories always followed the questions—stories about adoptions that fell apart at the last minute and women who got pregnant soon after they adopted—*because they finally relaxed and stopped trying so hard.* Gail answered the questions vaguely, with the fewest words that politeness allowed, and then she set down her knife and walked out, before the stories came, and before she gave in to the urge to tell Grandma about the girl in Morris.

Now Jon spotted Gail and waved her over, but she just smiled, waved, and looked away. She couldn't go back to the kitchen, but she also couldn't summon the energy to fabricate an opinion about the Blackhawks defense or the best Modest Mouse album. The wine made everything slant a bit, and the yard swarmed with children she didn't want to look at, darting around adults she didn't know. She could go help with the three-legged race, but it seemed well staffed with mothers. Heidi and Colin were already surrounded by strangers. She could go to the bathroom again, but she'd already been twice in the last hour. She'd probably be discovered if she hid in the car.

Finally, Gail stepped off the porch and drifted toward the petting zoo. She leaned against the fence erected around the animals and tried to focus on the rabbits and goats and chickens. She tried to ignore the children chasing them, and she mostly succeeded. She tried not to think about the book that went out to that nameless, faceless pregnant girl in Morris, and she failed miserably. Paige from the agency had told Gail nothing about the girl but her hometown. She never shared more than that, and she always reminded Gail to manage her expectations. That girl would be sorting through a stack of books, and there was no way to guess how she would decide.

Getting your hopes up in the early stages too often leads to disappointment, Paige always said.

The first three times the book went out, Gail had mostly managed to heed Paige's advice, but those first three times had been easier. The answer had come quickly, a quiet no from Paige, in two days, in four, in three. This time, though, after a week passed without a word, Gail had begun to imagine that girl in Morris thumbing through their book. Gail tried to guess what she saw in the carefully curated pictures, what conclusions she would draw from the painstakingly crafted sentences. She knew that she should think about something else. She shouldn't get her hopes up. And she should have told Jon about sending the book to Morris.

A little girl wedged in the corner of the petting zoo caught Gail's attention. She wore a frilly dress and couldn't have been more than three, maybe four years old—about the same age as Gail's child would have been if her first pregnancy stuck. The girl sat in the grass and held a chick in her lap. When it tried to escape, she scooped it back up. When it pecked her, she giggled. The chick settled into the folds of the girl's dress, and she bent over it, her hair draped down the sides of her face, murmuring to her little friend.

As Gail watched, she considered the minimum required stay at a first-birthday party. There should be a formula, a spreadsheet. She could imagine the inputs: *The number of your friends in attendance; the length, in years, of your relationship with the parents; the number of your own children writhing in the jump house. If you brought no children, the number of times you miscarried would serve as a key variable. The time elapsed, in months, since your last miscarriage might complete the algorithm. You could display the output in minutes or seconds.*

"I hate these things."

Gail turned to find Jon next to her, his brown, almost black eyes scanning the yard. His hair was tousled—he usually didn't touch a comb on weekends. He stood a foot taller than her, lanky in a manner that didn't appeal to many other women, but all his parts fit together in a way that had always seemed just right to Gail.

"Why can't they just invite their family and call it a day?"

"They're testing our fealty," Gail said. "Heidi's mom is probably tracking attendance."

"Seems like we should be able to buy our way out of it. A more expensive present? Maybe some savings bonds?"

"That's not how these things work. Tribute must be delivered in person."

"How are *you* doing?" Jon asked.

Gail leaned into the fence again and studied the girl. She'd have three children, two walking by now, if she had never miscarried. She indulged this math too often, and the equations never balanced.

"I'm OK," she said. The wine helped. That book in Morris helped. The little girl with the chick helped. Gail watched as a man wearing leather loafers, a deep tan, and expensive-looking sunglasses walked up to the fence behind the little girl.

"Time to go, Taylor," he said.

The girl looked up from the chick, stricken. "No, Daddy. Not yet."

Jon took another swig of beer and leaned his elbows against the fence, his back to the zoo. "Where were you? Earlier."

"In the kitchen. Slicing celery and getting grilled by Heidi's mom."

Jon raised his eyebrows. "About?"

He knew the answer to that, of course. "Heidi must have told her."

"Shit. I'm sorry." Jon's forehead wrinkled as he glared across the yard at Heidi. "She's got loose lips for somebody in HR."

Taylor's dad checked his enormous watch. "We have to be at your brother's soccer game in twenty minutes."

Taylor looked back down at her lap. "But I got a friend."

"C'mon," Taylor's dad said impatiently. "Let's go."

"Let's go," Jon said.

Gail glanced at her watch. "We'd miss the chicken nuggets and coleslaw."

Taylor looked up at her dad. Her lower lip quivered, and her face began to collapse. When the tantrum began, the other children and the animals scattered. The chick in Taylor's lap stayed put only because she folded the hem of her dress over it, trapping it. Heads throughout the yard swiveled toward the commotion. After everyone confirmed that their own progeny wasn't screaming, their eyes lingered, to see what would happen next. Jon glanced at Taylor only once, and then turned back to the yard.

"Let's get Indian takeout," Jon said. "Trade this mess for a date."

"Did you talk to Heidi *and* Colin?" Gail asked.

"I did. I even took a picture with Evan."

"Really? You held him?"

Jon drank again from his beer, shook his head. "I've got a cold."

"C'mon, Taylor," her dad said sternly. He looked around the yard, becoming fully aware of his audience. "It's time."

Tears streamed down Taylor's face, and she hyperventilated between wails. Gail could see the chick wriggle beneath the dress. Taylor's hands pressed the fabric tightly around it. She finally recovered long enough to shout, "I don't want to leave him, Daddy! Don't make me leave him!"

"You're right," Gail said. "Indian sounds good."

Jon drained the last of his beer. "I'm gonna take a leak, and then we'll make like Houdini."

Jon headed toward the house, and Gail turned her full attention to the standoff between Taylor and her dad. She couldn't help but root for Taylor. Her dad seemed like an asshole; the brother would probably survive if they arrived a few minutes late for his game, and Taylor's need to hold her little friend seemed so visceral. Taylor's dad leaned closer.

"Please, Taylor," he said more quietly.

Taylor began to settle a bit. Her lips trembled, but her voice was clear when she stated her terms. "I want to keep him, Daddy."

"You can't keep him," her dad said. "You know that."

"I'm gonna keep him," she said. She stated it as fact and looked up to gauge his reaction.

"I said no!" her dad hissed.

Something hardened in Taylor's eyes, and Gail's allegiance drifted toward the chick. Taylor leaned back and let loose a truly catastrophic scream. Her dad's eyes darted again, landing, finally, on the petting zoo lady who guarded the gate on a camp chair. Taylor's dad walked quickly to the woman, and his daughter tracked him, even as she screamed. He bent down and whispered something. The woman shook her head emphatically. He said something else, more urgently this time. The woman ignored him. He looked at his daughter, then tugged a money clip from his pocket. He peeled off a small stack of twenties. The woman glanced at the cash and then shrugged. She took the money, wadded it up, and crammed it into the pocket of her jeans.

Taylor's dad circled the fence, bent to his daughter, and whispered fiercely in her ear. She stopped crying immediately. She smiled. She got up, still holding the chick bunched in the fabric of her dress, and walked triumphantly to the petting zoo's entrance. Gail moved even before she decided to.

"You can't do that," Gail said to the man.

He picked up his daughter and squinted at Gail. His lip curled slightly. "I just did."

Gail tried to summon the words that might win the chick's freedom, even as she tried to figure out why it mattered so much. "It's not right" was all she could manage.

Taylor looked down at the wriggling lump in the fabric of her dress, and then up at Gail, her eyes, too, now drawn to slits. Her father drew a breath and leaned forward as if about to shout. Instead, he just shook his head, turned, and marched out the side gate, avoiding eye contact with everyone.

Gail leaned her head against the passenger window on the drive home. The wine left her with a dry mouth and a headache gathering at her temples. The smell of curry leaked from the bag of food at her feet. She wondered where Taylor's family would keep the chick. She imagined a tub in the guest bathroom, covered in shit, the chick's chirps growing weaker by the day. What would they feed it? How long would it last? Would Taylor tire of it before it died?

Jon was quiet as he drove, and for this Gail was grateful. For all the boneheaded things Jon sometimes said, he knew when to keep quiet and let her work through things. And, of course, he knew how parties like that could send Gail sideways for a few days. He had offered to go alone, and she probably should have let him.

After a while, though, the silence began to grate on her. It seemed to accuse her, to indict her for what *she* had failed to say. She should have told Jon about the book right when Paige sent it out. She definitely should have told him about it after the first week drifted past. But the fact was, after they sent each of the other three books, she had regretted telling him. Every time, he'd gone quiet. He avoided looking at her, his eyes darting like a cornered raccoon while they awaited the verdict. This time, as each day slid by without a call, it became harder to tell him, even as Gail knew that it became more important. Maybe all those questions from Heidi's mom made her want to tell him now. Maybe it was all those kids running around the backyard screaming and laughing that allowed her to accept that something good might happen this time. Probably it was the pinot.

"Paige sent out a book," Gail said quietly.

"Oh," Jon said.

The word came out hollow, as if he'd gotten the wind knocked out of him. Gail stole a glance at him. He stared hard at the road, as if he were driving through rain. Her skull ached. She shouldn't have had that third glass. She should have kept her mouth shut.

"To who?" he finally asked.

8

"Some girl in Morris. That's all I know."

"Where's Morris?"

"About an hour west. Small town off Eighty."

Jon chewed his upper lip. He fell back into silence, his eyes darting to the rearview mirror, to the side mirror, to anywhere but Gail. Finally, as they turned onto their street, he spoke again. "When did it go out?"

Gail tried to think of vague words to drape over the truth. Jon pulled the car into the driveway and shifted into park.

"Tomorrow will be two weeks."

At that Jon grew still, and they both stared at the garage door. Even Jon knew that two weeks was a long time. Gail tried to imagine what he was thinking, but he was so hard to read when he got like that. Gail had no doubt about how she was feeling, though. She had tried to fight it. She tried to distract herself with work, and she'd made lists of all the ways that things could go wrong, but as day five crept into day six, the hope became insidious, hard to suppress, and it wormed its way deep into her bones, like cancer.

Gail settled into bed, turned on the lamp, and opened her notebook. The sound of Jon's guitar leaked through the door from his office across the hall. She started by drawing a line through *Tell Jon about the book*. The little jolt—like an espresso or a sneeze—that she always felt when crossing an item off her list, was muted by guilt.

She made a note to pick up the dry cleaning. She flipped to her grocery list and added arugula and celery and avocados. She crossed out *chicken breasts* and added *pork tenderloin*. She made a list of the restaurants and butcher shops that she'd call the next day when she got to work. She turned to the last page, where she kept the list of baby names, because she liked to look at them. Because she couldn't not do it.

Gail was grateful for the music that seeped from Jon's office. He hadn't said a word after they came in from the car. They'd sat at opposite ends of the too-long kitchen table eating cold tandoori chicken. That book, the fact that she hadn't told him about it, sat at the table between them, spoiling their date. At least his guitar spoke.

Gail didn't recognize the melody. He might have made it up himself. She still loved to hear him play. The night they first met, at a mutual friend's party, after everyone was drunk, someone thrust a guitar into his hands. She hadn't really paid much attention to that tall, skinny guy with his bangs over his eyes. But once he started playing that Elvis Costello song she loved, she couldn't pull her gaze from his long, graceful fingers as they danced up and down the guitar's neck. When the song finally ended, she looked up at his face and found him staring at her. As he played that night, he shifted deftly from one song to the next and then back again, crafting a new song that was all his own. His ability to play by ear and to improvise thrilled her in a way that she could never find words to describe.

On their first date, they snuck into the Arctic Monkeys concert at the Metro, through a door that Jon's bartender friend had propped open. They danced in the first row of the pit, and Gail had felt a rush of something that frightened her. On their second date, when Jon bought standing-room-only tickets to the Cubs playoff game and then talked his way down to a pair of seats that remained inexplicably empty near the Braves' dugout, she began to feel a bit less frightened, but the rush remained. When he snatched a foul ball from the scrum in the aisle and then gave it to the kid with the glove in front of them, she began to see that he lived his life entirely by ear—he improvised everything in a way that she never could—and she began to love *him*, too.

Jon switched to the banjo. Gail couldn't stand the banjo, and she had nothing more to cross off or add to her lists, so she put her notebook on the side table and climbed out of bed. She padded down the hall toward the stairs but paused at the door to the nursery. She opened it, slipped into the darkness, and closed the door behind her.

She flipped on the light and let her eyes wander the room. The sea turtle rug waited in the center of the floor. Animals shaped like the letters of the alphabet circled the top of the wall. The changing table, the rocking chair, and the crib stood ready. Children's books lined the bookshelf. She'd organized them alphabetically at first, but it proved too messy. By color wasn't much better. She finally arranged them by height before accepting the fact that it really didn't matter.

Every object in the room had started as an entry on a list in her notebook. Jon hated the lists, but Gail had started when she was ten and had forgotten how to function without them. She had copied her grandfather, who kept a tiny spiral-bound steno pad in his shirt pocket, a nub of a pencil crammed into the coil. Her lists made sure that she never missed a homework assignment, never arrived for an exam unprepared. During high school, when Gail's mom fell most deeply into the booze, Gail's lists made sure that food was in the fridge, dentist appointments were kept, and the utilities got paid. When she started selling for the family knife-sharpening business, the lists helped her stay on top of the accounts and the calls and the proposal deadlines. She tried going electronic once, but the lists on her computer felt insubstantial, ephemeral, easily ignored. Before they started trying and failing to conceive a baby, the lists had been Gail's superpower, her secret weapon. But after her first miscarriage, they started to feel obsessive, even to Gail. Still, she didn't set them aside, because they helped her with the waiting.

She made individual lists devoted to children's books and clothes and supplies like diapers and wipes and creams. She devoted a list to the cribs they might buy, along with the pros and cons of each, the cost, the safety rating from Consumer Reports. After she found a negative review on *The Glow* or *Child-Mode*, she could draw a line through the name of the crib, striking the very same chord of satisfaction as completing a task. She made a list of potential themes for the nursery—nautical, polka dots, outer space. She finally settled on zoo animals. Another list cataloged paint colors, and on that list, she taped a tiny slice of the color swatches from Benjamin Moore, because it was hard to remember the difference between North Star and Smoked Oyster and Carolina Gull. Now, everything was in place, except, of course, for the most important thing, and for that she could only wait.

The waiting wasn't always so difficult. Gail's twenties didn't feel like waiting at all. In the beginning, when she was struggling to learn how to sell, her notebook was crammed with lists of lost customers, customers at risk, and eventually, as she learned the job, customers won. When she moved to downtown Chicago, to that apartment on Paulina Street, she made lists of parties she attended, the bands she saw at the Double Door, and the dates of the best summer street festivals. And after Jon moved into that apartment on Paulina, they hosted many of the parties, so the notebook held guestlists and mai tai ingredients and a recipe for hash brownies. When she and Jon got married at Salvage One on the Near West Side, her lists exploded with potential dresses and florists and caterers and DJs. And as they approached thirty, the friends who had flocked to their parties slid away with their first and second babies, so she listed the names of other people's children and new addresses in the far-flung suburbs like Buffalo Grove and Glen Ellyn and Oswego. It was hard to remember, after everything that happened, that Jon was the first to ask the question.

When should we have kids? he asked, like he was asking about takeout from Jade Garden or a movie on Netflix, like it was only a question of when, not if. He claimed that he had always wanted kids, but it took a while for Gail to decide that she was willing to try.

That first night of unprotected sex terrified her. The second was thrilling, the third an adventure. For a while, every month delivered another opportunity, each menstrual cycle another lunge at the brass ring. But then too many months piled up, and Gail discovered that a small, hard nugget of hope had begun to metastasize in her gut, even as her womb remained stubbornly empty. She listed her cycle dates and her basal body temperature and the state of her cervical fluid and, of course, the sex. She made lists of what she ate and her sleep patterns and how many times she went to the bathroom, and Jon's question gained weight even as Gail remained thin. Finally, when it became clear that things needed a shove, her doctor prescribed the shots.

The shots worked, and four years ago, Gail had become pregnant for the first time. When she told her friend Cindy, Cindy had given Gail the number for a Realtor in Elmhurst, where she lived, and that nugget of hope began to mutate toward expectation. The fetus was just the size of a grain of rice when they made an offer on their house, just a little bit bigger when it bled down her leg. Every setback rattled Gail badly, but the truth was, those failures not only crystalized her answer to Jon's question, they made her obsess upon it.

Gail probably would have settled into the rocker and ruminated on the one thing that was still missing from the room, becoming more and more annoyed by the muffled *plunk* of the banjo, if her phone didn't vibrate in the pocket of her pajama pants. And she probably wouldn't have answered if it hadn't been Paige from the agency.

"Hello?"

"Her name's Carli," Paige said.

Gail pressed the phone tightly to her ear. She opened her mouth to speak, but her tongue seemed to fill her throat.

"The girl from Morris. Her name's Carli, and she wants to meet you."

Jon

*

Gail sat on her hands on the seat next to Jon, her body still. Her long dark hair fell in a braid down her back. She sometimes reminded Jon of a bird because she was small and thin, and her eyes were large. And because she usually never stopped arranging things, like a wren, weaving twigs into a nest. She only stopped moving when she was anxious.

"What if she doesn't like us?" Gail said.

"Relax," Jon said, immediately regretting the word. It was like asking Gail to stop breathing. "She chose us."

Paige, from the agency, picked the diner—halfway between their home and Carli's. It was the real deal, Edward Hopper except all the stools were taken, and the booths along the windows were filled with noisy families. It smelled of pancake batter and burnt bacon. They sat in a window booth next to the street. Carli would recognize them from the adoption book, and they'd recognize her from her social media posts. The blue streak in her hair would stand out.

"She chose our book." Gail chewed her lip. "It's not the same thing as choosing us."

The book. Every couple who tries to adopt must create a book, an advertisement, a brochure about their lives. The book contained pictures of them and their extended family and their house and their town and their essay that told a birth mother that the only thing they wanted in the whole world was a baby. It promised that if she chose their book, her baby would become their child, and they'd raise it with love and care, and they wouldn't let anyone, or anything hurt it. Gail revised the book more times than Jon cared to remember. She swapped out the pictures, changed the wording; she even agonized over the font and the color of the cover. She asked him over and over again what he thought about the assortment of pictures, until he couldn't remember how he had answered the last time. He was so damn sick of that book.

Jon put his hand on Gail's knee and forced a smile. "We'll make her like us."

Gail checked her watch. "She's ten minutes late."

"She's eighteen years old. Ten minutes late is early."

"I brought some information about the school district. You think I should show her?"

"No. I really don't think that you should."

They fell silent as they waited, and Jon tried to listen to the conversations of the people at the surrounding tables and the sizzle of the grease from the grill, but the silence at his own table distracted him. Gail had grown quiet since she got the call from Paige, as she waited for something to go wrong. The silence reminded him of that trailer outside of St. Louis where his mother would retreat into the back bedroom for days at a time. The only sounds had been the pit bull barking next door, the whoosh of the stovetop when he lit it to cook himself canned ravioli, and the voices on the television that he sometimes responded to. He was eight when his mom's "nervous spells" grew longer and longer, until they melted into an unbroken silence. He finally went to live with his aunt Carol and uncle Mark, and although Aunt Carol talked all the time, and although they had raised him since he was eight, it wasn't their blood that thudded in his ears when Gail went quiet. Gail hadn't put anything about his mom into the book, which Jon found vaguely sneaky.

Out the window Jon saw an old brown pickup truck pull up at the curb. A large, middle-aged woman sat behind the wheel, her jaw flapping, her hands slashing the air. Paige had said that Carli's mom would probably drive her. The person in the passenger seat remained still, and although Jon couldn't see clearly through the glare on the windshield, it looked like a teenage girl. The girl finally got out of the truck and came around the front. Dirty-blond hair with a blue streak fell across her face.

"She's here."

The bell above the door jangled when she came through, eyes darting. Jon could feel Gail stiffen next to him. He waved, and the girl walked their way. A bulky sweatshirt hung well past her waist, making it hard to see if she was showing. Scrawny legs sprouted from her Converse high-tops. The bridge of her upturned nose was littered with freckles. Too much mascara made the rest of her face seem pasty.

She slid into the booth. "Hey," she said.

"Hey," Jon said. "I'm Jon, and this is Gail."

Her pale blue eyes flicked from one of them to the other. "Carli."

"It's so nice to meet you, Carli," Gail gushed. "I can't tell you how much we've been looking forward to this."

The way Carli tugged the sleeves of her sweatshirt over her fists told Jon that she had not been looking forward to this at all, that she'd rather be anywhere else, even in the cab of the pickup truck listening to her mother rant. The waitress appeared before anyone could say anything else.

"Can I get you somethin', hon?"

"Coffee. Black."

"Decaf?" Gail suggested quietly.

Carli's eyes settled on Gail, really taking her in. "No. Coffee. Black."

The waitress left, and Gail gathered herself.

"We were so excited to get the call. We're so grateful that you chose us."

Carli picked up the saltshaker, studied it, said nothing.

Gail faltered for a moment but pressed on. "Did the father help you choose?"

A barely audible snort and a twitch at the corner of her mouth. She shook her head.

"This must be really fucking hard," Jon said.

Carli shook a tiny pile of salt into her palm. Her eyes cut to the counter, out the window toward the truck, back to the salt in her hand. She nodded. "Yeah. It is."

Gail leaned into the table. "You must have so many questions for us."

Nothing.

Gail looked down at her hands and then continued more gently. "It's hard to put everything into that book. I mean, we tried to give you a feel for who we are and where the baby will grow up, but you can't put your whole life, your whole world into so few pages." Gail looked to Jon for confirmation and then at Carli. "This is such a big decision. Is there anything you want to ask us?"

Carli dumped the salt from her hand onto the table. She glanced briefly at Gail and then her eyes settled on Jon. "My mom told me to ask about the medical stuff."

Jon stiffened. Gail hadn't mentioned any medical problems. Surely Paige would have told her if there were problems. "The medical stuff?"

"The tests. The doctor visits. All that."

"Yeah?"

"You're gonna pay for that, right?"

Jon gripped the steering wheel on the way home from the diner and tried to make sense of what had just happened. What series of events had delivered them to Aurora to charm a pregnant teenager into giving them her baby? He wanted to become a father, but even when they were trying to conceive a baby themselves, he became terrified every time it seemed that they might succeed. He was afraid that he'd fail, like his mother did, and if he failed a child who was entrusted to him by someone else— well, that seemed a sin of a different sort.

"How do you think it went?" Gail asked.

Gail's knee was bouncing, and she kept tugging at her seat belt, so Jon chose his words carefully. "It's hard to say. I think it went as well as it could have. Given the circumstances."

"Do you think I came on too strong?"

"No, I—"

"She was so hard to read. I couldn't get her talking. And she only asked that one question."

"I think that—"

"I expected her to ask more questions. I mean she's deciding whether to let us adopt her baby." Gail was quiet for a long
moment. "I'd have more questions."

Jon worked to contain a smile. He tried to imagine the list
of questions that Gail would bring to *that* meeting. Of course,
he struggled to imagine the circumstances that would lead Gail
to give up a baby.

"If only I could have gotten her to talk."

"We did great, Gail."

"I should have shown her the information about the school
district."

"Gail. Some things you just can't control."

Gail changed into her running clothes and was gone for more
than an hour. Paige said she would call as soon as she heard
from Carli. She said that she'd call by the end of the day no
matter what. When Gail returned, Jon could tell by her closed-up
expression that Paige still hadn't called. Gail kept her phone on
the table during dinner. She picked at her salad. She pushed
her pasta around the plate. She looked at the phone more than
she looked at Jon.

"What time's hockey?" she asked as they cleared the table.

Jon had played on the Dumpsters, a beer-league team, since
shortly after he moved to Elmhurst. He needed the ice tonight—
the sweat, the exertion, the meaningless locker-room chatter—but
Gail's stillness told him that he needed to stay home even more.

"Seven thirty. But I think I'll skip the game."

"Why?"

"With everything. You know. With Paige calling."

"Go."

"But—"

"I'd rather you go. Otherwise you'll stare at me, while I stare at the phone. Eventually you'll say something stupid, I'll yell at you, and then we'll fight."

She was right, of course. Still, it didn't seem like the right time to leave. "But—"

"Go."

Hockey usually calmed Jon. The hiss of steel on ice, the slap of the sticks, and the heavy *thud* of the puck against the boards usually kept him in the moment. But that night, he fell climbing over the boards. He hooked a guy in the neutral zone—a senseless penalty with a minute left—and he sat in the box while the other team scored the game winner.

Jon checked his phone in the locker room, but there were no messages. He almost called Gail from the car but thought better of it. When he entered the mudroom, he stood still for a moment, listening, but all he heard was silence. When he went upstairs, he found Gail on her edge of the bed, bent over her brown leather notebook, making lists. She was pretty in a way that used to embarrass Jon. The dim glow of the dresser lamp painted her olive complexion even darker. Her eyelashes were impossibly long, and the shape of her mouth still sometimes caused him to miss a breath. A rubber band gathered her long brown hair into a ponytail. One of Jon's old T-shirts draped over her tiny body down to her thighs. Jon knew the answer to the question, but he couldn't not ask it.

"Did she call?"

"Not yet," Gail said. She kept her eyes on the page.

Jon stripped to his boxers and climbed in on his side. They used to wake tangled in the middle, but now they kept to the margins of their California king. The more obsessed Gail became, the farther away from each other they seemed to settle. It happened slowly, a bit at a time, like that frog on the Bunsen burner.

He wondered what list Gail could possibly be working. No list could help control what would happen when Paige called, but Gail gripped her pen tightly and scribbled. Jon hated the notebook. Gail always grew quiet when she made her lists, and Jon hated the silence. It reminded him too much of his mom. Jon and Gail still went back to St. Louis twice a year—at Christmas and Father's Day. It was always good to see Aunt Carol and Uncle Mark, and Jon could tell that Aunt Carol hungered for those weekends. But when he escaped back across the Mississippi to Illinois, his breath always came easier.

During their last visit, Gail sat in the family room with Uncle Mark, working a jigsaw puzzle and watching CNN, while Jon dried the dishes. Aunt Carol had let her hair go gray, and her face was starting to sag. She pushed up the sleeves of her cardigan, but one sleeve kept sliding down into the dishwater.

"Any news?" Aunt Carol asked. "About the adoption?"

"Nothing solid, yet. We sent out one book, but the birth mother chose someone else."

They worked in companionable silence, the splash of the water the only sound.

"I'm looking forward to it," she said. She looked up at Jon and smiled. "It'll be nice to be a grandma."

Aunt Carol would make the perfect grandma, spoiling her grandchild just enough, and reveling in every moment of it. But as Jon dried the pot in his hands, her words forced a question to his lips that he'd been struggling to swallow.

"What was she like?" Jon asked.

Aunt Carol stopped scrubbing the lasagna pan for a long moment. In the family room, Uncle Mark laughed at something Gail said. Finally, Aunt Carol's hand started moving again. "Who's that?" she said, as if he could be asking about anyone else.

"My mom."

Aunt Carol rinsed the pan and found a corner that needed more work. She grabbed the Brillo pad from the counter and locked her eyes on her hands as she scraped the charred cheese. Jon had broken their oldest unspoken rule, and Aunt Carol's whole body had gone rigid. It had been almost two decades since they last spoke of his mother. "I think you know exactly what she's like."

Jon put the towel over his shoulder, folded his arms across his chest. His mom still lived just a few miles away from Aunt Carol's house, in the very same trailer he'd left when he was eight. Sometimes, after a trip to the grocery store to pick up something for his aunt, Jon drove by. The shades were always drawn, the parking pad empty. Weeds hugged the side of the trailer instead of bushes. He didn't ever get out of his car. He didn't knock on that door. The last few years, he mailed a check to that address every month, and every month the check was cashed. He sometimes logged on to the Citibank website and stared at his mom's scrawled signature.

"I mean *before*." Jon had been avoiding the question since they started trying. But when they decided to adopt someone else's child, it had gained urgency. "Was she always like that, or did it start after I was born?"

Aunt Carol rinsed the pan again. Both sleeves had fallen into the water, but she didn't push them back up to her elbows. She inspected the pan, rinsed it again, and then handed it to Jon.

When she finally looked at him, her face was knotted up like a fist. Her voice when she spoke, though, was clear and certain.

"Some questions are like scabs, Jon. Best if you don't pick at them."

She dried her hands and then walked out of the kitchen, down the hallway, toward her bedroom. Probably to change her sweater. Jon dried the pan and tried to figure out what Aunt Carol wasn't telling him. Scabs? What the hell did that mean?

Jon watched Gail set the notebook and pen on the bedside table next to her phone. She turned out the lamp and curled onto her side, facing away from him. This was when Jon usually ventured across the middle of their bed and kissed her good night, but he knew that they weren't going to sleep yet. They were just waiting in the dark now.

Jon's fingers ached for his guitar. Music would help him wait. The strings under his fingers would help him make out the shape of the future and feel the best from the past. He remembered the day his uncle had taught him the G and D chords and patiently walked him through his first progression. Uncle Mark told Jon how hard it was when he was learning to play. He talked about practice and determination and muscle memory and calluses. He talked about strings and fingers and sounds. He helped Jon adjust his fingers on the fretboard again and again. It took Jon more than an hour to manage that first progression, and his nine-year-old fingers burned against the wire. But finally, he shifted from G to D in a way that felt just a little bit like a song, or at least part of one, and he looked up at Uncle Mark, who smiled through his beard and nodded. Jon did it again. And again. He could still feel the warm, heavy pressure of Uncle

Mark's hand on his shoulder as he bit his lip and struggled against the strings. That was the day that he started thinking of Uncle Mark as more than just an uncle. And sometime between that day and the day he met Gail, he had decided that someday he would become a father.

But Jon also remembered that morning Gail came out of the bathroom wearing a coy smile and carrying a plastic contraption with two red lines. He squeezed her tight and giggled into her ear, but even as he released her from that embrace, before they kissed and started to plan, anxiety tugged at him—the self-doubt, the suspicion that he was trying to do something that he had no right to try. But before the fear devoured him, Gail had bled, and then again, and again. He'd spent the last four years learning to hold both the hope and the fear at once. Lately, the fear seemed to have teeth.

It always started with the mundane. What if he dropped the baby? What if he fed it the wrong thing? What if it choked or spiked a fever, or he laid it down for a nap the wrong way and it never woke up? It helped to think that Gail would be there. Gail had read all the books and the websites; she had made lists. But inevitably he'd be left alone with the baby. And what about when it started to crawl? What if he forgot to close the gate at the top of the stairs? And, of course, it would learn to walk. What if it escaped and got hit by a car on Myrtle Avenue or just wandered off and got lost? And if all that wasn't terrifying enough, what if something happened to Gail? What if she got hit by a car or got cancer or fell down the stairs, and it wasn't just a few hours while she was at the gym or the store? What if he was expected to raise a child on his own, like his mother tried to do after his father left? What if the same dike that broke in her and flooded her with helplessness gave way in him? What if the terror that swamped him now was already eroding that dike, softening it, destabilizing the silt?

Gail squirmed, kicked off the comforter, and then settled to a tense stillness. Jon blinked at the ceiling. It was almost eleven when Gail's phone finally rang. At first, Gail didn't move, but then she answered it, just before the fourth ring.

"Hi, Paige," she said, her voice pregnant with expectation.

Paige talked, and Gail listened. Jon lay still, terribly aware that he was about to plunge toward fatherhood, or that Gail was about to dive into another tailspin. His body felt cold all over, because he wasn't quite sure which to hope for.

Gail

*

Gail drove Carli to the twelve-week ultrasound. It was their second doctor visit together, and like the other two, Gail took her to Panera afterward. They sat at the same table between the fireplace and the front window. Snow fell on the parking lot. Gail picked at a salad, while Carli plowed through a panini with a blueberry muffin and a bear claw in reserve.

The giddiness of that yes from Carli had quickly given over to a scramble through the paperwork and had then settled into waiting yet again. Gail had studied every dependent clause of that paperwork, and she knew how flimsy it all was. When she wasn't calling on accounts and negotiating contracts and selling new business, she spent too much time thinking about those loopholes and escape routes that those papers mapped for Carli. She went to all the doctor appointments so that she could learn about the baby's development, so that she could hear its heartbeat. She took Carli to lunch afterward so that she could come to know her, so that she could monitor the girl's pulse. Every visit, Carli gained a bit of weight, and her face filled out until

27

it was almost pretty. Gail couldn't decide whether Carli's eyes were gray or very pale blue. She couldn't help but stare at Carli's freckled, upturned nose and wonder what her child would grow up to look like.

During their first lunch, Gail had asked too many questions, and that earned her one-word answers and awkward silences. Then she talked too much—about children's books and nursery themes and about the average composite ISAT scores for the Elmhurst school district. Carli's eyes glazed over, and Gail felt foolish. This time, though, Gail couldn't seem to manage words, and Carli peered at her through that stripe of blue hair.

"What's wrong?" Carli finally asked.

Gail put down the fork and then picked it up again. She pushed a dried apple around the bowl. She felt like that apple slice—withered and curled in upon itself.

"Nothing's wrong," Gail said quietly, because nothing was wrong. Carli had avoided looking at the ultrasound monitor, but Gail couldn't take her eyes off it. The baby looked like ET with its too-big head and sticks for arms and legs and a bump that was probably its butt. The technician said that it was about the size of a lime, and he said that everything looked normal as far as he could tell. "It's just that I never got this far."

The sandwich froze halfway to Carli's mouth. "What do you mean?"

Gail squeezed the fork and looked out the window at the swirling snowflakes. "I was pregnant three times," she said. "But I lost them all."

The first, she lost at the gym. The second time, the baby was as big as a sweet pea, and she lost it in the car, driving to a customer. She had to pull over at a Burger King to clean herself up in the bathroom and sob and wait for the cramping to stop.

The third time, the baby was as big as a prune, and she lost it at home on a Saturday. That third time was the hardest, because she had made it to ten weeks and her expectations had grown faster than the fetus. She could almost feel that second heartbeat, and she had started to tell people. Once you tell people about a baby growing inside, you have to tell them when it dies, and then you have to make a list of who they told and make sure that all the people that heard about your exciting news hear about your little tragedy, so that when they see you at the Jewel they don't ask you how you're feeling with that sideways secret smile, because then you're sure to sit in the parking lot and weep while the lunch meat gets warm.

"I felt so empty. After." She bit her lip and pushed the apple around the bowl again. "Not just the space in my gut. It was like all my hopes had drained from me, too."

"I'm sorry," Carli said, looking straight at Gail. Her eyes were still for the first time since Gail had met her. "I didn't know."

Of course she didn't know, and Gail wanted to say that it was OK, that it wasn't her fault, that it was nobody's fault. But she was afraid that if she opened her mouth, she might just make that noise that she had made in the Burger King bathroom, so instead she closed her eyes and squeezed her fork.

"I finished my GED last week," Carli said.

Gail opened her eyes and stared at the girl, disoriented by the sudden swerve.

"It was just four tests, and they weren't that hard."

Carli was talking. About herself. To fill the silence. For Gail.

"I'll need it in the spring for Waubonsee."

Gail swallowed a smile and managed to spear a tomato. She had never thought to ask Carli about her plans for the future. "The community college?"

29

"Yeah."

"What will you study?" Gail bit the tomato, and juice flooded her mouth.

"I wanna be a nurse someday."

"I have a friend who's a nurse," Gail said, and for the first time she really looked at Carli, saw her as someone with a future beyond the due date, thought of her as more than just the girl who was carrying her child. "You'll make a good nurse."

Carli stared at Gail for a long moment as if desperate to believe those words. When she started talking again, about semesters and prerequisites and financial aid, Gail's mind drifted back to the hospital, to that monitor in the radiology department, to that squirming little lime.

The next morning, Gail arrived at work just after seven. The shop was housed in a low brick building on Central, next to where her grandparents' house had stood before it was razed for a parking lot. The Tomassi name, in green metal letters spotted with rust, had been bolted into the masonry many decades before. No matter where her first sales call took her, Gail came by the shop every morning, to solve problems and plan with her dad, but mostly just to hear the noise.

Gail said hello to Anna, her dad's cousin, who invoiced the customers and answered the phones. Gail dropped her bag in her office and then pushed through the door into the shop. Both lines were already singing. Boxes, each containing the knives of a single customer, were piled high on tall rolling racks at the head of the lines. Men stood at each machine, grinding or edging or honing or buffing, passing the boxes from station to station. Blades screamed against the stones, hissed through the honer, splashed through the wash, and clattered back into boxes. The grumbling motors supplied the bass line to it all. The sound of the shop was embedded in Gail's earliest memories. She visited often as a child. When she was a teenager, she begged her father to let her work the line, and finally, the summer after her freshman year in college, he relented.

Her grandfather insisted on training her himself. His hands were spotted and wrinkled and covered with scars and calluses. Black and white hair curled from his nose and his ears, and it framed a face as dark and smooth as a walnut. That first day, he wouldn't even let Gail touch a knife. He taught her about grind lines and plunge lines and ricassos and bevels. He explained bolsters and bellies and angles and choils. He showed her all the grinds and explained their uses. Flat grinds are shaped just like you would expect, with flat sides and a small bevel at the cutting edge, and they're used for dicing and mincing. The hollow grind features a concave curve from the spine of the blade to the cutting edge. They're sharp but fragile, and make for a good filet knife, he explained. The convex grind is just the opposite, bulging outward before tapering to the edge. They prove sturdy and are well suited to chopping and hacking. Gail stood at his bench, listening intently, recording everything he said in her notebook.

It wasn't until the second week that Gail touched steel to stone. Working their way down the line, her grandfather demonstrated how to use each machine. He taught her the demands of each type of blade and how to stay safe. After she mastered the entire line, he brought her to the stand-up grinder, and her real apprenticeship began.

It was just a large spinning stone—no guides, no guards—so it was dangerous in a way that the other machines were not. It was a mechanized version of what her family had been using to sharpen blades for generations, but now they mainly used it to fix damaged knives and to sharpen specialty blades. Gail's grandfather taught her to feel the vibration of the steel when she applied the right pressure. He taught her to listen for the sing of a blade held at the correct angle. Eventually, he let her repair a knife by herself and then another and then a third. She gained speed and developed a feel for the steel and the scream of the stone. As she repaired blade after blade, she fell into a rhythm that felt like it had always lived in her hands. And the magic of dull, chipped blades being made right again stirred something in her belly that she never told anyone about. When she dropped a salvaged knife into the box, she looked up at her grandfather and smiled. He smiled back in a way that told her that he felt it, too.

Frank said hello as Gail walked by. Javier just nodded. The rest of the men remained bent to their work. Her dad's office door stood open. He loved the sound of it all as much as Gail did. She closed the door behind her, though, so that they could hear each other talk. She moved a crescent wrench from the chair to a shelf and then sat.

"Morning," he said, not looking up. He usually spent his mornings scrambling to reroute the vans after a driver called in sick or helping to troubleshoot a stubborn piece of equipment that stood in the way of sharp edges. But things must have been quiet that morning because he was bent over a knife catalog, reading glasses perched on his bulbous nose. His scarred, calloused fingers turned the pages. His intelligent eyes, magnified by the lenses, darted from image to image. He ran a hand through his thinning salt-and-pepper hair and glanced up at Gail. "Thinking about ordering from that new place outside of Guangzhou."

"Forged steel?" Gail asked.

He nodded. "Marchesi tells me that they're holding up."

"Schmidt and Weber both renewed their contracts," Gail said. "I told both of them that Martin will be handling their account while I'm out."

"How'd that go?"

"Fine," she said. "They're butchers. They don't care who manages their account if their knives stay sharp. Becker's still complaining about the cleavers, but he'd complain about the cleavers if they were made of platinum."

He flipped a page in the catalog and asked about the only account that mattered. "Have you heard from Subway?"

"I did," Gail said. "Yesterday. They said that they've got cheaper options."

"They say that every year."

"This year they want to trim twenty-five cents per blade."

That made her dad look up. "Twenty-five cents? That's absurd."

They charged Subway two dollars per knife per week. Gail shrugged. "I hear those guys out of Skokie are trying to buy accounts because they're getting ready to sell their shop. Almost two hundred stores. That's a boatload of blades." Gail waited for her dad to do the math, the same math she'd been doing since yesterday. "But we can't touch that price, of course."

Her dad's eyes flicked toward the closed door. Gail heard Frank laugh, probably at something Javier said. "I think we have to," he said.

"Dad. That would eliminate our gross margin on the account. We'd probably lose money on it."

"Maybe so," he said. "But it would help cover our fixed costs."

Every asset in the building had been amortized decades ago. The vans were all leased. The only costs that really mattered were knives and labor. "All our costs are variable, Dad."

He looked back down at the catalog and said nothing. In her dad's mind their costs were inextricably tied to Frank's laugh, Javier's jokes, and Juan's sick mother.

"Maybe *we* should pay *Subway* for the privilege of sharpening their knives," Gail said.

"It's our biggest account, Gail. See if there's wiggle room, but we can't lose Subway."

Gail's dad usually deferred to her when it came to customers. But sometimes, when customers threatened to affect the men in the shop, he spoke in that quiet, tight-lipped way that told Gail that it might take a few days to change his mind. So she dropped it for now, but she didn't get up. He finished scanning the page of knives, flipped to the next, and then looked up. "What's up?"

"I went with Carli to the ultrasound yesterday."

He laid his glasses on the catalog and leaned back in his chair. He clasped his hands behind his head. "All good?"

"As far as I could tell," Gail said. She fought off a smile, but she could see from her dad's own smile that she had failed. "I saw the baby. The head. The tiny arms. It looked like an alien."

"That's great, Gail. That's really great." For a moment they both listened to the scream leaking through the door. "You've waited a long time for this."

"I have," Gail said.

He paused, and Gail could see him decide to say more. "I know that you plan to take four months," he said. "But you should think about what you really want."

"I thought about it," Gail said, trying to keep the edge off her words. "I want four months."

"Jon's doing well at work, right?"

Gail had been expecting this conversation, or some version of it anyway. The week before, when she told her dad that she was taking four months, he didn't really reply. He looked like he wanted to argue, but he held his tongue. She had considered taking more time, maybe going part-time. But, although her dad ran the shop tight, he had no clue how to sell—Gail's grandfather had always handled the selling. When he died, Gail was still a junior in college, and she had no idea how much her father struggled to fill the gap, how much the business suffered. It wasn't until graduation approached that her dad told how deep the hole had become. She'd never forget those first three years that she'd spent scrambling to dig them out of it.

"That's beside the point."

"Martin and Stephanie are both doing well."

Easy for him to say. All he saw were the new accounts they brought in. Gail had hired Martin three years ago, Stephanie just last year. Both were still learning the business. "They do well when I stay on top of them," she said.

Gail's dad glanced at the wall, at the black-and-white photo of Gail's grandfather standing next to his own father. "You saved the company when he died," he said. "There's no denying that." He shifted in his seat, and she could see him choose his words carefully. "I want you to come back after four months. That's what I want. I love working with you, but I love *you* more. I want you to decide what's best for you and your family."

Decide what's best. Gail fell still, and her lack of a ready answer caught her off guard. *Decide.* She didn't really decide to work at the shop after college. As much as she enjoyed those summers grinding knives, she had dreamed of a job at a marketing agency or a tech start-up. But back then she wasn't given a choice. The shop chose her. Could it really do without her now? And was that even what she wanted? She didn't expect to love selling so much, and she never expected to become so good at it. And wouldn't she go crazy as a stay-at-home mom? But then she thought of that lime squirming inside of Carli, and she wondered if she could really come back after four months. Could she drop her baby off at day care every morning, leave that baby for eight or nine hours at a stretch? If she stayed at home with the baby, she would miss that shot of adrenaline when she closed a deal, and she would miss the scrape and clatter of the shop, but what if she missed her baby's first steps or first words? She looked at the picture of the two dead men, stiff in their poorly fitted suits, staring at the camera expressionless. It was easier to have no choice.

"Let's just see how it goes," Gail finally said.

Then she stood, carefully avoided her father's gaze, and walked through the door, back into that delicious noise.

Carli

*

Carli was late for class, but she walked slowly. Waddled really. Past the commons. Past the two students sitting at a card table, registering people to vote. She had slept poorly—contractions every few hours, like something was twisting her intestines. She should have stayed home, but she missed class on Wednesday because her car wouldn't start, and she might miss more after the baby. She was barely hanging on to a B, and the class cost her almost four hundred dollars. Besides, the doctor told her to ignore the contractions until they were ten minutes apart—or until her water broke.

Everybody stared when she entered the classroom. Partly because she barged in late, partly because she was so fat that she could no longer zip her jacket, but mostly because they were already bored to tears by whatever Professor Aronson was going on about. This was Carli's first class at Waubonsee Community College, and she had met nobody. Nothing like a twenty-pound bubble of fat and fetus to get between you and your new friends. Aronson had given up trying to coax class participation after the first few weeks—now he just droned on and on. She shuffled to the closest open seat and wedged herself in. Professor Aronson never stopped talking.

Carli took out her notebook and squinted at the whiteboard: Maslow's hierarchy of needs. She hadn't done all the reading— she'd had four shifts behind the cash register at Giamonti's that week—but she had scanned the chapter on Maslow. She worked to remember it her own way while Professor Aronson babbled.

The first three levels were easy. *(1) Physiological needs.* Carli was always hungry. She ate a whole pizza at work the night before during her break. Food came first. *(2) Safety needs.* In the beginning, when Andy started delivering pizza at Giamonti's, she had felt safe with him. The first time they hooked up, she didn't yet know about his addiction. He made her laugh, and the way he smiled revealed a kindness that she wasn't used to. When he was tweaking crank, though, he became unpredictable and manic, and some of his friends really scared the crap out of her. When Carli finally broke it off with Andy, the night after he punched her, and just a couple of weeks before she realized she was pregnant, her *(3) love and belonging needs* took a hit. Not that he ever really loved her, but when he wasn't high, the gentle way he treated her made her feel warm and almost safe. Her friends drifted off about the time her baby bump arrived. Her mom hated her, and her sister didn't seem to care one way or the other. *Love and belonging* were going to need some work. *(4) Esteem needs.* Probably why she wanted to become a nurse, why she sat in this classroom for three hours every week, listening to Aronson talk about all this crap that she'd never need to know. She had read the paragraph about *(5) Self-actualization* four times, but still had no idea what to make of that tiny triangle at the top.

It was probably more guilt than her esteem needs that kept her coming back to class. She promised herself that she'd get her life together. She promised the baby. Once she decided to give up her baby, she couldn't just go stock shelves at Walmart or pack boxes at the warehouse or find another meth-head like Andy to nuzzle. She'd be letting the baby down, but double. She wondered why Maslow didn't devote a slice of his pyramid to guilt.

Halfway through class, Carli felt another contraction building, and the pain raced right past anything that she'd felt the night before. It started at her hips and moved inward as if it were hungry. Stupid to come to class. She bit her lip hard and leaned over the desk, pretending to take notes, but then it really hit, and she let out a little yelp. Even with her eyes closed, she knew everyone in the classroom was looking at her.

"Carli?" Aronson said. "You OK?"

Carli couldn't answer, so she kept her head down on her desk, her hands clutching her stomach. And then the water flooded her pants.

When the contraction finally, begrudgingly eased its grip, Carli tried to figure out what to do next. She considered waiting until the end of class so that she could let everyone leave before her. But then she heard water drip from the seat of her chair and splatter on the floor, and she felt the nearest students stir. She grabbed her backpack, stood, and plodded toward the door, trying to ignore the wet. Professor Aronson stopped talking.

"Jesus Christ," the kid behind her said with disgust. Carli didn't look at anyone, didn't even breathe, until she made it to the hallway.

She found a bench near the commons and sat down, the water already going cold. She thought about driving herself to the hospital, but if another contraction like that hit her on the highway, she'd find the ditch. Her sister wouldn't answer her phone. Her mother was an hour away. Then she remembered that the Durbins were paying. She pulled out her phone and dialed 911.

Gail

*

Gail walked past dumpsters of spoiled vegetables and goat meat. The alley, even with its trash and rats and stink was familiar, comfortable. Gail had first come to Greektown with her grandfather when she was just a child. He'd taught her the names of the men in the offices above the restaurants, and he'd taught her that although she could use the front door of a restaurant in the suburbs, in Greektown, professionals came in from the alley, through the kitchen. To do otherwise would show incompetence, weakness.

Chicago's Greektown was just a handful of restaurants clustered around the corner of Halsted and Adams. But the men who owned them—and they were all men—owned hundreds of other restaurants throughout the city. Thai and Italian and Indian and Mexican—all owned by the Greeks. When Gail's grandfather decided to go after restaurants in a big way, he went to night school to learn to speak Greek. He called himself Georgios when he came to Greektown. He told those men that his mother was Greek—said her family hailed from Naxos—even though she was really Sicilian. Scores of Greeks showed up at his funeral. They all winked at Gail's father in the receiving line. *We knew he wasn't one of us,* they said. *But he tried so hard that we had to give him the knives.*

Gail pushed through the screen door into the kitchen of Hera's Greek Restaurant. It was almost three—that magic hour of prep between a late lunch and an early dinner. The only patrons in the restaurant would be a small group of old Greek men sipping ouzo at the bar and repeating stories they had worn out long ago. There was no shouting in the kitchen, like during a lunch or dinner rush. But everyone was moving, and the knives spoke. A half-dozen men, dressed in white shirts and checkered pants stood at cutting boards throughout the kitchen, chopping, slicing, mincing. The muted clatter of a well-run kitchen in the afternoon, the *tap, tap, tap* of six different knives, was one of Gail's favorite sounds, second only to steel on stone.

The man nearest to her turned, although his knife kept chopping carrots. His hooded eyes peered from either side of a beak-like nose. Costas didn't call himself a chef, but he ran this kitchen. "Gail," he said in greeting. When he wasn't yelling at people during the rush, he was stingy with words.

"Costas," Gail said. "How are my knives?"

He shrugged. "They go dull."

"Good. I'm counting on it," Gail said. She started walking toward the stairs. "I'm here to see Stavros." Her grandfather taught her to never *ask* to see the owner or the chef. That would earn her a spot at a table or at the bar, waiting until someone came to tell her that the boss *just can't make the time today.*

Best to just walk in as if the boss had demanded your presence, he always said.

She threaded her way through the kitchen, saying hello to each man by name. She kept a notebook in her glovebox devoted to lists of the staff in the kitchens she visited most often. The narrow stairs creaked as she climbed them. When she reached the top, she knocked on the first door to the right and heard something like a grunt. She pushed the door open and found Stavros bent over his big oak desk. The mounds of paper stacked across its surface made him look smaller than he really was. The crown of his head gleamed bald, but the gray tufts of hair everywhere else—his eyebrows, his forearms, his knuckles—made up the difference. Just like every other time she had visited Stavros, his fingers clattered the keys of the adding machine. His eyes scanned an invoice. His lips moved as his finger traced the column of numbers. Gail sat in the only chair and waited. Stavros looked old that first time that Gail visited with her grandfather, but he hadn't seemed to age in the decades since. The walls were lined with waist-high shelves, every shelf stacked with invoices. Stavros now owned seventeen restaurants across Chicago, but two decades later, his filing system hadn't changed a bit.

He finally reached the bottom of the invoice and looked up. His eyebrows twitched, but the rest of his face registered nothing. "Ms. Tomassi," he growled.

Long ago, Gail had stopped reminding him that her name was no longer Tomassi, because to Stavros, she would always be a Tomassi.

"You come here to raise my prices again?"

"Not this time, Stavros," Gail said. "My grandfather told me to stick it to you at Christmas. Those were his dying words, in fact. He said you're a soft touch around the holidays."

He leaned back in his chair. "How's your father?"

"Stubborn," Gail said. "Just like all you old men. He'll be calling you over the next few months, by the way. To check in. That's why I stopped by. To tell you that."

"What? I get the ugly Tomassi?"

"You won't have to look at him. He'll just call."

Stavros nodded. "I see. You got better things to do than visit an old Greek?"

"Actually, I do," Gail said, and she couldn't help but smile just a little. "I'm becoming a mother."

Stavros's eyes darted to her stomach and then back up to her face. Gail let him squirm with confusion and discomfort for a moment before putting him out of his misery.

"We're adopting," she finally said. "The birth mother is due any day now."

Stavros's face settled back to its familiar mask. "This baby. It's Italian?"

Gail felt a flash of heat and wanted to say something sharp about the fact that ethnicity didn't matter, that they would forge a family from the baby they were given, that they would remain ever grateful for that gift. But Stavros was old, so she said it in a way that he might understand. "It will be," she said. "Just like my grandfather was Greek."

This finally pried a smile from Stavros. "I'm happy for you," he said. "I was beginning to worry."

Gail's phone vibrated in her pocket, but she let it roll to voice mail. She knew that checking her phone would send Stavros back to his invoices and Gail back into the alley. Before that happened, she wanted to know what he knew. "How are your cousins?" she asked.

By this she meant the tight-knit community of Greeks who owned so many of Chicago's restaurants. Some of them were cousins, most of them weren't, but Stavros knew what she meant. He shrugged.

"Some are good. Some, not so much. Diakos is buying those burrito places from his brother-in-law." Diakos was Gail's customer. His brother-in-law was not. Gail made a mental note to add Diakos to her call list. "And I hear that Karras has some new Italian friends." Which meant that Karras was talking to another knife-grinding company for his two dozen restaurants. Another item for her list.

Gail's pocket vibrated again, and with a lurch she realized who it might be. She yanked the phone from her pocket. Sure enough. Paige. Her hand shook as she answered. "This is Gail," she managed.

"Carli's going into labor."

Gail squeezed the phone and peered over the old man's shoulder at the sun filtering through the blinds. It was happening. After everything they had been through, it was finally happening. She felt weightless yet unable to move. Warmth flooded her stomach, and she couldn't speak.

"Gail? You there?"

"Yeah. Yeah. I'm here. Mercy?"

"Yep. Go through the doors on the north side of the building. Maternity is right past orthopedics. I'll see you there soon."

Gail hung up the phone and stared at it. When Stavros spoke, he startled her.

"Was that what I think it was?"

Gail looked up at the old man, and his face had creased into the first full-on smile that she had ever seen from him. She stood and tried to steady herself. "It was," she said, her voice crackling with everything. "Seems the bambino is coming today."

Jon

*

J on hunched over the long granite table in the main conference room, perched fifty-three stories above the Loop. The
room could accommodate almost twenty, but today they were
just three—Jon, the client, and Adam, the account manager.
Jon wore his headphones and locked his eyes on the screen. His
fingers danced across the keyboard of his laptop. The other two
were arguing about some changes to the project, about expectations. He was just there in case they had detailed questions,
and in the meantime, he would make the changes that they
were arguing about.

He was listening to Hendrix. When he was reworking existing
code, adding new features, he listened to Jimi or Page or Knopfler sometimes. Rock respected structure, but the best guitarists
used it as a starting point and then added what was needed with
an unusual bridge or variations on the theme or a solo when all
else failed. When he was working with data, he usually played
classic twelve-bar by Stevie Ray or B. B. King, because data was
all about the structure. When he was designing something, he

favored Reinhardt or Montgomery, because jazz kept him loose, open to any possibility. When he was coding a new system, he drifted toward Earl Scruggs or Ralph Stanley because in those bluegrass bands, the banjo players seemed to do all the work, laying down the beat and the rhythm and the melody all at once.

Today was mainly just typing. He had built the shape of the interface in his mind the night before while riffing on a Béla Fleck solo. Listening to music helped him to focus, but playing music helped him to imagine. Whenever he got stuck on a particularly tricky design problem, he made time at night to play. Sometimes it took an hour, sometimes just ten minutes, but something about the feel of the strings under his fingers, the way the notes shaped themselves into coherent music, helped his mind drift toward the contours of a solution. And once he could see the shape of it, the rest was just typing.

Jon's phone vibrated in his pocket. He let it go to voice mail. He was working the hard part and tried to wall off the distraction. It stopped and then started again—his fingers froze. He fumbled the phone out of his pocket. Gail.

He tugged off his headphones. "Hey," he said.

Adam glanced Jon's way but continued talking to the client, pressing his point.

"It's happening," Gail said.

"What? Carli?"

The client looked at Jon now, too.

Gail laughed in a breathless, joyful way that Jon hadn't heard in a very long time. "Yes. Of course, Carli. She went into labor an hour ago. It's finally happening."

"OK," Jon managed. He closed his laptop and crammed it into his backpack. It was happening. "Wow." It was happening today. "I'm leaving. I'm coming."

"She's at Mercy."

Jon stood. He felt Adam and the client staring at him. He couldn't feel his hands or his feet, and the air filled with static. "I'll—I'll meet you there."

"No. I'm headed home," Gail said. Jon could hear the smile in her voice. "Pick me up at home. We're going to do this together."

They found the maternity ward right away, but it took Jon a while to explain to the nurse at the desk who they were and why they should be kept apprised of Carli Brennan's status. It probably didn't help that he felt like he was explaining it to himself. She directed them to the waiting room, and Jon slouched into a chair next to Gail, opposite the large windows overlooking the parking lot.

"Did she say how far apart the contractions are?" Gail asked.

"Ten minutes."

"So, it'll be a while," she said. Gail had read a slew of books on labor even though she wouldn't be pushing. "What about her cervix?"

"Her what?"

"Did they say how dilated she was?"

"I didn't ask."

"The cervix dilates to allow the baby's head to—"

"Gail—"

"Unless of course the baby's breach, and then they'll have to perform a C-section, and if that happens there's a chance that—"

"Gail," Jon said more sharply. Gail's eyes were dilating. Jon grabbed her hand and gave it a squeeze. He was nervous enough. He couldn't have her flipping out on him. "We've done everything we can. Now we just have to wait."

"Right. Sorry. I just can't believe that it's finally happening."

Jon tried to surrender himself to Gail's excitement. He'd been trying for months. He tried to ignore all the insecurities that had swelled with each passing day. He smiled in what he hoped was a reassuring way and said the truest words he could summon. "I can't believe it's happening, either."

This seemed to satisfy Gail, and she pulled her leather notebook from her purse and turned to a page that Jon knew contained a list titled something like *People to Call When the Baby Comes*. She started with her mother. Jon checked his watch. They'd have at least forty-five more Eleanor-free minutes.

"You couldn't have a waited a bit?" Jon asked after she hung up. "Until the baby was born? Maybe the first-birthday party?"

Gail smiled as she searched for the next number.

"Please tell me that your dad's coming, too."

"That's the only reason I called her."

Eleanor had grown easier to stomach since she'd gone dry. And most of what she said was so ridiculous that Jon found it hard to take her seriously, but she could always crawl under Gail's skin, and then Jon would have to deal with that. Gail called Jon's aunt next. Jon could faintly hear Aunt Carol's excited chatter, and that made him smile.

Next she called the girls. Every single one of them had been Gail's friend first, and she had woven them all together. Cindy, Gail's best friend since second grade, Gina from college, Allison from yoga, Kara from that beach volleyball team almost a decade ago. The apartment on Paulina Street had been their gathering place, where they all drank too much and stayed up too late and laughed too loudly. Allison and Gina both met their husbands there. For so long the girls were embedded into the texture of Gail's life, but when they moved to the suburbs with their children it was like the fabric unraveled. Maybe Gail's childlessness rendered her irrelevant. Maybe all those children made the girls difficult for Gail to stomach. It was hard for Jon to know what caused it, but at some point, the girls stopped calling Gail, and Gail stopped calling the girls, until Cindy was the only one Gail still talked to.

While she worked through the list, Jon scanned the waiting room and tried to place the melody filtering through the speakers. He winced—a smooth jazz version of a song by the Velvet Underground. The sleet tapped a staccato beat against the window. *Women's Day* and *Redbook* sprawled over *Condé Nast* and *Men's Health* on the coffee table. Three kids with their grandparents—another evidently on the way. Several men alone, checking their phones, knees bouncing. C-sections? At the other end of the room, next to the window, a middle-aged woman peered at Jon, but when their eyes met, she took a sudden interest in the parking lot. She wore a Wisconsin Dells sweatshirt, black sneakers, and a dour expression. It took Jon a moment to place the face: the brown pickup truck outside the diner. He stood.

"Where are you going?" Gail whispered, her hand cupped over the phone.

"I'll be back in a minute."

As he approached, the woman studied the cars through the window. "Excuse me, ma'am," Jon said.

She didn't look at him. She was thick, like an oak, and her disheveled hair, a color somewhere between red and dirt, was pruned short. Her mouth turned down at the corners in a way that suited the rest of her face. She kept steady watch on the cars in the lot.

"My name's Jon Durbin."

"I know who you are," she growled.

Jon waited for her to say more, but she seemed to have finished. "Well. I just thought I'd introduce myself."

Jon was about to turn away when she spoke again. "She's gonna regret this."

At first Jon thought she was talking about Gail, but he realized she meant Carli, of course. And she was right. He'd been so consumed with Gail and himself that he hadn't given much thought to what Carli was about to go through. The aftermath would be hard.

"It ain't right what she's doing. You don't just give your baby away."

Jon tried to summon words that might help. "We'll make the baby happy," he said.

She turned from the window, her eyes narrow, her lips thin. "How you know that?"

Jon opened his mouth, but his own uncertainties tangled his tongue, and no words came out.

"You think just because you got money you can make the baby happy?"

"That's not what I—"

"It's a mother's job to make a baby happy." Her eyes cut to Gail. "A real mother."

Jon cocked his head. "What was that?"

"You heard me."

And he suddenly smelled her, too. Under the cigarettes and the sweat, he smelled the mothballs and the trailer and the canned ravioli, but he forced himself quiet.

"I said she ain't a real mother."

Jon's hands curled into fists. "You know nothing about her."

Jon turned to go, but she spoke again. "I know enough."

The words flew from Jon's mouth before he knew what he'd say. "So . . . getting knocked up . . . that makes Carli a real mother?"

The woman's jaw jutted. "Listen here, you son of a—"

"No," Jon said. He took a half step toward her. He spoke low and fast. "You listen to me. You don't know shit about my wife. You don't know a damn thing about the mother she'll be."

Her eyes flicked back to Gail. "Maybe there's a reason she can't make her own baby."

"Maybe there's a reason that a daughter of yours shouldn't raise one."

The woman's mouth dropped open, but before she said anything else, before Jon could say anything else, he turned and walked stiff-legged back to his seat. Gail finished her call and hung up. He sat down. His pulse hammered, and Carli's mom glared at him from the corner. He kept his face as neutral as he could, but he stared right back.

"Is that—"

"Yes."

"What did she say?"

"Nothing, really."

"Should I go—"

"No," he hissed.

"I feel like I should go say something, introduce myself."

"I really don't think that you should."

Gail looked at Carli's mom for a long moment. "Jon. What did you say to her?"

Jon looked from Gail to Carli's mom and back to Gail. His legs still trembled with rage, but he forced a smile. "Nothing, really."

Paige

*

aige ambled into the waiting room and took stock of things. Marla Brennan claimed one corner, looking, as always, like she was trying to shit a cinder block. The Durbins staked out the other. Hopefully they hadn't talked to each other. Everybody always worried about that first meeting, but it was usually at the hospital that things went to hell.

She gave the Durbins a quick once-over. Adoptive parents often didn't realize how important it was to put their best foot forward on the big day, no matter how many times she told them. Gail got the message, though. She wore a long black skirt and an ivory silk blouse. And she even managed to unscruff her husband a bit—no holes in his jeans, and his plain, black T-shirt bore no references to Space Invaders or Blue Öyster Cult. She met so many couples in her line of work, and she always tried to figure out how they fit together. With the Durbins, the pieces didn't seem to lock tight. Gail could use a cheeseburger or four, but she was beautiful in that dark, Sicilian way. He was all elbows, knees, and shaggy hair. Even with bonus points for the three-day stubble, he only brushed against handsome. Paige decided to start with the Durbins.

"Hi, Gail."

Gail looked up from her notebook. Her eyes were darting, but she managed a smile. "Paige!"

Jon peered through his bangs. "Hey, Paige."

Paige settled into the chair across from them. "How you guys doing?"

"Nervous," Gail admitted.

Jon just nodded.

"That's only natural."

"How is she?" Gail asked.

"I checked in with the nurses," Paige said. "I think we've got a bit of a wait ahead of us."

"Do you have the adoption petition?"

Paige patted her bag. "Right here."

"And when will you—"

"Henry will file it tomorrow."

"What about the home study?"

"Next Friday."

"What about—"

"Relax, Gail. It's all handled. This is your big day. Try to enjoy it."

Gail looked as if she wanted to argue, but nodded.

Paige glanced at Marla and then turned back to the Durbins. "Carli's mom is over in the corner."

"Yeah," Jon said. "I introduced myself."

Shit. Paige took a long look at him. He stared back with an intensity she hadn't seen from him before. "How'd that go?"

Jon shrugged noncommittally. "What's she doing here?"

Gail looked at him, puzzled. "She's her mother."

Jon frowned. "I mean why isn't she in the delivery room with Carli?"

Paige was wondering the same thing. "I'm not sure," she said quietly, and then smiled in that way intended to help adoptive parents see that she was an experienced professional, trained to handle anything, to control the uncontrollable. "But I'm going to go sit with her and find out."

Marla just grunted at Paige's initial questions, so Paige pulled her yarn and needles from her bag, sat with her, waited her out. The mothers of birth mothers always responded in one of three ways: supportive, sad, or pissed off. The purple vein pulsing at Marla's temple, the way she squeezed a crumpled coffee cup in her fist, told Paige she was dealing with anger. Gail's parents arrived. Paul and Eleanor, if Paige remembered right. Marla studied the four of them for a long time, and then glared again out the window.

"It ain't right what you done," Marla said at last. She waved her hand toward the door, toward the Durbins. "All of this. It ain't right."

Paige counted three breaths before answering. "Carli came to us, Marla. She said she wasn't ready to be a mother."

"I guess she was ready to fuck."

"It's not my place to comment on that." Paige looked sideways at Marla, tried to figure out what would work with this one. "All of that aside—do *you* think Carli's ready to be a mother?"

Marla turned from the window and glared. "It ain't your place to ask that neither."

"It was an honest question," she said. She softened her voice. "I want to know what you think."

Marla tugged at her sweatshirt and looked at the door. "I don't guess that anybody's ready," she said. "Least not till they have a baby."

Paige could sense Marla remembering, and her gut told her that those memories were hard ones. She decided to let Marla stew in them, and they sat quietly like that for several long minutes.

"He came over."

"Who? Jon?"

"He thinks his shit don't stink."

Paige looked up at the Durbins. Gail scowled at her mom. Jon sat two chairs away, studying his phone. Gail's dad was taking photos of plants.

"They're good people," Paige said quietly.

Marla opened her mouth and closed it several times before she spoke. "I don't give a shit what kinda people they are. They're taking my grandbaby."

Gail

*

Gail's mom sat next to her, too close, bent over her nails with a file, sharpening her talons. She still dyed her hair, of course. But the color of it just served as counterpoint to the toll that the gin had extracted upon her face before she finally quit. She layered makeup over the veins that snaked across her nose but couldn't quite cover the crow's-feet that clawed at her eyes.

But the day was one for new beginnings. Her mom had left messages all week, checking to see if Gail had heard anything about the baby. Gail hadn't returned any of those calls, but now she resolved to be patient with her mom. Maybe becoming a grandmother would allow her to start over, too. Besides, her mom was the price of her dad's presence. He sat opposite, his glasses perched on his nose, struggling with the settings on his camera. He practiced shots of the potted fern across the room and studied the results on the display. His thick calluses made the tiny buttons and knobs difficult.

"How'd you pick Mercy?" her mom asked. She looked around the waiting room, her mouth puckered as if she'd eaten something sour.

"It's halfway between Elmhurst and Morris," Gail said.

Gail creased her notebook open and uncapped her pen. Her hand needed to move. It would help her breathe.

"Morris? Is that where Carla's from?"

Breathe. "Her name's Carli."

Gail paged back and forth between two lists. *Things We Still Need from the Store* and *Baby Names*, but everything was crossed off the first, and she needed fewer names, not more. Dominic was her boy name, but she still vacillated between Amelia, Harper, and Maya if they got a girl. Jon was adamant that he didn't want to learn the gender until the baby was born, but he couldn't seem to muster an opinion about names. She was leaning toward Maya, which meant *generous* in Old Persian, *love* in Nepalese.

"Carli? I thought her name was Carla."

Breathe. "No. It's Carli."

"Where the hell is Morris, anyway?"

"An hour west. Out past Joliet."

Gail turned to a blank page. Her fingers gripped the pen, but her hand didn't move. Nothing more to plan. No decisions to make. No tasks to manage. But her hand needed to move.

"Carli. From Morris. I guess that figures."

Breathe. "Can you keep your voice down, please?"

"Why?" her mom asked without lowering her voice. "What's the big deal?"

"That's Carli's mom over by the window."

Her mom looked up from her nails and swiveled to get a good look. "The fat hippie?" she whispered.

"No, that's Paige from the agency," Gail said, working to contain a smile. She had to admit that something about Paige's quilted knitting bag, her shapeless flowered shift, and her frizzy, gray hair made her look like an aging hippie. "Carli's mom's in the sweatshirt. Please don't stare at her."

Gail's mom studied the other woman. "She looks rode hard and put away wet."

"Eleanor," Gail's dad said without looking up from his camera.

"I'm just saying."

"How far along did they say she was?" her dad asked.

"It'll be a while," Gail said.

"You took your sweet time," her mom said. "Five hours I pushed you. Felt like you were clinging to my uterus."

"Eleanor."

So much for new beginnings. Gail's hand started to move. She titled the list *Now*. She described the clothes that everyone was wearing. She cataloged the magazines on the table. She listed the types and colors of the cars she could see in the parking lot. She invented names that Benjamin Moore might assign to the color of the rain: *Quicksilver, Granite, Wrinkled Gray, Sharkskin*. She recorded how each part of her body felt. *Head: too large. Hands: sweaty. Stomach: heavy. Shoulders: knotted. Eyes: watery. Feet: ticklish. Arms: empty.* None of her lists drifted into the past or the future. She listed *now*, because *now* was what she had planned for, *now* was what she had waited for. Paige was right—this was her day, and she wanted to experience every detail of it. And Gail had been wrong—she *could* make a list out of waiting.

"How long are you taking, Jon?" Gail's mom asked.

Jon looked up, dazed, from his phone. "What do you mean?"

"From work. How long are you taking off?"

"Oh. Two weeks."

"You excited?" her mom asked.

The raccoon eyes flitted from Gail's mom to the ground to the door and then back to her mom. "I am." He slipped his phone into his pocket and picked up his coffee from the table. "A little nervous, too, I guess."

"Of course you're nervous. You should be. This is the biggest day of your life."

Jon leaned forward, his elbows on his knees. He looked down at the swirl of cream in his coffee. Gail could see the cup shake just a little.

"Mom," Gail said.

"Everything's about to change. Ev-er-y-thing. I remember when I had Gail, it hit me like a freight train."

Jon forced a smile that wasn't a smile.

"I thought I was ready," she said, nodding at Gail. "But when that slimy little—"

"Mom, I don't think you're helping."

"I'm just saying. Nothing's ever going to be the same once that baby comes through that door."

They waited three more hours. Jon mostly stared at his phone. Gail's mom told stories about her own pregnancy that Gail didn't want to hear. Gail's dad remembered how to use his camera, and Gail did her best to remain in the present. It helped when her parents left for a coffee refill. She knew all the things that could go wrong, but that was one list that she refused to make. When a nurse in scrubs finally bustled through the door, she made eye contact with Gail for the briefest moment, but she gave nothing away. Gail grabbed hold of Jon's hand, and only by squeezing it could she stay in her chair.

The nurse walked to the far corner and sat down opposite Carli's mom. Gail stopped breathing and strained to hear, but she could make out nothing. Carli's mom got up and followed the nurse back through the door. Paige put her knitting into her bag. First the scarf she was working on. Then the yarn. Then the needles. Gail resisted the urge to go pack the bag for her. By the time she hoisted it to her shoulder, Gail had grown dizzy. As she approached Gail and Jon, a grin emerged.

"It's a girl," Paige finally said.

A sound somewhere between a laugh and a hiccup escaped from Gail's mouth. She leaned into Jon, and he squeezed her tight.

"It's a girl," Gail whispered.

"Everyone's healthy?" Jon asked.

"Yes. Everyone's healthy."

Jon kissed Gail's neck.

Gail whispered again, "It's a girl."

"I need to go do the paperwork." Even Paige's eyes were misting. "I need her name."

"Maya," Jon said suddenly.

Gail looked at him. He blinked and managed a smile. This was the first opinion about a name that he'd been able to muster, but it felt right. Love. Generosity. She turned back to Paige. "Maya."

"Maya." Paige let the word hang in the air for a moment, as if testing it. "Maya Durbin. That's pretty."

Paige carried her knitting through the door. Gail couldn't manage any more words, but none were required. Their baby was born. After everything they had gone through, their baby was born. Gail could feel her through the walls and the doors. She was alive, and she was well, and her name meant *love,* and her name meant *generosity.* Gail squeezed Jon's hand, and he squeezed back tightly. Their daughter was Maya.

Carli

*

Carli lay in the recovery room, listening to the awful chirps from the machines and staring at the photograph on the opposite wall, a close-up of a mother's lips touching a baby's forehead. That picture told her that she was in the wrong fucking room. Twice, she almost asked the nurse to take it down, but she couldn't quite form the words.

She sucked ice water through a straw and tried to focus on the pain. Every time her mind started to wander, she shoved it back toward the pain of the delivery, because that pain was clear and safe. The contractions had come in waves, like her gut was churning broken glass. She tried to focus on the memory of the hairy mole on the forehead of the nurse who was in her face, yelling at her to breathe and to push, as if she was screwing up even that. The contractions hurt so much that in comparison, the needle in her spine felt like cool relief, and although the pain became fuzzier after the epidural, the weight of it still crushed her to the bed. As she lay there, sucking on the straw, her mind kept wandering, and she shoved it again back toward the pushing and the screaming. She couldn't let it get near the murmurs of the doctors after the pushing stopped, after the warm, wet slurp of the birth. She couldn't let it sneak toward that tall, skinny nurse who slipped from the room with a bundle in her arms while Carli's body still quivered, pushing out the afterbirth. Now, everything below her belly button tingled numb, but just under that numbness lurked the fierce ache that waited for her when the epidural wore off. But the worst had already hit her—the epidural didn't do a thing for the emptiness.

The recovery-room nurse appeared at the door with her kind smile, and Carli was finally going to ask her to take that picture down, but Marla followed with her jaw locked and her eyes hard. Carli tried to concentrate on the machine noises. The nurse looked from one of them to the other, and her smile faltered.

"I'll give you two some time," she said quietly as she left the room.

Carli glanced at Marla, tried to read her, but her face was locked into a mask that told Carli nothing. Marla's gaze drifted from the machines to the extra bed to the television. Her eyes settled on the picture of the woman kissing the baby's head. When she spoke, her words sounded all chewed up.

"So it's done, then."

"Yeah." Carli's own voice seemed far away, like somebody else talking.

"Where's the baby?"

"Huh?"

"Where's the baby?" Marla asked again, and now the words had a rumble beneath them that Carli knew too well. Marla finally looked at her, and the mask had fallen away. Her nostrils flared, and her eyes drilled Carli. Carli turned away.

"I asked you where your baby's at."

"I told them I don't want to see it."

"I didn't ask you what you told 'em, and I don't give a shit what you want."

"I can't," Carli said, but Marla probably didn't hear her because she said it quietly, and when Carli turned back toward the door, Marla was gone. Carli closed her eyes, tears began to leak, and the empty place throbbed.

Several minutes later Carli heard loud voices down the hall, and the loudest was Marla's. And then it got quiet again. When Carli opened her eyes, she was startled to see Marla back in the doorway, holding a pink bundle in her arms. Carli tried to ignore what Marla carried, but she couldn't pretend it away.

"I can't," she whispered.

"You will."

Carli turned her head back toward the empty bed.

"Before you give her away, you're gonna look at her."

She heard Marla move closer, and Carli knew that she wasn't going to leave until Carli looked at the baby. And then she heard a crinkly sound, and she turned, and she looked, and the baby's face was just a foot away, and its eyes were squeezed shut, and she could see a little bit of its tongue between its lips, and she smelled just a whiff of vanilla cream soda. Carli forced herself not to reach out and touch the baby's face, and she forced herself to roll back over and stare at the empty bed across the room. After what seemed like a very long time, she finally heard the door swing shut. Carli clutched the sheets in her fist and tried to summon the memory of those moments just before the epidural, when she had felt like she was splitting apart. But that face changed everything. The pain had become useless. That face made everything real in a way that terrified her, and she knew that the pain, even at its very worst, wouldn't be able to help her forget.

Jon

*

After an hour passed with no word, Jon felt as if he were floating, like he was back in that trailer waiting for his mom to stir, playing her Joni Mitchell albums to ward off the silence and the sound of that pit bull. Jon paced the room, looked out the window, came back and sat down. When an hour became an hour and a half, Gail texted Paige but got no reply. She chewed the end of her pen but wrote nothing more in her notebook. Eleanor paged through a *Reader's Digest*. Paul fiddled with his camera. As the two-hour mark neared, Gail became very still.

"It isn't supposed to take this long," Gail said quietly.

Jon felt the urge to touch her but somehow knew that he shouldn't. He felt like he should say something, but he knew that it would come out wrong. Gail thought it was taking too long, while Jon worried that it was all happening way too fast.

Jon stared at the chair where Carli's mom had been. She seemed so familiar, in that way of a dream or a distant memory. He looked out the window at the rain and then back at the chair. He tried to remember without trying too hard to remember, because that sometimes worked. And then it hit him. Aqua Bay Resort. Carli's mom looked like the woman who glared at him every time he went to the office at Aqua Bay.

He couldn't remember why they went there in the winter— the Lake of the Ozarks was deserted in the off-season—but he remembered that the word *resort* didn't fit, and he remembered the smell of the mouse shit and cigarettes and the greasy feel of the brown shag carpet on his bare feet. It might have been in pursuit of a man or a job or just another one of his mom's loopy ideas that never panned out. He remembered the bright blue paint peeling off the little cabin and the screen door that had no screen and the slate gray of the lake, but he couldn't remember whether it was November or December. He remembered the heap of groceries his mom bought the day they arrived— mostly mac and cheese and hot dogs and canned ravioli—and the mounds of dirty clothes that grew as the pile of groceries shrank. He remembered the glare that the hulking woman in the office gave him when he went to buy Skittles from the vending machine with the change that he picked from the bottom of his mom's purse. He couldn't remember how he knew that his mom had recently gone off her meds, but he knew.

The TV broke the first week, but his mom didn't call the office to have it fixed, because by then she had gone quiet and still, huddled under the covers, just watching him move about the cabin. Jon wore all the clothes his mom had packed for him. He wore them three times before their stench became too much. Then he just wore his underwear, and he wrapped himself in an extra blanket he found in the closet. When he wasn't cooking or eating or looking out the window at the cold, gray lake, he wrapped himself in the blanket and wedged himself in the crack between the bed and the wall, because the squeeze of it felt almost like a hug.

Jon knew that they were getting low on food when all he could find in the pile of wrappers and trash on the counters was canned ravioli. That night, when someone pounded on the door, Jon thought it was that terrifying woman from the office looking for money, so he stayed wedged in the crack between the bed and the wall. His mom stirred but didn't get up. When the door opened, the cold air tickled Jon's face. He heard the covers rustle, but for a moment nobody said anything, so he didn't yet know who had come for them.

"Where is he?"

And then he knew it was Aunt Carol. He still didn't say anything or move, and he didn't know why. Jon's mom didn't say anything, either, but the bed creaked, and Jon imagined her propping herself up, to get a better look at her sister.

"Goddamn it, Melissa," Aunt Carol shouted. "Where the hell is he?"

Nothing but silence for a long moment. "He's here," his mom whispered, her voice hoarse from disuse. Those were the first words he'd heard from her in a week. "He's here somewhere."

Jon didn't know what made his aunt Carol eventually look in the crack between the bed and the wall, but he'd always remember the way his aunt's face melted toward relief when she saw him staring up at her from the gloom. And he would never forget how strong her arms felt when she lifted his skinny little eight-year-old body and squeezed him tight to her chest. And Jon often remembered looking over his aunt's shoulder at the rage on his mother's face—the first real emotion she'd seen from her since they arrived at Aqua Bay.

Jon knew what would come next. After a long, quiet car ride back to St. Louis, they dropped his mom off at the trailer with a garbage bag full of her dirty clothes. And then Aunt Carol drove Jon and his own garbage bag to the tidy little ranch house on a cul-de-sac that she shared with Uncle Mark. She sent him to the shower with a clean towel and brand-new pajamas that fit him just right. When he crawled into the bed in the guest bedroom, the sheets felt so clean and crisp that they didn't feel like sheets at all. When she came in to make sure he was asleep, he didn't open his eyes. He didn't move even when Aunt Carol's papery lips brushed his forehead, because he knew that they would, because that's how it always happened.

Aunt Carol didn't wake him up until a little before noon the next day, and that's how he knew it was the weekend. If it was a weekday, she would have gotten him up at seven thirty and sent him to the school near her house. Some of the kids would remember him from the last time, but none of them would talk to him much, because they knew that he would only stay a couple of weeks. That's how long it would take for his mom to get herself cleaned up and back on her meds and her refrigerator filled, so that Social Services wouldn't ask too many questions.

When he came out to the kitchen still wearing his pajamas, Aunt Carol was making a grilled cheese sandwich, because she knew that was what he would want. He sat at the table and watched.

"Do you want one sandwich or two?" she asked.

"Just one."

Jon fiddled with the placemat. Aunt Carol flipped the sandwich.

"How are you feeling this morning?"

"I'm OK," he said over the sizzle. And then, although he wasn't quite sure why, he said, "I miss my mom."

Aunt Carol faced the stove, but he could see her stiffen. "I know, honey," she said. "It must be hard to be away from her."

"She's been gone awhile."

Aunt Carol stopped moving for a long moment and then checked the underside of the sandwich. She slipped it onto a plate, brought it to the table, and set it in front of him. She sat down across from him, blinking. Her face looked a lot like his mom's—the same too-small nose, thin lips, and eyebrows that almost met in the middle. The main difference was that Aunt Carol's face moved, twisting more often into the shape of what she was feeling. Jon bit into the sandwich, closed his eyes, and bit into it again before he even swallowed. He was so hungry, and it was so good, that he didn't hear what Aunt Carol said next. She had to repeat herself.

"What did you mean, by that—when you said she's been gone awhile?"

While he chewed and swallowed, he tried to think of the right words to describe what he meant. "It's like she's there, but she's not."

Aunt Carol squinted at him. Jon tried to find more words to help her understand.

"Sometimes she's really still and quiet, watching me all the time. Other times she can't stop talking or moving, and she doesn't look at me or listen to me at all."

Jon took another big bite, and he began to wish that he'd asked for two sandwiches. Aunt Carol's eyes got shiny.

"Which one is your mom?" she finally asked.

"What do you mean?"

"The quiet one or the one who can't see you?"

"Neither," Jon said immediately.

"Neither?"

"In between is my mom."

"In between?"

Jon nodded. "When she stops taking her pills. Or when she starts. For like two days."

Aunt Carol's face collapsed. She swiped her eye with the back of her hand.

"For two days she can see me, and she can move, and she touches me and talks to me and listens to me, and we play games, and she plays her guitar, and we sing together, and one time we made one of those construction-paper chains that was so long it probably could have gone around the whole block."

Jon studied Aunt Carol, hoping that his words would stop her tears. Aunt Carol pulled her knuckles out of her mouth long enough to say, "Two days?"

Jon nodded. A smile tugged at the corner of his mouth as he remembered how his mom looked in those two precious days. "She sparkles." He put the last bit of the sandwich into his mouth, chewed, and swallowed. "I save it up for the rest of the time." He peered at his aunt, to make sure that she understood. "I save up the sparkle."

By the three-hour mark, Gail had closed her eyes and gripped the arms of her chair as if she meant to break them. Jon went to the bathroom and emptied his bowels yet again. When he came back, he sat down next to Gail, put his hand on top of hers.

"This is how it happens," Gail whispered.

Jon glanced again at the door. Yes, this is how it was going to happen.

"It's taking too long. All the websites say this is the most dangerous time."

"Gail—"

"Right after. This is when they change their minds."

"Why are doing this?" Jon asked. "Why do you always do this?"

But Gail just stared at the door. She didn't say anything more. She sat very straight in her chair and just stared at the door.

Just before midnight, the door finally swung open, and Paige came through, looking wrinkled, holding a bundle in a pink blanket. Jon's pulse doubled its pace. Gail opened her eyes and sucked in a breath. They all stood. Nobody said anything. Paige handed the bundle to Gail, and she peeled the blanket from the baby's face. "This is Maya."

The face blotched red, and tiny wisps of wet hair jutted from under the pink cap. Her nose was turned up at an impossible angle, her eyes were closed, her mouth open. She looked like she was about to sneeze, but she didn't. Paul's camera clicked and whirred, and Jon heard Paul ask them to look up and smile, but Jon couldn't tear his eyes away from the baby's face. Eleanor mumbled something, and the shutter clicked, and Paige said that maybe they should sit down, but they didn't. Gail looked at Jon. Tears drained into the corners of her smile. "Wanna hold her?" she asked.

Jon said nothing, and a bubble of fear swelled in his throat. He reached out, and Gail placed Maya into his arms. Her head fit into the crook of his elbow, and she was lighter than he expected, like her bones were hollow. He swallowed, and the fear still clogged his throat. But alongside it wedged something like a giggle or a warm shower or the bass line at the start of a

Doors song. Paul badgered him to look up for a picture, but Jon ignored him. His daughter. The future roared. He finally looked up, not at Paul, but at Gail, and she asked him, "What do you think?"

He looked back down at Maya. Maya. Four letters that just a week before blended in with the Emmas and Sophias and Evas that Gail had pressed upon him. When Paige asked, he'd blurted it out without thinking. It just felt right. Now his baby was named Maya, and Maya had a face, and that face was specific. It demanded his attention, and it belonged to his daughter. And that name added weight to the bundle in his arms. He was terrified that he would drop her or fail her. He looked up at Gail, and he summoned a smile.

"She's ours," he managed. Even to Jon, his terror sounded a lot like wonder.

Gail pressed close. Eleanor wiped tears with a tissue. Paul focused and clicked. Paige stood apart from the rest of them, folders of paperwork clutched to her chest, staring hard at the door she had just come through.

Gail

*

All the nurses, doctors, and machines with blinking lights made Gail feel safe in the hospital. After Paige told Gail that Carli had been discharged, she felt even safer. Gail had insisted on a closed adoption—she just couldn't imagine sharing a child with another mother—so they would never see Carli again.

Gail held Maya, and Jon held Maya, and they fed her, and they stood at the glass with their noses pressed against it. Gail's mom and dad stopped by, but thankfully they didn't stay long, so Gail and Jon only had to share Maya with the nurses. Gail couldn't wait to get Maya home, but when, after a day and a half, the hospital let them take her, it all seemed terribly abrupt. They signed the discharge papers, and a nurse gave them the baby and said they could go.

"That's it?" Jon asked.

"That's it," Gail said.

The sliding glass doors whooshed open, and they walked through with Maya. Just like that, they were out in the world.

"It just seems like there should be some sort of training process," Jon said. "Some sort of certification."

"We'll figure it out. Where'd you park?"

Jon stood on the curb scanning the sea of cars, looking utterly lost. "This way," he said. "I think."

They walked up and down three rows of cars but couldn't find theirs. "Did you park in the garage?"

He shook his head, scanned the lot, changed directions again. Gail followed, carrying Maya. She couldn't help wondering how they would care for this little human if they couldn't even find their car in the parking lot.

"It's just that we've been here so many times over the last few days," he said. He held the key fob up on the air, pressed the unlock button. "There should be a manual at least."

"For finding your car?"

"No. A baby manual. A how-to. Frequently asked questions. Something."

Gail smiled to herself. She'd read dozens of books about what to expect, what to buy, how to get your baby to sleep through the night, how to potty-train. She learned how to cure diaper rash and colic and scabies even. She'd read the FAQs on hundreds of websites. She left a few of the thinner books on Jon's nightstand, but they all found their way back to her own unread. She was certified. She could probably write the manual that Jon was asking about, but he wouldn't read that, either.

"We'll be fine."

Finally, their car chirped from two rows over. Jon loaded the gear into the trunk. Gail settled Maya into her car seat, and Maya immediately began to cry. Gail strapped her in. She cried louder. Gail loosened the straps. Maya screamed.

"What's wrong?" Jon asked.

"She's crying," Gail said. "That's what babies do."

But even as Gail said this, she unbuckled the straps. She lifted Maya out of the seat, made sure that nothing was under her, lowered her back in. She only cried louder. Gail buckled the harness again, adjusted the straps. "She'll probably stop once we get moving."

Gail climbed into the back seat next to Maya. When the car started moving, Maya kept screaming. Jon peered into the rear-view mirror. "Is she hungry?"

"I fed her right before we left. Keep your eyes on the road."

Tears streamed down Maya's scarlet face. Gail tried to slip her pinky into Maya's hand, but her fists squeezed tight. Gail knew it was all perfectly normal for Maya to cry, but she wondered if it was normal that she wanted to cry, too.

"Does she need to be changed?" Jon asked, his eyes twitching in the mirror.

"I changed her right before we left. Drive."

With every cluster of traffic, with every red light, Maya renewed her protests. Jon kept glancing up. "Can you just try feeding her?"

"Fine," Gail snapped. She pulled a bottle from her bag and poured water from the thermos. She dropped the nipple onto the floor. She scrabbled through her bag for another. She'd heard babies cry before, but the truth was, none of the books she read, none of those websites prepared her for the knot in her stomach when the crying baby was her own. She finally found another nipple and attached it to the bottle. She shook it and tried to ease the nipple into Maya's mouth, but Maya's lips remained stubbornly closed. When Gail took the bottle away, Maya screamed even louder. Jon accelerated.

When they careened onto Myrtle Street, Gail saw the sign that someone had planted in the front yard next to the redbud tree. WELCOME HOME, MAYA!, it shouted, the pink letters almost matching the blossoms on the tree. Pink balloons bounced in the wind. Gail relaxed just a little bit. Jon parked, hopped out of the car, and opened the back door. His hands shook as he unbuckled Maya and lifted her out. He cradled her to his shoulder and patted her back, but she screamed. He walked back and forth on the driveway, whispering into her ear.

Gail unlocked the front door. Jon paced back and forth in the front room, then the dining room, patting Maya's back, whispering. He tried funny faces. She screamed. He handed her to Gail, and Maya wailed. They checked her diaper, but she was dry. They tried another bottle. She screamed. They took her temperature with the ear thermometer and with the one that swiped across her forehead, but they both read normal. Maya's face grew purple from the screaming.

"Should we call the doctor?" Jon asked.

"And tell him what?" Gail asked. "That our baby is crying?"

"I don't know," he said. "She was never like this at the hospital."

"Jon, we can do this," Gail said, for herself as much as for Jon.

Jon played his guitar and Maya screamed along. They tried laying her in the crib, but that didn't last long. They tried the rocking chair. Gail sang to her, and Jon even tried the Cookie Monster hand puppet, but she just cried louder.

An hour and a half after they arrived home, Gail held Maya in the sunroom and stared out the back window at the buds on the maple. She considered the unthinkable: calling Cindy, or worse yet, her mom, for advice on their first day home. Maya was still screaming when Jon came up behind Gail and wrapped his arms around them both. Her crying slowed as he swayed all three of them back and forth and hummed "Helplessly Hoping." She settled to a whimper as Jon kissed her on the crown of her head. Just before Jon whispered "I love you" into Gail's ear, a blessed silence settled upon the house.

Carli

*

Carli put Band-Aids on her nipples before she put on her bra. Nobody had warned her about the leaking, and her first day home, two warm wet circles of milk had soaked through her shirt while she watched TV. It took her a while to find pants that fit. All the maternity clothes that Gail bought for her were too big, and her jeans from before were all too small. She finally settled on a pair of black sweatpants. Black, in case she bled.

When she came down the hall into the front room, she found her sister, Wendy, and her boyfriend, Randy, sprawled on the couch, their legs tangled on the coffee table. The curtains were closed against the sunlight to protect the hangover they were inevitably nursing. Randy was playing a video game—first-person shooter by the looks of it—while Wendy painted her fingernails. Randy was tall, quiet, his red hair buzzed short. Wendy looked a lot like Carli—the same dirty-blond hair, freckles, the blue eyes set just a little too far apart—but everyone had always called Wendy the pretty one. Carli knew it was Wendy's confidence, her arrogance really, that made people say it.

"Marla just left," Wendy said, her voice husky from lack of sleep. "Which is good for you, because something must have crawled up her ass."

Randy chuckled, but maybe he just belched. His thumbs danced across the game controller, and his eyes never left the TV.

Wendy was ten when she first started calling their mom Marla. It was the day that Marla kicked Wendy out of the car for spilling a soda and made her walk the last mile home. Wendy never called her Mom again after that, and Carli, just eight at the time, followed Wendy's lead. Marla never said anything about it—she pretended not to care—but Carli sometimes saw Marla stiffen a bit when she heard her first name like that.

"Where you goin'?" Wendy asked.

"Pickin' up my check," Carli said.

"Stop at Seven-Eleven on the way home. I need a pack of Camels."

"And a Red Bull," Randy said. He hacked up something solid and swallowed it back down. He never took his eyes off the screen.

Carli cranked the dead bolt and opened the door. Wendy looked up, squinted into the light. "And stay the hell away from Marla. She's got that look."

Carli gripped the black pipe railing and eased herself down the three concrete steps. Stairs made the stitches pull. When she lowered herself into her Corolla, she sucked her teeth. Eighteen years had taught Carli to expect little from Wendy, but they were sisters, and as she drove to Giamonti's, she couldn't stop thinking about everything that Wendy didn't say, what she never asked. It was like she had done her best to ignore all the puking and the eating and Carli's bulging belly. She never asked about the strange lady in the Subaru who picked her up and dropped her off. She didn't say anything about the hospital or the baby or the leaking milk. For Carli, everything had changed, but *I need a pack of Camels* was the best Wendy could manage.

Carli turned into the strip mall and pulled up in front of Pay Day Loans so that nobody from work could watch her struggle out of the car. As she walked past the empty storefronts where Kinko's and Blockbuster used to be, she tried to walk normal, but it was hard to remember what normal felt like.

When she looked through the tinted glass, past the row of empty booths, she saw red hair behind the counter and froze. Marissa. Andy was with Marissa before Carli, and she turned nasty after Carli and Andy hooked up. Carli's hand rested on the door handle, and she thought about coming back the next day, but she needed that check. She pulled the door open, and the bell rang. Marissa looked up and saw Carli. Her dull blue eyes brightened. One corner of her mouth lifted a bit.

Carli avoided looking at the clowns as she made her way to the counter. Tommy Giamonti's wife decorated the place back before she died of colon cancer, and Tommy wouldn't let anybody change a thing. Nobody could explain why she chose the clown theme, but between all the beer mirrors hung pictures of clowns. Photos and drawings, color and black-and-white, large and small, all of them clowns.

"How you feelin'?" Marissa asked when Carli got to the counter.

"Fine," Carli said. "Is Matt in today?"

"Nope. Rick's the manager."

Marissa *and* Rick. She should have called first. She walked past the counter, through the empty, greasy kitchen. She heard pans clattering in the dish room. She made her way to the tiny office in back near the time clock. Rick rattled the keys on the adding machine with one hand and traced a column of numbers on a sheet of paper with the other. He wore his red Giamonti's polo shirt and black jeans. His wispy yellow hair strained to cover his bald spot. His face, as always, bloomed as red as his shirt, as if he was angry or had been holding his breath. When he finished with the numbers, he leaned back in his chair against the file cabinet and looked her up and down. "Well. If it isn't the handmaid herself."

Carli worked to keep her hands away from her belly where the empty place was beginning to stir. "I came for my check."

"'Course you did," Rick said, but made no move to get it. "Everything turn out all right? Ten fingers? Ten toes?"

"Can I please just have my check?" Carli said. She focused on the Corvette calendar above Rick's head.

"Sure. Of course." He started to work the small safe. "Just wanted to make sure everything went OK. You know me—always trying to make sure that the customers are satisfied."

Carli looked away, toward the ovens, and then back to find an envelope in Rick's hands.

"Should I put you back on the schedule?"

Carli thought about the stitches and the dull ache that coated everything, but she also thought about her tuition bill and credit card minimums and her car payment. "Yeah. Any day but Wednesday. I got class on Wednesday."

"Right." His lips twitched. "College girl."

He tossed her the envelope, but she missed it, and it fell to the floor. Rick swiveled back to the adding machine and resumed pounding the keys. Carli eyed the check before bending awkwardly to get it. She stretched against the pain. Just as she picked up the envelope, she felt a sharp pull at the stitches, and she swallowed a breath. When she stood and walked toward the front, she felt blood trickle down her leg. She walked past the register, past Marissa, without a word.

"I saw Andy last night," Marissa said to her back.

Carli said nothing and kept walking. The clowns leered.

"He asked me if you really gave away his baby."

The leg of Carli sweatpants was warm and wet and sticky. She pushed through the door. Marissa said something else, but it was drowned out by the sound of cars rushing by on Division.

Jon

*

Jon looked for Gail. He padded around in his socks, searching all the logical places, trying to keep quiet. The old house made noises that he'd never noticed before. He was finding the floorboards that creaked, the steps that groaned. He thought Gail might be sitting in the nursery watching Maya nap, making sure that Maya was still breathing. She wasn't there, but he stood at the door for several minutes, watching Maya nap, making sure that Maya was still breathing. Gail wasn't in the kitchen fixing something to eat. She wasn't in the front room, consulting her lists or making new lists. She wasn't in the office, sorting through paperwork, filing things away. He finally found her in the bedroom, lying on the bed, hair spread across the pillow, hands folded across her stomach. Her eyes were closed, but he could tell by her breathing that she was awake.

"What's wrong?"

She smiled but didn't open her eyes. "Nothing. Nothing's wrong."

"You need me to get anything from the store?"

"No. We have everything."

And the way she said *everything*, the way she licked the syllables, drew them out as if they were three separate words, told Jon that she didn't just mean formula and diapers and lunch meat and milk. And the way that her lips settled back into a relaxed, gentle smile, convinced him that, for the first time in a long time, nothing was wrong, there was nothing to solve. He lay down on his side of the bed, careful not to let it creak. Gail shimmied over and snuggled in next to him, her head tucked into his armpit, her leg across his. He couldn't remember the last time she'd ventured to his side of the bed.

"She's perfect," Gail said.

"I thought that she was never going to stop crying."

"They do that."

He'd known, of course, that babies cry. All their friends' babies cried, and the babies in the Jewel cried, and there was that baby on that flight from Chicago to San Francisco who didn't stop crying for four hours. But it had always just been noise, an annoyance, and he'd always thought embarrassment turned the parents' faces red. But when Maya started to cry in the car, his whole body seized up and his breath came in gulps, as if he had emphysema, or rabies. His jaw still ached from the clenching. Every scream sounded like failure.

"It's amazing, isn't it?" Gail, asked.

"Huh?"

"She's right in there. In the next room. And she's ours."

He still couldn't get used to the feel of her in his arms, so light and so heavy at the same time. Her skin was so soft and so thin. She squinted at him as if she recognized him, as if she was blaming him for something already.

"And scary."

"Yeah." Gail snuggled in closer. "A little scary, too."

That baby was counting on them for everything. Foc
clothes, shelter, college. And what if he lost her or dropp
her? "You sure you don't need me to get anything?"

And just then it started. A tiny whimper and then a cou
and then it gathered to a full-throated scream. Gail gigg
"Just Maya."

They both got up and walked into the nursery. Gail plu
Maya from the crib and carried her to the changing table. "]
her hands while I change her."

Jon gripped her tiny hands, while Gail peeled off th
per and wiped Maya down. He knew that he should be v
ing, that he needed to learn how to do it, but Maya's fi
wrapped around his pinky and distracted him. They we
tiny grown-up fingers, perfectly shaped, and she squee
pinky tighter than he expected. The neighbor's golden re
barked. He wriggled his finger, tried to ease it from her g
Maya held on tight. And then Gail was done, and he had
his first training session entirely. He picked up Maya a
her carefully, tight enough to keep her from falling, bu
tight that he would break her.

"You get the next one," Gail said.

"Yeah," he said. "See, I've never really done that befc
if she squirms off the table?"

"She won't," Gail said. "You won't let her."

Jon eyed the changing table. It was way too high.
just lay Maya on the floor until he figured things out

"My parents are coming over tomorrow morning
Jon groaned.

"I know," Gail said. "She was like a bill collector. C
two hours."

"We could have blocked her number."

"I held her off for a day. Best I could do."

"We could move," Jon said. "Run away. Somewhere she can't find us."

"Mexico," Gail murmured. "Or Canada." Gail pulled her phone from the pocket of her jeans and frowned. "Paige called."

"What does she want?"

"I don't know. You feed Maya, and I'll find out."

Gail left, and Jon looked helplessly around the room. Finally, he set Maya back into the crib where she'd be safe. He grabbed a bottle, scooped formula into it, and ran to the bathroom to fill it with warm water. He could hear Maya begin to squeak and raced back, shaking the bottle as he went. He set the bottle on the windowsill next to the rocker and then rushed to the crib in time to pick Maya up before she started to cry. He sat down in the rocker and held her awkwardly on his lap. He eased the nipple between her lips, and she sucked greedily. He wondered what Paige wanted. He wondered how he was going to manage when Gail left the house, because she would leave the house eventually, probably for hours at a time. He wondered if this was the panic that sent his dad west before Jon could crawl. But Maya's eyes closed, and she sucked, and one of her tiny little hands rested on his forearm. Then she patted his arm just a bit as if to say, *Daddy, everything's going to be OK.*

Carli

Carli climbed the stairs carefully, gripping the rail. The blood had dried crusty, and her sweatpants stuck to her leg. When she pushed through the front door, she found Randy still scorching earth. Wendy had moved on to her toenails.

"Did you get my cigarettes?" Wendy asked.

"I forgot," Carli mumbled.

"What about the Red Bull?" Randy asked, leaning forward, eyes locked on the TV, thumbs pumping.

Carli ignored him and walked down the hall to the bathroom, where she stripped, careful not to look at herself in the mirror. She stepped into the shower, and scrubbed her thighs and calves, her tears mixing with the blood. When she was clean, she stood under the water with her eyes closed until it ran cold.

Back in her room, she put her sweatshirt back on and another pair of black sweatpants. She wanted to lay down on her bed and curl into the fetal position, but she knew that she would only cry some more and squeeze that empty place just beneath her ribs. She might not get back up for a long time, so she forced herself to pack her backpack. Her phone vibrated on the dresser. She saw it was Marla, so she ignored it, because she couldn't deal with that right now.

Wendy didn't look up from her toes as Carli passed through the front room. "Where you going now?" she asked.

"I'm gonna study."

Wendy made a face. "Have fun. And don't forget my smokes this time."

"And the Red Bull," Randy said.

"And call Marla. She keeps calling me asking where the hell you are."

Carli started going to the Denny's up by the interstate a couple of weeks into the semester. It was impossible to study at home. And Denny's was all truckers and old people, so she could eat and study without seeing anyone she knew. She turned off her phone and slipped into her regular booth, grateful for the padded seat. Anita, her usual waitress, drifted over, chewing gum, her eyes glazed. She pulled a pen from her helmet of black hair and flipped open her order pad.

"The regular?"

Anita was another reason Carli came to Denny's. Anita didn't ask unnecessary questions. "Yeah. The regular."

Anita drifted back to the kitchen without another word, scribbling the ticket. Carli cracked her textbook open to the chapter on social psychology. She had a lot to catch up on before her next class. Anita brought her a cup of coffee, and Carli picked up where she left off.

The section about *social roles* was easy reading. Carli had been living this section since third grade when her best friend, Kelly, moved to Morris. Kelly was short and loud and smiled a lot, and her last name was Benedict, so she sat near Carli in nearly all their classes. The textbook said that each social situation entails its own set of expectations about the "proper" way to behave, and ever since Kelly arrived, she set those expectations for Carli, Andrea, and Madison. She set expectations about how to wear their hair and which shoes were cool and which boys were OK to talk to at recess. In high school, she set expectations about which parties were worth attending and which boys were worth sleeping with. Kelly did not expect Carli to get pregnant, and she certainly didn't expect Carli to stay pregnant. Kelly made it clear without saying anything that she didn't expect to spend much time at parties with somebody wearing maternity clothes. Carli learned to expect fewer and fewer responses to her texts and calls until they dwindled toward none. Andrea and Madison fell away with Kelly, just as Carli expected. She still wasn't sure what to expect now that the baby was born and gone.

Interpersonal perception—how people form beliefs about one another—was just as easy to digest. Everyone she knew had been forming beliefs about her for the last seven months. Kelly and Andrea and Madison and Marissa and Rick and Marla and Wendy and Randy and even Anita, leaning against the counter now, whispering with one of the other waitresses, had formed their beliefs. A whole bunch of beliefs were formed on Wednesday when she waddled out of class dripping water on the floor.

She also knew too much about *fundamental attribution errors*—the idea that people blame mistakes on your character rather than your circumstances. Wendy thought she was a fuckup. Madison thought she was a fuckup. Marla thought she was a fuckup. Pretty much everyone she knew thought she was a fuckup. She had a little more trouble sorting through *self-serving bias*—the idea that individuals tend to credit their character for their success and blame their situation for their failures. She couldn't think of any recent successes, so she set that part aside. Mrs. Axelrod, her high school counselor, had prattled on about intergenerational teen pregnancy and broken homes before Carli earned her GED and dropped out, but Carli never bought into that bullshit. Truth was, she agreed with Marla and Wendy and Madison and the rest: she was a fuckup.

Carli was swimming through a dense section about self-perception and introspection when Anita finally delivered the plate of eggs and toast and hash browns. "Who's watching the baby?" Anita asked.

Carli blinked up at her. Just like that, Anita had ruined it. Carli would have to find a new place to study. She searched for an answer, and Anita waited. "My mom," she finally said. "My mom's watching the baby."

Gail

*

That first afternoon passed in a blur. Before Gail knew it, she was sitting in the armchair in their bedroom, feeding Maya her last bottle before bedtime. She read *Goodnight Moon* while Maya lazily sucked the formula. When the bottle was done, Gail put it and the book on the floor, and settled in to hold Maya until she slept. The sunlight had given way to dusk, but the small lamp on her dresser glowed yellow. Jon sat propped on the bed in a T-shirt and boxer shorts, watching them. Maya yawned and squeezed her eyes tight. She squirmed, pushing her arms against the blanket, working to get comfortable.

Gail's own arms were still, relaxed, more relaxed than they'd been in the years they'd been waiting. She felt like she was finally taking her life off pause. They had moved to Elmhurst too soon. She knew that now. Ever since they moved from Paulina Street she'd fallen into an endless loop of lists and anxiety and waiting that consumed her in a way that she hadn't fully felt until Paige placed Maya into her arms at the hospital. As Gail accepted that eight pounds, when she smelled that ripe pear smell, it was like life sharpened, like it shifted back into balance, like all her expectations had hardened into certainty. Maya would free her to reconnect with friends and start running again and read a novel instead of another book about what to expect or another website about grief. She felt greedy as she sorted through the possibilities.

When Paige called earlier to see how they were doing, Gail wanted to tell her that everything was different now. The porch was where she would feed Maya when the weather was nice, and Maya would play there when she was older, and she might even kiss a boy on the swing. The TV would now play more Barney than Blackhawks. The kitchen, where two people used to eat by themselves, largely in silence, would now echo with squeals and laughter. The table would be smeared with mashed peas and carrots. They would sing "Happy Birthday" and talk about homework and soccer and ballet and boys.

She wanted to tell Paige that the nursery seemed especially transformed by Maya's arrival. While they waited, it had seemed so terribly empty, an open sore, reminding her that she couldn't bear a baby of her own, that she must wait for someone else's baby. She wanted to tell Paige that when she placed Maya into the crib for a nap, the nursery felt suddenly full and complete. The green of the tortoise on the rug, and the yellow on the giraffe that formed the letter X on the border around the top of the room, and even the stripes on the Cat in the Hat's hat seemed perfect.

Instead, Gail just told Paige that they were fine.

Gail slowed her rocking as Maya's breathing slowed. She looked up at Jon, who was watching her, watching them. He still looked terrified. He seemed afraid that he would break Maya, afraid that he'd fail. It reminded her of when he taught himself "Sultans of Swing." He struggled with that one. His usual dexterity seemed to desert him. It took him two weeks of You-Tube videos and constant noise from his office before he finally conquered it, and for those two weeks he wandered the house cursing Mark Knopfler and muttering about selling his guitar. She would be his YouTube for this. She would help him melt the fear. She would convince him that he wasn't his mother.

Gail stopped rocking, stood, and carefully placed Maya into the bassinet at the foot of their bed. She squirmed a little, but then settled. Gail climbed into bed and snuggled up next to Jon, where he lay in the middle. They'd spent too long curled on their opposite edges—ever since those raccoon eyes had started flitting about, Jon had crept away from the center. This, too, felt right—meeting in the middle again.

"Beautiful," he whispered.

"Huh?"

"Sitting there. You and Maya. So beautiful."

Gail smiled into his shoulder. For the first time in a long time she *felt* beautiful. They lay quietly. Gail matched her breathing to the rise and fall of Jon's chest. She thought about her notebook on the bedside table. Every night she reviewed her lists, checked things off, added new items. Not tonight, though. There were still a few calls to make, a few loose ends to tie up, but for now, they could wait. All the important things were lying in the room with her. She closed her eyes and breathed Jon's musky scent, and for the first time since they moved from Paulina, she fell asleep in his arms.

Jon

*

That first night home, Maya woke every two hours. They took turns feeding her, but they both woke up every time, and every time it took Jon a while to get back to sleep before the next squall came. Gail seemed to expect this. All the books must have told her to expect it, but Jon had read none of the books, so he wondered how long it would last.

The hospital was so polluted with the odor of disinfectants and latex that he couldn't properly smell Maya there. At home, though, Jon could filter the familiar smells of their house from the smell that was Maya. Milk Duds. He turned on the tiny lamp on the dresser while he fed her. He studied her features, trying to sort out what she'd look like when she was older. Other people's babies all looked the same to him. It wasn't until after a year or two that they became distinct humans. But the slope of Maya's nose and the furrows on her forehead when she took the bottle couldn't belong to anyone else. And those fingers. They gripped his pinky so tightly that it almost hurt.

Halfway through the night, Jon finally saw the point of a bassinet. They didn't quite argue about it, but in the previous months he had asked Gail again and again why they needed two places for the baby to sleep. Her explanations made no sense, and after a while, she just smiled and said, "Trust me." It seemed foolish to park a crying baby *closer* to their bed, but now he knew that he would wake at Maya's slightest noise, no matter where she was in the house. Best to have the baby handy when he rolled out of bed, groggy. Besides, with Maya in the room, he could smell the Milk Duds as he drifted off to sleep.

The last shift came a little before dawn, the gray light prying through the blinds. Jon was exhausted, like after a hockey game with a short bench, but he was starting to make out the shape of what would come next. Maya's fingers tugged at him. And when he put Maya back in the bassinet and fell back into bed, he spooned up against Gail. All night they had touched. Gail's hand against Jon's hip. Their knees kissed. Both of them far from the edges.

Carli

*

Carli studied too long. She drank too much coffee, which just made it all worse. Still, her eyes kept closing. She could hear every fork click every plate and every mug clatter onto its saucer. And the laughing. Everyone in the restaurant seemed to be laughing, but when she opened her eyes, the people at the other tables all looked angry or sad, like late-night Denny's people always looked. She started to pack her books into her backpack when Anita came toward her. Anita was laughing— that's who it was—but she wasn't carrying Carli's check, she was carrying a baby.

"I have to go," Carli said. Anita must have thought that because Carli just gave birth that she'd want to see someone else's baby.

Anita smiled down at the infant. "She's beautiful. Look at her."

Carli zipped her backpack and ignored the pain as she scooted across the bench of the booth. "I really have to go."

"Look at her," Anita said. She blocked the end of the booth with her body, with the baby. Anita seemed confused, hurt even. "Why won't you look at her?"

Carli tried to push her way out, tried to stand, but Anita shoved her back into the booth with her hip. She wasn't smiling anymore.

"Before you give her away, you're gonna look at her," Anita said, but now Anita's voice was Marla's. Carli looked at the baby, and it was *her* baby, the same blotched, squinting, delicate face that Marla had thrust at her in the hospital. Carli started shaking, and she couldn't take her eyes off that face.

"Get up," Anita said in her not-Anita voice, but Carli couldn't move. She just stared at the baby's face.

"Get your ass up now!"

Carli woke and saw Marla staring down at her. Carli was still shaking, and in the half-light of dawn she could see the angry cut of Marla's mouth, but she could also still see that baby's face, like a bright light had burned it into her retina.

"Where the fuck were you last night?"

"Denny's," Carli said. She didn't tell Marla that after Denny's she went to the ten o'clock movie in Batavia. The latest Batman. Batavia so that she wouldn't see anybody she knew. The late show to be certain that Marla was asleep when she got home. Batman so that she didn't have to think. "I was studying."

"Why didn't you answer my calls?"

Carli said nothing. There was nothing to say.

"Get up," Marla said again as she turned to the door. "Get dressed. We need to talk."

Carli pulled on sweatpants and a sweatshirt and then drifted into the kitchen. Marla was at the table, wearing a flannel shirt, hunched over a mug. Carli sat down gingerly across from her.

A folder lay on the table. The logo on the front had green arms holding a blue baby.

Marla lit a cigarette, inhaling deeply. "How you feelin'?"

Carli tried to remember the last time Marla asked how she was feeling but came up blank. How *was* she feeling? She got four hours of sleep, her whole body ached, her crotch felt like it had been weed-whacked, and her breasts were leaking useless milk. Worse, though, was the emptiness. She eyed the folder.

"Fine," she said.

Marla set her cigarette in the ashtray, opened the folder, and took out a single sheet of paper. Carli knew it was the only piece of paper left in that folder, but she read the top of the page anyway: *Final Consent.*

"You were one when I left your dad. Wendy was three."

"Marla—"

"Let me talk," Marla growled. Carli blinked at the piece of paper that Marla clutched between her tobacco-stained fingers. "Your dad came home drunk like he always did, but instead of hitting me, he hit Wendy. Because she was crying too loud."

Carli had always assumed that it was her dad who did the leaving. Marla never talked about him. She and Wendy had stopped asking about him long ago, because whenever they did, Marla always fell into a sullen silence.

"I worked three jobs when you was little." Marla grabbed the cigarette, took a long drag and blew the smoke toward the ceiling. "I wasn't ever around."

Marla held the cigarette between her lips, folded the paper, first in half, and then in half again. "I didn't get to be a mom," she mumbled. "Not really." She looked down at the paper, folded it once more, and then looked back up at Carli. "I ain't gonna miss out on being a gramma."

Marla took a deep pull on her cigarette and held the edge of the paper to the glowing tip. Carli wanted to reach out and snatch it from Marla's hands, but she couldn't move. It went black and then red, and then a yellow flame finally fluttered. As the paper burned, the empty place inside of Carli twisted and curled at the edges right along with it. Marla held it until the fire licked at her fingers, and then she dropped it into the ashtray where it crinkled, the flame died, and the ashes, black and orange, flaked and settled into a heap.

"You woulda regretted this if I let you do it."

"I don't think I'm ready," Carli whispered.

Marla looked at her for a long time, and the line of her jaw seemed to soften just a little. "Ain't nobody ready, Carli."

"Marla. I—"

"You got a choice." Marla stood, tucking her cigarettes and lighter into the pocket of her jeans. "Either get that baby back or find some other place to live."

Gail

*

G ail heard her parents climb the porch stairs a little after
ten. Jon was up in the nursery trying to change Maya's
diaper all by himself. She couldn't bear to watch.

"They're here," she yelled.

"Awesome," came the muffled reply.

They rang the doorbell, and Gail forced herself to take a few
deep breaths before opening the door.

"You're going to need this," her mom said, handing her a
coffee from the cardboard tray. She wore a velour tracksuit,
but her makeup was caked on like usual. "You look exhausted."

"Thanks," Gail said.

"Hey, buddy," her dad said, giving her a peck on the cheek.
He wore a button-down shirt and his church shoes, a nod to the
solemnity of the occasion. He handed her a present with a pink
ribbon. "You look great."

"Thanks, Dad."

"You're supposed to look tired," her mom said. "Serves you
right. You didn't sleep through the night for the first eight months."

And she had colic, and she had chicken pox twice, and it took her six months to potty-train. Gail had heard it all before.

"By the end of the first week, I was ready to put a pillow over your head."

Jon came down the stairs with Maya, and Gail's mom smiled. "Of course, that was before husbands changed diapers. And I was recovering and nursing. Let me see that baby, Jon."

Jon handed Maya over, and Gail's mom sat down on the couch and cooed softly. *I was recovering and nursing,* her mom said. *Unlike you,* she didn't say, but that's what she meant. Gail put the gift on the coffee table and sat down across from her mom, resisting the urge to pluck the baby from her.

Gail's dad settled on the couch next to her mom. He studied Maya for a long moment, as if memorizing her features. Then he rubbed her palm between his calloused thumb and forefinger. "She's got good hands, Gail."

Then, to Jon, he asked, "How are *you* doing?" Her dad had a gentleness about him, careful from decades of handling sharp edges, and people often said things to him that they wouldn't say to others. Gail kept her eyes on the baby but tuned to Jon's answer.

"It's—" He paused. "It's not what I expected—"

He sounded like he was going to say more. Gail waited to hear what he had expected, and how Maya stacked up against those expectations, but Gail's mom cut him off.

"I love her eyes," she said, bent over the baby. "They're beautiful."

Maya squinted up at her doubtfully.

"How can you tell?" Gail asked. "They're not even open."

"They look like Jon's."

Gail's dad shifted uncomfortably.

"And her nose." She looked up at Gail. "She's got your nose."

"Mom. Stop."

"What?"

"Eleanor," her dad said quietly.

"What?"

"She's adopted, Mom."

"Of course she's adopted. I'm just saying that it's not obvious."

Gail tried to steady herself.

"It's all right if it's obvious, Eleanor," Jon said. "She's beautiful just like she is."

"Of course she's beautiful. I'm just saying that nobody can tell. People will see the three of you and not even know."

"And that would be better?" Gail's voice felt brittle. She took another breath, gripped the cushion of her chair. "Nobody knowing?"

"Gail," her dad said.

"No, Dad. We waited a long time, and I won't have Mom ruin this, too."

"We *all* waited a long time," her mom said, looking pointedly at Gail.

"What does *that* mean?" Jon asked.

"I'm just saying. I was fertile in *my* twenties."

"Eleanor," her dad said, finally raising his voice.

Gail clung to the cushion. Her mouth worked, but the words wouldn't come.

"So," Jon said. "If we didn't wait so long, you'd be holding a real granddaughter. Is that it, Eleanor?"

They all froze and stared at Jon. He stood up.

"Gail's right," he said quietly, almost to himself. "Try as you might, we're not going to let you ruin this."

Gail's mom sat stunned as Jon lifted the baby from her lap. He settled Maya into Gail's arms, and their eyes locked. When he spoke again, Gail felt like he was talking only to her, like her parents weren't even in the room. "I think that we're exactly the family that we were meant to be."

Gail rocked Maya to sleep for her nap. She could tell it wouldn't take long. It seemed that her mom exhausted Maya, too. While she rocked, she remembered the look on her mother's face when Jon put her in her place, and she smiled. He'd never done that before—by unspoken agreement it had always fallen to Gail to push back against her mother.

Maya was dead asleep when Gail lowered her into the crib. She didn't even stir. Gail made her way to the bedroom, where Jon lay on top of the covers, his eyes closed, his mouth open, breathing evenly. The early-afternoon sun slanted through the front window. Gail paused at the door for a moment, then gathered her hair and tied it in a knot on the top of her head. She walked to the window and lowered the blinds. She undressed and stood next to the bed, watching Jon breathe. She climbed onto the bed and straddled him, careful not to wake him. She lowered herself to his ear and licked it. He stirred. She kissed his lips, and he smiled, but his eyes remained closed. His hands found her thighs bare and his eyes popped open.

"You weren't asleep, were you?" Gail whispered.

"No." He smiled. "I was just resting my eyes."

He shifted as she peeled off his T-shirt. She kissed him again, and his hands searched. She grabbed him by both wrists and pinned his hands next to the pillow, shaking her head. His smile widened. She kissed his chest and his belly, and then pulled off his jeans and his boxers. He was ready. She climbed back on top and she guided him inside of her slowly. It had been a long time.

His eyes closed, and his face tightened with concentration. Up and down gently until they found that fit, and then she dropped onto him with all her weight and arched her back. He propped himself up, reaching for her breasts with his mouth, but she pushed him back down, held him down with her hands on his chest. His hand groped, and she grabbed his wrists again, pushed them under the pillow. The tingling warmth started near her knees and pushed up her spine, toward her neck. Faster and slower and then just faster, and Jon's eyes squeezed tight and his mouth fell open. They both somehow managed not to make a sound, and they both strained with it and against it. When they finished, she lay against him, crouched on top of him, her cheek against his sweaty chest, feeling, more than hearing the pounding of his heart. He wrapped his arms around her, and this time, she let him.

They lay like that for a long time, their breath slowing. Jon stroked her back and kissed the top of her head. Finally, she slipped off him, dangled a leg over his, snuggled her head into his shoulder.

"Motherhood becomes you," he said.

It felt nice to lay naked and warm against each other again. It had been too long.

"Remember Paulina?"

"Yeah," he said. She could hear the smile in his voice. "I remember Paulina."

"I want to go back there."

Jon shifted, but said nothing for a moment. "I thought you liked it here."

Gail smiled. He could be so literal.

"I'm not sure that would be such a good idea—with a baby," he said. "Parking. Schools."

"I don't want to move," she said. She thought about takeout from Jade Garden and how they used to finish each other's sentences and the easy, natural way they had. That's what she wanted, the way they fit with each other on Paulina, without effort, without the heavy silences and puzzled looks. "I want it to be like Paulina *here*."

Jon kissed her on top of her head. "Me, too," he said, and she could tell by the way that he squeezed her tight that he understood. "Me, too."

Carli

*

Carli hung up the phone and wrote up the ticket: a large sausage and a medium pepperoni for delivery. She stamped it with the time and set it on the ledge of the window to the kitchen.

"Order!"

Phil, the cook, grabbed the ticket, glared at her like he always did, and disappeared to make the pizzas. The dinner shift had been easy for a Saturday—more delivery orders than eat-in—and Carli already had most of the mess cleaned up. She usually scrolled through her social media feeds in between delivery orders, stalking Kelly and Madison and Andrea, watching life go on without her. But she had turned off her phone hours ago because of Paige's persistent texts and calls, so mostly she just stared out at the headlights on Division and tried to avoid the eyes of the fucking clowns. On Carli's best days, she could laugh at the clowns, but tonight, their toothy painted grins seemed to laugh at *her*.

She tried not to think about what Marla had done to her that morning. Carli hadn't given the final consent a second thought until Marla pulled it from the folder. It was just another piece of paper she would sign. It wasn't another decision to make. She'd made all the decisions seven months ago, closed the doors on all of them. She'd been leaning against those doors to keep them shut ever since.

When Carli found out she was pregnant, she wasn't sure how to broach it with Andy. She texted him first—she thought it might help to give him some time to digest the news before they spoke. He didn't reply, and when she called him, he didn't answer. That night, Andy didn't show up for his shift. A few days later, she heard that he quit Giamonti's and was helping his cousin clean carpets. They never really talked about it, but it in the end it didn't matter. The fact was, she knew before she sent that first text that he wasn't the kind of guy who could manage satisfactory answers to the questions that she never got to ask him.

Almost a year before Carli became pregnant, Andrea had found herself in the same situation. Carli drove Andrea to Ottawa for her appointment. She didn't remember what the front of the clinic looked like, but it was sandwiched between an art gallery and Caribbean Tan. She couldn't remember what the protestors looked like, but she couldn't forget the hard edge to their voices as they shouted at Andrea, and the horrible pictures on the signs that they waved. She couldn't remember how long she waited, but she remembered that only the receptionist spoke in that waiting room, and everyone avoided eye contact. She remembered everything about that long, quiet ride home. Andrea turned off the radio as soon as she got into the car. She stared out the passenger window at the cornfields that lined Route 80. When Carli asked if she was OK, she didn't answer. When Carli dropped her off at home, she didn't say anything— she just climbed out of the car and slammed the door. When Carli was making her own decisions, every time she thought about that clinic in Ottawa, those awful pictures and that silence kept her from dialing.

In a way, Carli made the decision to give the baby up for adoption before she even knew that she was pregnant. At the end of her junior year, she got her scores from the SAT that all the kids had to take. She shoved the envelope into her back-pack and forgot about it. Mrs. Axelrod didn't call her down to meet until right before summer vacation. That was the first time they ever really had a meeting—usually she just checked to make sure that Carli was taking enough classes to graduate. And before that day, nobody had ever asked what kind of career Carli had in mind, which was just as well, because Carli had always thought in terms of jobs, not careers. It took her a long moment of silence to work up the courage to say *nurse* out loud. Mrs. Axelrod talked about bell curves and percentiles and free college. She talked about Carli's above-average intelligence and unlimited potential. When Mrs. Axelrod said, "But I'm sure that you already knew all that." Carli didn't say anything. *Unlimited potential. Above-average intelligence.* Carli did *not* know all that. She had taken standardized tests every year since first grade, but if Marla ever looked at the results when they came in the mail, she'd never said anything. And when Carli's teachers said things like *I expect more from you, Carli,* it had always felt like they were yelling at her for screwing something up rather than challeng-ing her to reach her potential. Throughout the summer, Carli couldn't stop thinking about that talk with Mrs. Axelrod. Those three words—*nurse* and *college* and *free*—rattled around in Carli's head. She couldn't stop seeing that line with her name attached to it, slicing across the skinny part of the bell curve. The word *nurse* snagged in her throat, but it tasted good.

It was August, just before Carli's senior year started, when she brought it up with Marla. Wendy and Randy were out, and Marla was in the den, stretched flat on the recliner, watching *Hardcore Pawn.* She gripped a Mountain Dew in her fist, and an ashtray with a lit cigarette balanced on her stomach. Carli sank into the couch.

"No way he's buyin' that shit," Marla said.

The pawnshop owner, a bald, bearded man with a diamond earing, was ignoring the jewelry on the counter. Instead, he was squinting at the skinny man with acne and bad teeth who stuttered through an explanation about where he got the loot.

"They never buy from the meth-heads."

Carli watched for a while, trying to think about how to ask her question using the fewest number of words. "Can I see your W-2?"

Marla picked up her cigarette and took a drag from it. For a moment, Carli wondered if Marla heard her over the television. She was about to ask again.

"Whattaya want that for?"

"For school?"

"Bullshit." Marla drank from the Dew. Her eyes darted toward Carli. "I pay my property tax. That's all your school needs to know."

"I need it for the FAFSA."

"The FAF-what?"

"The financial aid form for college."

Marla barked a laugh. "You ain't goin' to no college. What the fuck is wrong you?"

"Mrs. Axelrod says—"

"Who the hell is Mrs. Axelrod?"

"My counselor." Her words, Mrs. Axelrod's words really, tumbled out in a rush. "I scored real high on the SAT, and she says that with my test scores and merit aid and need-based aid I can probably go to college for free."

Marla picked up the remote from the arm of the chair and pressed Pause. The pawnbroker froze on the screen, his eyes pinched to slits, his mouth open, his finger pointing at the customer.

"There ain't nothin' free. That lady's blowin' smoke up your ass. Probably wants my social so she can load you up with loans for me to pay."

Carli stared at the pawnbroker, tried to think of words that Marla might hear. "I just need—"

"You *just need* to get your head out of your ass. And you *just need* to shut the hell up so I can watch my show."

Marla held the remote in the air, glared at Carli with her eyebrows raised, waiting to make sure that the conversation was done. When Carli said nothing, Marla hit Play and turned back to the TV. Carli climbed off the couch, walked quickly to her room, and slammed the door.

She didn't sleep that night. She trembled with rage, but you can only stay mad for so long before it wears you out, so toward dawn, she started making decisions. She decided that she would search the attic and the cellar and Marla's room to see if she could find the W-2 herself. She decided that when school started, she would meet with Mrs. Axelrod again, to see if there was another way. And she decided, no matter what it took, no matter what she would have to give up, she would never end up like Marla.

*   *   *

Almost a month after that night—after she had searched unsuccessfully for the W-2, but before she met with Mrs. Axelrod again—that heavy, greasy feeling in the pit of her stomach and a puddle of vomit in the school parking lot sent her to CVS for a pregnancy test. When she told Marla she was pregnant, Marla called her a stupid bitch and didn't say another word to her for a week. During that week, Carli scoured the Internet. She studied pictures of smiling couples trying not to look desperate for a baby. As she sorted through those pictures of beautiful homes and well-scrubbed people, she tried to imagine raising a baby on her own, and all she saw was a dingy apartment with cigarette butts in coffee cups and Mountain Dew cans on the windowsill. She saw Marla. The fourth night, she made that decision, and then firmly shut the door on it.

The Open Arms Adoption Agency showed up first in the search results. She filled out the "Contact Us" form, and Paige called her back an hour later. When they met the next day, she liked the way that Paige listened as much as she talked. Her eyes remained glued on Carli while Carli spoke, and when Carli finally asked *her* questions, Paige answered them with a gentleness that startled Carli. She left the agency's office with a stack of books. Carli tried to sort out what each couple was saying and what they weren't saying in those pages. She narrowed it down to four and then three and then two. She googled the towns and the school districts and asked Paige a ton of questions. Finally, she chose the Durbins. After she met Jon and Gail at the diner, she cried for hours, not because of anything particularly horrible about Jon and Gail, but because she had to cry. And then she called Paige. With that call, she closed the final door.

Carli took two more phone orders, and on both, she had to ask the callers to repeat themselves. She couldn't stop thinking about that morning. Marla probably wouldn't really kick her out of the house, but there was no telling with Marla. That would sort itself out one way or the other, but she couldn't stop thinking about that baby's face in her dream. Her gut burned like that paper in the ashtray. Carli had made all her decisions, and she was edging her way toward a different life, a better life, but now Marla was trying to force her to decide all over again. And worst of all, she couldn't stop smelling vanilla cream soda.

The bell jangled, and a little boy stumbled through the door, followed by his mom carrying a car seat. Carli recognized the spiky blond hair and the tattoo of vines and flowers that wrapped the mother's bare arm down to her wrist. This family came in about once a week, sometimes for lunch, sometimes late, like tonight, never with a dad. The mom always looked exhausted, and she always yelled at the little boy. She pushed her son into the booth near the window and set the car seat on the other bench. Carli grabbed menus and made her way to the front of the restaurant. She forced a smile, placed the menus on the table. "Hey there."

"One second," the mom said without looking up from her phone. "Make up your mind, Lucas—pepperoni or sausage?"

Carli tuned out the pizza argument and allowed her gaze to linger on the baby. The little girl grinned at Carli while at the same time eating her own fingers. Her eyes locked on Carli's and they wouldn't let go, and the empty place fluttered.

"Congratulations," the mom said.

"Huh?" Carli grunted, tearing her attention away from that face.

She nodded toward Carli's stomach. "Last time I was in here, you were about to pop."

Carli stared at the woman for a long moment before she could make her mouth work. "Thanks," she mumbled.

"Boy or girl?"

And suddenly Carli felt like she should explain everything, but she wasn't quite sure what she would say. She'd have to tell the lady that the baby belonged to other people now, and that would get complicated. She was certain that the woman's face would harden, and then Carli would be forced to sit down in the booth across from the woman and sob.

"It was a girl."

Was. Not *is.* She said *was,* and the word tasted like a rotten tooth, but the woman didn't seem to notice. Instead, she glanced at her own daughter and then glared at her son. "You got lucky. Girls are easier."

Paige

*

Giamonti's opened for lunch at noon on Saturday, so Paige waited until twelve fifteen to call. A girl that wasn't Carli answered the phone, so Paige just hung up. She filled a travel mug with tea and trudged reluctantly to her car. When she first started as a social worker, she made the rule: no weekend work. It was the type of job that could take over your life if you let it. But Carli wasn't answering, and if Paige didn't find her, she'd just stew on it all day, and her Saturday would be ruined anyway.

Twenty-four hours of emails and calls and texts—to Carli, who never went anywhere without her phone. She was probably checking Instagram when she birthed Maya. Hell, she might have been texting somebody while she conceived her. But now she was refusing to answer her phone. So Paige had to follow her GPS southwest out of the city to where the corn grows, in order to collect the signed final consent. Thing was, Paige didn't like her odds.

Her career numbers were nothing to sneeze at. One hundred and twelve successful adoptions spread across almost two decades in the business. Paige counted herself responsible for several dozen saved marriages, hundreds of graduations, thousands of birthday parties, and innumerable tantrums about crusts that weren't cut off peanut butter and jelly sandwiches. Just eight times things went sideways. Better than 93 percent. An A on any grading scale. An absurd batting average. She didn't know another social worker with better numbers, not that it was contest.

But it wasn't the numbers that mattered the most to Paige. Every success reminded her why she did this thing. When new parents held their baby for the first time, she could always feel the room vibrate with the energy of a new family being formed. She had a drawer full of pictures of her kids as they grew. That's what she called them, *her kids*, even though she usually only spent a few minutes with each. Most of them never even knew Paige's name, much less the critical role that Paige had played in their lives. But Paige knew.

Paige kept another drawer of pictures. It wasn't as full, but those photos made her just as proud. Her girls, the birth mothers she helped through the process, sent her pictures when they graduated from high school or college or when they got married. The adoptions were always hard for the birth mothers. That deciding. That letting go. When she did her job well, she could help her girls make the decision for the right reasons, and she could help them adjust to the idea that other people would raise their children. Her favorite photos in that second drawer showed her girls holding the children that they were finally able to raise themselves.

For all the success, Paige remembered every one of those eight failures viscerally, and she always remembered the warning signs. If this one ended up in the loss column, Marla would be the red flag. Usually the mother of a teenage birth mom was

all up in Paige's business, fingering the books, asking questions about school districts, demanding answers about the process. All that noise proved comforting. When the birth mom's own mother was quiet, that was when she had to worry. And Paige didn't hear a peep from Marla throughout the pregnancy—until that night at the hospital.

Paige passed the rest area that came right before the Morris exit. The Chicago suburbs sprawled into farms far from the Loop, but it's difficult to say that you live in a suburb if you pass a rest area on the way to the city. The only other time that Paige came out to Morris was in the middle of the pregnancy. Carli's car had broken down, and Paige needed the paperwork that the birth father signed, so she made the drive. When Marla answered the door that day, Paige introduced herself. She offered her hand in greeting. Marla just glared down at her hand and then turned without a word, leaving Paige to wait on the front step for Carli.

All the houses on Carli's block looked depressingly the same. White clapboard shacks with concrete stairs planted in front. Only the degree to which the hedges covered the front windows and the age of the cars, some measured in decades, differentiated each. Paige pulled up in front of the house with Marla's old battered pickup truck in the driveway. Carli's Corolla wasn't there, but it could be in the shop again. She texted Carli one more time and waited in vain for a response. She called her, but it again rolled directly to voice mail.

Paige heaved herself out of the car and made her way to the house. When she knocked, she expected to wait, but the door opened almost immediately. Marla loomed, sporting a Dale Earnhardt sweatshirt and jeans. Her lips twisted around a sneer. Paige pasted on her standard-issue social-worker smile.

"Good to see you again, Marla."

"She ain't here."

Paige forced her smile steady. "Can you tell me where I can find her?"

"It don't matter."

"I'm sorry?"

Marla's coffee-stained teeth flashed. "Yeah. You are."

"How do you mean?"

"I told you at the hospital. What you did ain't right." Marla shook and snorted. "Glad you finally realized it yourself."

Paige should have kept driving when she didn't see the Corolla. Rookie mistake. "Can you tell her I came by?"

"She ain't gonna sign it."

Paige went still inside. Marla knew about the final consent. Paige had been counting on the fact that Marla wouldn't take an interest, that she would think that the process was done. Either Carli told her about the final consent, or somebody taught Marla how to use the Internet. Paige widened her smile.

"Thank you for your help, Marla." She turned to go.

"We want to reclaim the baby."

Goddamn it. She was even using the right words. Paige turned back to Marla and studied her more closely. "Carli hasn't told me about that. Why don't you have her call me?"

"I'm telling you now. I'm her mother."

"With all due respect, Marla, you're not Maya's mother. I work for Carli. Have her call me." She turned to go again.

"Bullshit."

"Come again?"

"You work for the fucking Durbins."

Paige felt the urge to set Marla straight, to tell her that she didn't take sides, but the hard glint in Marla's eyes told her that she would hear none of it.

124

"One way or the other, we're gonna get my grandbaby back."

With that, Marla slammed the door. Paige stood on the concrete steps for a long moment before turning to trudge back to her car. *One way or the other.* If Carli reclaimed, Paige knew from experience the long odds that she and Maya would face. And she knew that taking Maya from the Durbins would kick loose whatever it was that held Jon and Gail together. None of that mattered, though. The fact was, she didn't take sides. And the law sided with Carli. It didn't matter what Marla or the Durbins or Paige herself wanted to happen. During Paige's first few failures, she had made the mistake of hoping for a certain outcome. Long before the eighth loss, she had learned to push hope aside. Hope just made adoptions more complicated.

Paige started the car and tried not to think about Gail. This whole thing was going to shit—she could feel it. Maybe Carli would finally return her call, and they could talk this through. As she pulled away from the curb, she reminded herself not to hope for it.

Jon

*

Late Sunday morning, Jon sat on the bottom porch step, waiting for Gail. The stroller stood at the ready, and Maya slept, wrapped in a blanket on Jon's lap. Throughout the weekend, a steady stream of women came to see the baby. Kara came to see the baby. Gina and Allison came to see the baby together. Gail's aunt and her cousin came to see the baby. Jon called Aunt Carol, and she and Uncle Mark would drive up later that week to see the baby. Sunday, they would venture out into the world.

Jon couldn't fathom why they needed so much stuff to go six blocks for three hours. Gail had packed three pacifiers, five bottles, ten diapers, two packages of wipes, three burp towels, a camera, two changes of clothes, and a rattle that Maya didn't even know how to use yet. They would need a trailer when Maya started to crawl.

Jon studied the other houses on the block. The McKennas' youngest, who had just turned one, could become a friend of Maya's. The Jensens' three-year-old boy already had the look of a bully. The McConnells had three older girls who seemed likely babysitter candidates. The Pratt woman was pregnant, but Jon didn't know much about the Pratts. The fact was, he didn't know much about any of his neighbors. They learned the central truth about the suburbs early: until you have kids, you don't really exist. They had gone to the block party a few weeks after they moved in. Every woman Gail met asked her which kids were hers. Her answer was universally met with awkward pauses and quizzical looks. Each woman drifted off to check on her own kids or to return to one of the tight clusters of women near the jump house. Jon and Gail retreated back inside after an hour, and they avoided the next three block parties entirely.

They should have stayed in downtown Chicago, in that apartment on Paulina, until they were parents. Jon knew it when they moved, and although they never talked about it, he was pretty sure that Gail came to realize it, too. They had been happy on Paulina. They fit together there, even if the start had taken some adjustment. It was Gail's apartment before Jon moved in, and at first he felt like a fugitive in a foreign land. Cindy had moved out a few weeks before—to Elmhurst with Ted—but Jon could still smell her sickly sweet perfume, and he occasionally found blond hairs on his black jeans. Gail had simply smiled and shaken her head when Jon suggested he bring his couch with him. Gail's furniture tended toward pastel cushions and painted wood. Bowls of shriveled leaves and twigs that Gail called potpourri lurked on the coffee tables.

It helped to unpack his CDs and add them to the shelf that held Gail's tepid collection, but T-Bone Walker and John Lee Hooker seemed uneasy leaning against Whitney Houston. It helped when he set up his computer in Cindy's old room and propped his guitars and his banjo against the wall next to it.

It helped even more when he plugged in an air freshener to smother the stink of Cindy's Malibu Musk.

Their first party was an awkward affair, with his friends clustered around the keg and Gail's chattering loudly in the kitchen. Over time, though, their friends began to mix, and by the end of that first year, their parties were populated by *their* friends. Soon enough, they were arguing about who knew Greg first and who brought the Steve Miller CD to the shelf. Paulina became the meeting place, in part due to its strategic location. Almost equidistant from the Vic, Schubas, and the Double Door, they all met at Paulina before shows to drink and smoke. As they pushed through their twenties, the weed fell away with the concerts, and they all sat out back on the deck, drinking, laughing, and listening to the bands that they used to see live.

But Paulina wasn't always crowded with friends. Most of the time it was just Gail and Jon, and that's the part he remembers most vividly. They always seemed to be touching. Cooking stir-fry together in the too-small kitchen, watching Netflix all tangled up on the mauve couch, sprawled across the bed with the Sunday *Times*, nudging each other to point out something of interest. They touched last thing before one of them left and first thing when one of them returned. It felt so natural that he didn't really notice it until they moved to Elmhurst. After Gail got pregnant that first time, before the miscarriage, she called the Realtor on the sly. Before Jon realized what had happened, movers were carrying their stuff into the house on Myrtle. As that first year wore on, they seemed to forget how to touch each other. Maybe it was the size of the house compared to the Paulina apartment, all that space they suddenly found themselves not quite sharing. Maybe it was because they'd grown older. Probably it was the grit of the expectations that had sifted into the cracks between them and seemed to expand with each month, with each failure.

Jon worried a bit that a baby might come between them, driving them further apart, but he was wrong. He marveled at the changes that Maya had brought. Gail hadn't opened her notebook since Maya was born, and she seemed able to breathe deeply again. She was becoming the old Gail, the Gail from Paulina, in the way that she laughed and the relaxed slope of her shoulders and the easy way she moved around the house. More to the point, she no longer seemed to shrink from his touch. And when he wasn't expecting it, he found her hand on his forearm or felt her fingertips whisper across the back of his neck. He hadn't realized how much he missed the Gail from before all the waiting and failing and trying again until she came back. The baby *had* come between them, but like a magnet, pulling them back to where they used to be.

Gail finally came out on the porch and locked the door behind her. She wore makeup, a sundress, and a smile. "It's a nice day," she said.

It *was* a nice day. Almost seventy. It would drop back into the fifties the next day. "Seems a shame to ruin it with a trip to Ted and Cindy's."

"Nice try," Gail said. "We're already late."

Jon strapped Maya into the stroller and shouldered a backpack full of the gear that didn't fit in the basket underneath. As they set off, he felt like he was acting in a play. He'd seen hundreds of families pushing strollers down their street while he sat on the porch reading the paper or answering emails or drinking coffee, but he'd never really imagined manning the stroller himself. The handle felt too big in his hands. And when they walked through the little downtown by the train station, everything seemed new and strange. When they first moved from the city, he'd been disoriented by the town's cloying cuteness—the vintage movie theater, the bowling alley, the ice cream shops and nail salons in every other storefront. The bars attracted a strange mix of middle-aged alcoholics and students from the college. He and Gail only really liked one of the restaurants. The record store closed a few months after they moved in. Nothing in Elmhurst had seemed relevant. As he pushed his daughter down York, though, the smell of fudge drifted from the candy store, and he wondered which ice cream shop would become their favorite. And on the opposite side of the town center, as they turned onto Cindy's street and approached her yellow two-story, all the debris on the lawn—the bikes, the soccer ball, the Wiffle ball bat—seemed suddenly necessary.

Gail pulled Maya from the stroller and rang the bell. Ted opened the door wearing his barbecue apron and his toothy grin.

"There she is!" Ted said, cupping the side of Maya's face in his hand for a moment. Maya squinted at him.

"She's nice-sized," he said, as if measuring a fish. "What? Eight pounds?"

Gail smiled, accepted a kiss from Ted on her cheek. "Seven pounds, fourteen ounces."

"Come in, come in."

"Is that them?" Cindy shouted from the second floor. She turned the corner and rushed down the stairs. Cindy wore bangs, now, and sensible shoes. She was always a little heavy, but four babies had each left her with a few more pounds.

"She's beautiful," she whispered.

Gail surrendered Maya to Cindy. She blushed, and her mouth squirmed as she tried but failed to suppress a smile. She glanced quickly at Jon and then back at Cindy.

They drifted into the kitchen, where Cindy's youngest—Jon could never remember whether it was Teagan or Ryan—sat in a booster chair, eating chicken nuggets, his face painted with ketchup. The counters sagged under catalogs and sippy cups and half-eaten food, and the floor of the family room was littered with brightly colored plastic toys.

"What color beer can I get you?" Ted asked.

"I'm easy," Jon said. "Whatever you're having."

"Is that your baby, Aunt Gail?" the child in the booster chair asked.

"She is." Gail smiled. "Her name's Maya."

Cindy bent down to give the boy a good look at Maya. He reached out with sticky hands to touch her, but Cindy pulled Maya away.

Ted handed Jon a bottle. "I'm thinking the ladies can handle the dwarf. Why don't you help me burn meat?"

Jon followed Ted out to the patio and settled into a frayed wicker chair. He took a long swallow of his beer while Ted lit the Weber with a whoosh. He scraped the grill and wiped it down with olive oil while Jon watched Cindy and Ted's two oldest play tetherball in the back of the yard. Aidan and Olivia. He could remember the names of the older ones. Maybe because they'd been around longer. Maybe because with age, they had become more distinct. Like people. He couldn't remember the last time he'd seen someone play tetherball.

Ted sat next to Jon and took a drink from his own beer. "Used to be a charcoal guy," he said. He tilted his bottle at the kids. "Till they came along."

Contentment leaked from Ted. Even back when Ted and Cindy had just started dating, Ted had seemed like a dad—the mock turtleneck sweaters, the corny jokes, the receding hairline. It was probably what attracted Cindy to him in the first place. Back when they had all gathered at the Paulina apartment, Ted never quite fit in—he lingered at the edge of the circle. But on his cluttered backyard patio, wearing his apron, with a spatula in one hand and a beer in the other, although he hadn't changed a bit, he fit perfectly into the center of it all.

"How's she sleeping?"

Jon grunted. "Like a baby."

"So she shits and screams every two hours?"

"Exactly."

Ted nodded toward the house. "I haven't seen Gail like that in years."

Ted could see it, too.

"Yeah," Jon said. "She's waited a long time for this."

"I'm happy for her. For both of you."

Jon knew that he was supposed to say something in response, but he couldn't quite figure out what that was, so instead, he took another drink.

"How 'bout you? How you doin'?"

Ted was persistent.

"I'm good," Jon said. "It's great."

Ted laughed. "Sticking with the party line . . ."

Damn right, he was sticking with the party line. Jon knew that anything he said would find its way to Cindy and then Gail and then right back into his lap. "It's awesome."

Ted took a long drink and leaned back in his chair. "Let's pretend I'm not your wife's best friend's husband for a minute."

Jon glanced at Ted and then down at his beer. He tugged at

the label on his bottle and tried to find the words that could get at it, the words that he'd tell Ted if he'd tell Ted anything real. "It feels like the terror is fading."

Ted grunted and smiled, but for a long time he didn't speak. "It fades," he said. "Sometimes you won't even feel it. But it never really goes away."

Ted felt it? Ted, who was practically born a fully formed father felt it? And it never goes away? They both drank their beer and avoided eye contact. Never is a long time. Finally, Ted glanced at the grill and got up. "I'm getting the meat. You need another beer?"

"Yeah. Sure."

Gail came out as Ted went in. She still looked embarrassed by her good fortune. "Can you hold her for a minute?"

"Of course."

"Cindy's making the potato salad, and Paige just called. I need to call her back."

Jon reached up, took his daughter, and settled her into his lap. Gail kissed him on the lips before she went back inside. The weight of Maya in his arms was starting to feel right. Maybe she was getting heavier, or maybe he was just learning what to expect when he held her. He breathed in the Milk Duds and thought about what Ted said. He let the idea wedge itself next to that sweet scent, next to the expectations that had been sneaking into his life over the last few days. *It never really goes away.*

Maya woke, yawned, and stretched. Jon bent over her and wiggled his pinky into her fist. She gripped it like she always did, but this time those fingers pulled him off-balance, and something shifted. Maya cracked her eyelids and seemed to look at him for a long moment. Her pupils were gray, like granite or steel. She squeezed his pinky insistently, as if tugging him toward the future, and all at once Jon could see her hand in his own, walking uptown for ice cream. He could see those fingers around the chain of a swing, gripping a pencil, texting a friend, plucking a guitar string, accepting a ring. He could even see the tiny fingers of Maya's own child wrapped around *her* pinky. The screen door slammed, and Ted set a full bottle of beer on the table. Maya's eyes creased back to slits. That pit bull's growl settled toward silence, and Jon was left to wonder how his father could just walk away from his own tiny fingers.

Jon was halfway through his second beer, watching Aidan push Olivia on the swing, when he heard the screen door open and close quietly. He felt the stillness. He swiveled his chair and saw Gail near the door, hugging herself, staring out at the kids. Her eyes looked hollow and her head tilted just a bit, as if she was listening for something.

"What's wrong?" Jon asked.

Ted looked up from the grill, spatula in hand, ready to fix something.

Gail blinked rapidly. "We have to go."

"Nonsense," Ted barked. "I've got six pounds of meat dripping grease on these flames. You aren't going anywhere."

Jon stood. Gail didn't turn to him. She didn't laugh at Ted. She didn't move at all, only blinked. The way her mouth hung slightly open, the way her eyelids fluttered, made Jon's throat close up. He held Maya close and breathed in the Milk Duds.

Cindy opened the screen door, drying her hands on a dishtowel. "What's this I hear about you leaving? I just finished the potatoes."

Gail finally tore her eyes from the kids at the back of the yard and turned toward Cindy. She tried to smile, but her lips couldn't manage it. "I'm sorry. We have to go."

Cindy peppered Gail with questions that she wouldn't answer. Ted tried a couple of jokes, but nobody laughed. Cindy stopped asking questions when Gail began to tear up. Ted finally turned off the grill. The children gathered around the stroller to watch Gail pack it back up, looking with confusion from their mom to Aunt Gail and back to their mom. Jon just held Maya until Gail pulled her from his arms without a word and strapped her into the stroller.

Ted, spatula still in hand, stood next to Cindy on the front stoop as Jon and Gail headed down the driveway. Gail pushed the stroller this time, and the wheels clicked loudly across each crack in the concrete.

"What did Paige say?" Jon asked when they were out of earshot.

"She can't find Carli." Gail stared past the end of the block. "She's called a dozen times, but Carli won't answer her phone."

"So what?"

Gail's mouth twisted like it did whenever she was trying to be patient with him but failed. "She hasn't signed it yet. The final consent."

Jon remembered the piles of paper that he had signed himself and the too-long wait in the hospital while Carli signed papers. He remembered the accordion file full of paperwork that Paige handed to Gail when they finally went home that first night, and he remembered the *thlump* of the three-hole punch the next day and the snap of the three-ring binder as Gail locked all the papers into place. He remembered Gail prattling on about the paperwork, but he never really listened to her because that was all Gail's job. So, as the stroller clattered across the cracks of the sidewalk, even though he tried, he couldn't remember ever hearing the words *final consent.*

"You have no idea what I'm talking about, do you?"

Jon said nothing because Gail's voice leaked venom. And because she was right.

"It means Carli still has rights. She can still reclaim the baby."

Gail walked faster, and the rhythm of the wheels striking the cracks accelerated with her. Jon had fallen two steps behind when she spoke again.

"It means that Maya's not our baby yet."

Carli

*

Carli sipped her coffee and nibbled on a blueberry muffin. She hunched over a table near the bathroom at Liberty Street Cafe, an old two-flat turned coffee shop down by the river. Her shift didn't start until four, but she had to get out of the house to avoid Marla. She couldn't go back to Denny's, and the kids she knew from high school usually went to the Starbucks out by the expressway, so she had ventured down toward the river. If she had to deal with anyone at Liberty Street, it would probably be somebody's mom or dad or grandma, but the only other customers so far were two old men in feed caps and denim. They were talking too loudly about soybean futures and asking each other to repeat themselves. She didn't recognize the woman behind the counter, either. This might become her new regular place.

She was slogging through Kohlberg's stages of moral development, and none of it made much sense. Kohlberg studied men, which probably explained why Carli found it so goddamn confusing. She highlighted what she understood, underlined the parts to come back to. Her phone vibrated on the table. Paige again. Carli ignored it. She was still calling every hour or so. Carli had stopped listening to the voice mails. They were all the same. Seventy-two hours had come and gone, and Paige wanted that final consent. Just a formality, she said. Housekeeping. She kept calling, but Carli wasn't ready to tell her that Marla had burned it, that she needed a new one. Or not.

Maybe the caffeine kicked in, or maybe the charts in the next section were easier to digest. Maybe it was because Carol Gilligan had only studied women when she developed her of ethics of care. Whatever it was, the reading got easier. Women develop through three levels, it said. At the first level, girls make important decisions based upon what's best for them. Wendy and Kelly spent most of their time at that level and probably always would, and Carli couldn't deny that she was sitting in Liberty Street Cafe reading a book about psychology because of what she wanted for herself. At the second level, women make their decisions based upon what's best for others. This was where Carli's head started to swim with thoughts of Gail gripping her pen, bent over her notebook, making lists of things for the baby. And she thought about that wrinkled face that Marla had thrust at her. The empty place started to throb. Lots of women never make it to the third level, the book said, the place where women *balance their moral choices between their own needs and care for others. Do no harm to yourself and do no harm to others.* The phone vibrated again, and Carli sent it to voice mail without looking at the number.

Do no harm to yourself. Do no harm to others. Which others? Gail? Marla? Paige? Jon? The baby? If she did what Marla wanted, that textbook would go away for a long time and maybe never come back. But she could feel the blood pump through that empty place with each beat of her heart. And if she did what Paige wanted, that empty place might get bigger and more painful until it was all she could feel. She underlined, and she highlighted, and she studied the text until her eyes burned, but that third level seemed to raise more questions than answers.

Do no harm to yourself and do no harm to others. Maybe Marla was right. Maybe all this stuff she was trying to learn in college was bullshit. In the end, there was only one baby. The phone buzzed again. A text from Paige. Carli checked the time—ten minutes until work. She turned off the phone and packed it with her book into her backpack. Her head ached, and her eyes itched, and the empty place seemed to unfold when she stood. There was only one baby. Someone would be harmed.

Carli counted the drawer and then wiped down the counter and all the tables. The dinner rush started at five, but the delivery calls always trickled in around four thirty. So when the first call came, Carli tucked the receiver between her shoulder and her cheek and grabbed a pad and pen.

"Giamonti's."

"Is this Carli?"

Paige's voice. Carli's eyes darted to the caller ID. Paige's number. Carli coughed.

"No," she said, forcing her voice higher. It sounded fake even to her. "This is Marissa."

A long pause. Paige recognized her voice, of course. They had talked on the phone so many times over the last seven months that it only took that one word. "Is Carli working tonight?"

"No," Carli said in her Marissa voice. "Not tonight."

"OK. I'll try her cell phone again." Another long pause. "Thank you."

Carli dropped the phone into the cradle as if it were hot. She stared at it. The clowns watched from the walls. She couldn't avoid the decision much longer.

Paige

*

The bell rang when Paige entered the restaurant. She arrived a little after eight, so the dining room was empty. Carli didn't look up, but Paige saw her stiffen. Her hair hung limp, as if she hadn't washed it in a while. She bent over the counter, doodling on a pad of paper. She had probably been expecting Paige since Paige called, dreading her arrival. She made her way past the tables to the counter.

"What's with the clowns?" Paige asked.

Carli looked up at the walls. She shrugged. "I dunno. They've been here ever since I can remember."

"I've been trying to get hold of you."

Carli looked back down at the pad, and her hand moved more quickly. Paige saw her pen press more firmly into the paper.

"I know," she said quietly.

"I went by your house."

"Marla home?"

"She was."

"How'd that go?"

"Probably about like you'd expect." Paige tried to decide how much to say, how hard to press. "She said you weren't going to sign the final consent."

A tiny shrug. Carli drew lines from a circle to the rectangle next to it. Paige couldn't take her eyes off the pad.

"She burned it," Carli whispered.

"The final consent?"

A tiny nod.

"I have a copy in the car," Paige offered quietly.

Silence. Stars and trapezoids and diamonds. This could go either way. Paige knew that if she gave Carli a shove, she could probably tip the balance, but she resisted the urge. It wasn't her job to take sides. "Marla and Gail have both made it clear what they want," she said. "What do you want?"

Carli's hand stopped moving. When she finally looked up, she blinked, looking confused and startled, as if nobody had asked her that question in a very long time. Paige remembered with visceral clarity a day twenty-four years earlier when her aunt had finally asked her the same question.

Carli shrugged. "Marla said that she'd help me."

Paige knew exactly how that would work out. Marla would watch Maya once, maybe twice. She would change some diapers, give her a bath or two. But then Marla would remember how much an infant demanded—all the crying and stink and constant attention. She would make excuses, make herself scarce, and Carli would realize how alone she really was. With an effort, Paige forced herself back toward neutral. "She might. For a while."

A small smile. A nod.

"I called Gail this afternoon."

Carli's smile withered. "What did she say?"

"Not much. I did most of the talking."

"What did you tell her?"

"The truth. I told her that I couldn't find you. I told her that I didn't know what would happen next."

The paper ripped a bit under the tip of the pen, and Carli shifted her attention back to the circle and rectangle. "She must hate me," she whispered.

"Carli. You have to decide what's right for you. Not Marla. Not Gail and Jon."

They were silent for a long time. The circle that Carli had attached to the rectangle now had two eyes and a little mouth. Carli was rounding the corners of the rectangle, shading it.

"But how do I do that?" Her forehead creased as she scribbled. "How do I decide?"

Right down the middle. Don't take sides. Right down the middle. "If you're anything like me," Paige said. "And I think maybe you are. You've been trying to think this through. Pros and cons. Pluses and minuses. All that. But you can't think your way to a decision like this. Trust me. You have to feel for it."

Carli's hand finally stopped moving, and she set down the pen. Paige wanted to grab that hand and squeeze it tightly. Carli looked drawn and exhausted, like she'd have trouble enough choosing the toppings on a pizza, much less face the choice in front of her. Paige wanted to help her decide, she wanted to make the decision for her, but, of course, that wasn't her place. "I need to get back to Jon and Gail soon. It's only fair."

Carli nodded. "I know."

"Sleep on it. Let yourself feel it. Call me in the morning."

Carli nodded again, and then turned and walked through the swinging door into the kitchen. Paige wanted to follow her.

She wanted to wrap that confused little girl in her arms and tell her that she knew exactly how she felt. Instead, she turned and walked toward the exit. She tried to ignore the painted smirks of the clowns, and she tried to stay balanced on that skinny invisible line. Right down the middle.

Gail

*

It took Gail a long time to get Maya to sleep that night. It may have been the way that Gail's hand trembled while she fed her the last bottle. Maya might have felt Gail's heart hammering against her rib cage. Maybe she could hear the blood rumbling through Gail's ears. When she was finally able to settle Maya into the bassinet, Gail climbed into bed and lay curled under the covers, her eyes wide.

Jon hadn't come to bed yet—he'd been on the computer since they got home from Cindy's—which was just as well, because he'd want to talk about it, and he'd say the wrong thing, and she'd get pissed. She stared at the notebook where it lay on the bedside table holding its useless lists. What a joke. All of them—the lists of childproofing supplies and vaccinations and medications and hypoallergenic cleaning products and emergency contacts—but especially the paperwork lists. The paperwork for the home study and for the FBI and for the Department of Children and Family Services and for the state and for the agency. She had lists of paperwork that she and Jon had to sign and paperwork that the birth father had to sign and paperwork that Carli had to sign. Way at the bottom, only one item remained on those lists. The rest had a single neat line drawn through them. What a pathetic attempt to control the uncontrollable. Gail could control nothing. An eighteen-year-old girl, with hormones flooding her system like a marsh at high tide, controlled everything.

That notebook sat too close to Gail's nose, and the stink of the leather, of dead cow, stirred the bile in her stomach. She allowed her mind to drift toward the unthinkable, and she imagined that bassinet empty and their house so terribly quiet, and the acid rose to her throat. And then her mind started to pick at the aftermath of her miscarriages, when she had felt so empty. But Maya wasn't a grain of rice or a sweet pea. She was eight pounds of living, breathing baby. It would be so much worse, and when Gail started to pick it apart, she found that it *was* unthinkable, and her mind refused to think it.

The breath whistled through Maya's nostrils right there at the foot of the bed. Every ounce of her baby told Gail that Carli would sign that paper. She was just busy. She had forgotten about it. She might be studying for a test. Her phone battery was always running low. Maybe she had lost her phone entirely.

Gail reached for the lamp and turned it on. She sat up against the headboard and picked up the notebook and pen. She opened it to the first blank page. She licked the tip of the pen and then bent over the notebook, carefully printing the title of a new list. She held the paper flat with one hand and gripped the pen tightly as she wrote. It wouldn't change anything. She knew that, of course. But it would help keep her mind away from the places that it shouldn't go. She drew a line below the words and then licked the tip of the pen again. *Perfectly Good Reasons Why Carli Hasn't Called Back.* Because there *was* a perfectly good reason. Because she would call. She would sign the final consent. Because she had to.

Jon

*

Jon sat in his darkened office, Cheap Trick leaking from the speakers, his hands awash with the blue light from the monitor. He kept rereading two sentences. First: *I wish to and understand that upon signing this consent I do irrevocably and permanently give up all custody and other parental rights I have to such child if such child is adopted by _____ and _____.* But the same web page showed him the birth-parent rights and responsibilities and all the way at the bottom of the list, number thirteen: *You have the right to decline to sign a Consent, Specified Consent, or Unborn Consent even if you have received financial support from the prospective parents.* He learned that Carli was not allowed to sign the final consent until seventy-two hours after the birth. He learned what Gail had already told him: his baby wasn't yet his baby.

He searched for and found the adoptive-parents rights and responsibilities. He found that he had the right *to be informed of the rights of birth parents*, and he had the right *to be treated with dignity and respect.* He searched for the right to appeal, but he found nothing—just *dignity and respect*, whatever the hell that meant.

Jon vaguely remembered Paige telling them all this a year and a half ago, at the beginning of the process, and he probably signed something all those months ago that said that he clearly understood the risks. But adoption paperwork was like mortgage agreements—you had to sign it all or else you wouldn't get the house or the baby, and if you tried to read it, you wouldn't understand it anyway.

Google helped him remember what he'd forgotten. It helped him learn what he'd never taken the time to know. Reclamation, they called it. He found a story about a sixteen-year-old birth mother in Iowa who reclaimed her baby and then left it with the seventeen-year-old father while she went to work. The baby died hours later. He found a lot of adoption sites. They all had logos made of hearts or abstract drawings of parents' arms wrapping babies. They assured birth mothers that they had the right to reclaim their baby, and they reassured adoptive parents that it seldom happens. Just 4 to 6 percent of domestic adoptions end with a reclamation. If he had read those numbers at the beginning of the process, they would have seemed puny, irrelevant. Now, they loomed enormous and reckless. He changed his search terms, followed every link, even forced himself to read through the Illinois Adoption Statute, but he could find nothing about a right to appeal.

Finally, he turned off the music and the monitor, pushed himself out of the chair, and walked into the hallway. He saw a finger of light underneath the bedroom door. He opened it, expecting to find Gail buried under the covers, but instead she was sitting up in bed, bent over her notebook. He stood in the doorway, exhaustion clawing at him. For a long moment, she scribbled in the book as if he weren't there. He heard the tip of the pen scratching the paper. He watched her clenched fist drift across the page. For the love of God, what was she doing? What list could possibly help with this?

"She's going to sign it," Gail finally said, her voice in the wrong key. When she looked up, her eyes looked flat, like the heads of screws. "She has to."

Gail

*

Gail peeled the onesie from Maya and threw it into the trash can by the door. Jon had dressed her in the outfit with the ladybugs that Gail's mom had brought when she visited. What an idiot. She reminded herself to do the same with the other clothes from her mom so that she wouldn't have to think about her mom and her baby at the same time. She slipped Maya into the caterpillar onesie that Cindy gave her at the shower, pinching the tiny snaps. She tickled Maya's feet, and Maya squirmed on the sea turtle rug. She leaned down and kissed Maya's forehead, greedily breathing in those pears.

"They'll be here in ten minutes," Jon said quietly, contrition muffling his words. He stood in the doorway of the nursery, buttoning his shirt, his hair wet. Gail's parents were coming for lunch. Her father wouldn't take no for an answer, Jon had said. But Jon should have known better. He should have forced no for an answer.

Gail plucked Maya from the floor, stood up, and held her close. She walked to the window and looked down at the redbud tree, bending in the wind, clinging fiercely to its pink blossoms. It just bloomed last week, but the wind was already tearing the flowers from the branches, scattering the petals like trash. The pink balloons drooped from their ribbons, battered by the wind against the bottom of the welcome sign.

"What are we going to tell them?" Jon asked.

"There's nothing to tell," Gail said sharply, because there was nothing to tell.

Jon had been picking at this thing all day, like it was a chicken carcass and he was trying to find a morsel of meat, but there was none there. Carli was busy working, or she was studying for class, or she was just sitting in front of the television, too lazy to call Paige back. Paige would find her, though, and Carli would sign the piece of paper. In the twenty-four hours since Paige called, Gail had forced herself certain.

Gail had replayed every moment in all those waiting rooms with Carli. She parsed every sentence that she could remember, but there wasn't a morsel of doubt to chew. Gail could feel the weight of Maya, her baby, in her arms, so much heavier than a grain of rice, or a sweet pea, or a prune. Carli would sign the paper, because the baby in Gail's arms was real, and Maya was hers, and no piece of paper, with or without a signature could change that.

"It seems like we should tell them something," Jon persisted. "Just in case . . ." But his voice trailed off.

Heat climbed Gail's back, and she blinked rapidly. Jon still didn't get it: there was no *just in case*, because they had waited so long, and they tried, and they failed, and they waited, and she bled, and they grieved, and they waited, and they tried, and she bled, and rinse and repeat and cry in between. The baby in her arms, the baby who weighed almost eight pounds when she was born but felt so much heavier now, was her baby. Jon could pick at it all he wanted, and Paige could keep calling him with her updates, and they could both talk about *just in case*, but Maya was her baby. Carli would sign the paper, and this would all be just a funny story that she'd someday tell their friends whenever Jon accused her of being uptight like he always did. To tell anyone about that unsigned piece of paper would just give that piece of paper weight and color and odor and an importance that it didn't deserve. Because Carli was going to sign it, because she had to sign it. Besides. If Gail was going to tell someone, her mom would be the last person in the entire world she would tell.

Her dad had been calling since their last visit. She had let all his calls roll to voice mail, because she knew that her dad wouldn't come without her mom.

"After what she said last time, I don't know why you even returned their call," Gail said. "You shouldn't have told them they could come."

"Your dad sounded worried," Jon said. "And he said your mom was sorry."

Sorry. Her mom was sorry when she missed Gail's recitals and ruined Gail's prom and got so drunk at Gail's wedding that she made out on the dance floor with one of Jon's groomsmen. She was a nasty drunk, but she was nasty sober, too, and careless always. If it weren't for her dad, Gail would take Maya out to Starbucks and wait for Jon to call to say they had left. Yes. Her mom was sorry. On that they could all agree.

"I've been doing some research," Jon said.

Gail kissed Maya on top of the head and worked to contain her rage. A few hours on the Internet and suddenly he was an adoption expert. He was poking around websites that Gail had long ago memorized. He was reading all the documents that he had signed last year without reading. He was investigating options that Gail knew weren't any more viable than that grain of rice, or that sweet pea, or that prune.

"She's going to sign it," Gail said.

"I know she will," Jon said, but his raccoon eyes darted to the floor, and his shoulders hunched when he tried to shove his hands deeper into his pockets. Gail could tell that he didn't believe a word of it. "Can I hold her?" he asked.

She said nothing for a long moment, and his question hung heavy in the air. He seemed to search the floor for somewhere firm to stand. "No," she finally said.

He looked up, startled, and Gail tried to gather words to explain, but they darted around inside of her head like the squirrel in the redbud tree. She knew that the words she might manage wouldn't sound right. They wouldn't say what she meant, and they wouldn't tell him what she felt. She didn't have the energy for the fight they would spark. She was almost relieved to hear the doorbell.

Gail's mom stood in the entryway wearing a dress, looking as stiff as the cardboard tray that held the coffee. Gail's dad wrapped Gail and Maya in a warm hug and kissed Maya on top of the head. He sat in one of the wingbacks. Jon took the seat next to Gail on the couch, forcing Gail's mom into the other wingback, and for this, at least, Gail was grateful. And Jon talked. He talked about diapers, and the taxonomy of infant poop. He talked about how the baby monitor sometimes picked up crying or conversation from the McKennas' baby monitor next door. He said that the lack of sleep reminded him of finals week his freshman year of college. He paused for a moment, perhaps to let Gail say something, but she had nothing to say. Instead, her dad looked meaningfully at her mom, and her mom glared back at him. She cleared her throat anyway.

"I'm sorry about the other day," she said, looking down at her hands. "I think you might have interpreted what I said in a way that I didn't intend."

Like a politician after a racist Twitter rant. Gail got up from the couch and carried Maya over to the front window. The wind was blowing hard, and she couldn't summon the anger that her mom's careless words usually fueled. So she stared at the redbud, feeling helpless as the April wind clawed at its few remaining flowers. Her dad murmured something to her mom.

"I'm sorry, Gail," her mom spat, as if the words tasted sour. "I was wrong."

Just three blossoms clung to the tree, and Gail couldn't watch them go, so she turned. Better to see an empty tree when it was all over, better, even, to look at her mom. "It's OK," she said quietly. "It doesn't matter."

Gail's mom recrossed her legs and sprayed Gail's dad with an *I told you so* glare. Her dad's face softened with relief. Jon looked terrified.

"Can I hold her, Gail?" her dad asked, pushing up from his seat.

"No," Gail said too loudly. His face collapsed, and he sagged back into the chair. "Not right now," she said more gently.

And then her phone rang. She shifted Maya to her shoulder and pulled it from her pocket. Paige. A rush of relief warmed her, and she answered. Carli must have signed it.

"Hey, Paige."

Jon's eyes locked on her, demanding too much, so she turned back to the window. Just a few petals left.

"Hi, Gail. I found Carli."

"She signed it?"

The phone was quiet for a moment, and Gail wondered if she lost the connection, because there was no reason for silence. Her vision went black around the edges, and all she could see was that tree clinging desperately to one final shred of color. She was about to lower the phone from her ear, to confirm that she had lost the connection, because that was the only plausible reason for the silence, when Paige finally spoke.

"She didn't."

Gail closed her eyes and waited for the explanation. She didn't ask why, because Paige would tell her why, and then it would all be OK.

"She's not going to," Paige said quietly. "She wants to reclaim the baby."

Gail dropped the phone and there was a shriek like a blade held to the stone at the wrong angle with too much pressure and she was twelve again and her grandfather took hold of her wrists and adjusted the angle and reduced the pressure to keep her from ruining the blade but the noise got worse not better, and when she opened her eyes it was Jon grabbing her wrists not her grandfather and his face was red and his eyes were wide and he was saying something but she couldn't hear him because the noise was so loud and she knew that the tree was bare and the shrieking grew ever louder and Jon pulled hard and his mouth opened wide and she could finally make out what he was shouting over the terrible noise.

"You're squeezing her, Gail! Stop squeezing her!"

And he tried to pry the baby out of her arms, but she couldn't let go. She tried. But she couldn't. She just couldn't.

Carli

*

When Carli woke up and told Marla what she had decided, she could tell by the smug look on Marla's face that Marla thought it was the trash bags that had swung the balance. Carli would let her think that. She wouldn't tell her that the decision was made last night, before she opened the front door, before she even got out of her car. After Paige left, she had spent her whole shift trying to sort out what she would regret the least. She thought about selling her textbook and throwing out her school ID, and she thought about that grubby apartment with Mountain Dew cans on the windowsill. She thought about the promise she had made to the Durbins, and she thought about packing boxes at the warehouse with her mom for ten-hour shifts. But Paige was right, thinking got her nowhere. She couldn't turn the decision into some sort of math problem, adding regrets, subtracting pain. Thinking just turned her in circles and made her eyes burn. Thinking just allowed her to avoid the real problem.

She didn't stop thinking until she drove home from Giamonti's and sat in the driveway, staring through the windshield at the glow of the lamp in the front room. She finally allowed herself to poke and prod against that empty place and found that it wasn't empty at all. She stopped thinking and allowed herself to feel. She had built that wall to shield herself from the feelings—the pain, the guilt, the shame. But as she sat in the car, staring at the glow of the lamp in the window, she realized that those were just the symptoms of the real problem. The real problem grew right along with every pound she had gained. It jostled her every time the baby kicked. It bulged against that wall she had built, even as the baby bulged against the drum-tight skin of her belly. The real problem boiled down to this: over nine months, although she managed not to admit it to herself, she had fallen in love with her daughter. Love had seared that baby's face into her memory, and love smelled like vanilla cream soda. Once she allowed herself to feel, the decision made itself.

When she finally went inside, the front room was littered with a half-dozen black garbage bags, each knotted at the neck. A Bowflex commercial blared from the den, and a flickering blue light spilled through the doorway. She knew without checking that those bags contained all her clothes. She closed the front door and picked her way through the bags and down the hall-way to her room. She crawled under her blanket and fell into a deep, dreamless sleep.

As soon as she woke up, but before she told Marla what she had decided, she dragged the garbage bags into her room and unpacked her clothes. Then, she dropped her psych course, before moving her computer into the laundry room to make room for the crib. She would take more shifts at Giamonti's to pay for stuff, and the rest of the time she'd be with the baby. She promised herself that she'd enroll again next semester—she'd find a way to make it work. And she promised the baby. Carli pushed her bed away from the wall. She planned to put the crib between it and the window. Carli smelled smoke and looked up to find Marla leaning against the doorframe.

"You talk to Paige yet?" Marla asked.

"I did."

"What did she say?"

"She said she'd get the paperwork started." Carli glanced up at Marla and then back down at the bed. She pushed it a little bit farther from the wall and then moved to the other side of the room. She cleared off the little shelf, dumping everything into one of the black trash bags: pictures of people who used to be her friends, some books from high school, the trophy that she won that year her neighbor signed her up for soccer. She would need the shelves for the baby supplies.

"Rhonda's gonna bring the crib over when she gets off work," Marla said.

"OK."

"We'll need to go to Walmart to get diapers and shit."

"OK."

"When's Paige bringing the baby?"

"I'm not sure. She's calling the Durbins to work it out."

Marla grew still. "Work what out?"

Carli wiped down the shelves with a paper towel. "Paige said the Durbins wanted time to say goodbye."

"Fuck the Durbins. And fuck Paige. Call her and tell her you want your baby now."

Carli put the paper towel into the bag and tied the top into a knot. "No."

"What did you just say to me?"

Carli stood up and put the trash bag on the bed. She turned to Marla, looked her right in the eye, held her gaze. "I said no." Her eyes burned, but she managed not to blink. She promised herself yet again, that no matter what, she wouldn't turn into Marla. "Paige will work it out."

Jon

*

Jon listened for Gail. Their bedroom door was closed, and he stood in front of it for several moments listening, but he heard nothing. He went downstairs. He listened for her footsteps as he loaded the dishwasher, and he listened for the creak of the hardwood after he came in from taking out the trash. After he filled a glass with ice and gin and splashed some tonic into it, he climbed the stairs and paused again near their bedroom door, listening. Nothing but silence.

He drifted to his office, fired up his computer, and half-heartedly clicked through a dozen sites, looking for a different answer than the one that Paige had given when he called her back. He was searching for that wrinkle, that crease that always lay at the center of any intractable problem. But Paige assured him that the law landed squarely on the side of the birth mother. The law strained to keep families together, she said. He and Gail and Maya weren't a family yet, she didn't quite say. *Dignity and respect.* She wanted to come for Maya right away, but after some shouting, Paige made a phone call to Carli. When she called back, she agreed to noon the next day.

They'd been through this too many times. Nothing quite like this, but every month after they started trying, started failing, really, they'd been through a version of this. He and Gail were wired so differently. Most of the time they compensated for each other, traded weaknesses for strengths. But having a baby proved different. If Jon had never said anything, they'd probably still be living on Paulina. Gail would be growing Tomassi Grinding during the week and shrinking her marathon times on the weekend. But he did say something, and once they started trying, once they started failing, Gail became obsessed. Her expectations would race ahead of her every time, even as the fear crept up Jon's spine. But then they'd fail, and her disappointment, her grief, mapped to his silent, shameful relief. And every time, they shared the silence. Gail would climb under the covers and lay very still, and Jon would leave his banjo and guitar in their rack. Silence became their soundtrack.

The silence, though, was better than the noise that would follow it. Gail would clean out the attic or rearrange the furniture in the living room or pack the children's books away yet again. She'd do it loudly, aggressively, angrily. And the racket wouldn't stop until he was stupid enough to say something—and eventually, he was always stupid enough to say something—usually something hopeful or encouraging even though he knew what that would get him. And then she would scream at him, he'd yell back, they'd fight, and then grow silent again. Every month in the beginning, when her period came, telling them that their efforts had amounted to nothing. Every six months when the sweet peas and prunes bled from her. That's what she called them—sweet peas and prunes. Three times they endured *that* nightmare, but each time, things would ease back toward normal when she was ready to try again. He didn't see any path back to normal this time, though, and he felt no relief. Maya wasn't a sweet pea or a prune. Maya was their baby. This time, the silence sounded like a scream.

When he was coding or playing banjo, he could always imagine what would come next. It didn't always turn out exactly the way he expected, and the details were never sharp and clear, but he could always feel the general shape of it. He couldn't imagine Gail handing the baby to Paige, and they couldn't pack Maya into a basket and leave her on the doorstep with her things like a fairy tale in reverse. So that meant he'd be the one to hand her over. He could see the shape of that only too clearly, and the edges of that cut sharp. He couldn't fathom the rest of it, though. Their lives after Maya remained unmapped. He couldn't imagine what they would say, where they would stand, or how they would find each other. Not just the next day, but the next week and the next month and the next year. All of it a blank. Nothing.

Jon drained the last of the gin. He thought about pouring another, but if the noise came tonight, he couldn't afford to be drunk. He turned off the monitor and pushed himself up from the chair. When he opened their bedroom door, the small lamp on the dresser glowed, and Gail was curled up on her edge of the bed, facing the window. Jon went to the bassinet and leaned into it, inhaling the Milk Duds. Maya's breath came even and quiet. Her head was turned to the side, and her fingers curled into a tiny fist. Jon kissed his own fingers and touched them lightly to her cheek.

He turned off the lamp, stripped to his boxers and T-shirt, and climbed into bed. Gail didn't stir, but she was awake, of course.

Jon felt the need to say something, but with every moment that passed, words seemed more futile. Gail shifted, but only to pull the covers higher up over her face. There were no not-wrong words left. They lay there in silence for a long time. The words *dignity and respect* rattled around his brain. He shifted to Gail's side of the bed and wrapped his arms around her. He needed to hold her to feel solid, to bear the silence. He kissed the back of her head and nuzzled his face into her hair. She murmured something that he couldn't quite make out.

"What was that?" he asked.

Her voice, when she spoke again, was loud and brittle. "I said don't touch me."

Jon froze for a moment, struggling to process what she said, what she meant. Finally, he rolled back to his side of the bed and stared up at the ceiling. He lay still, unable to see the shape of anything, forced to endure the scream of the silence.

Gail

*

When Maya squawked awake, Gail climbed out of bed and pulled her from the bassinet. She sank into the armchair while Jon went to mix a bottle. Already Maya didn't feel right in her arms, the weight of her just off, the shape somehow different. Jon returned and handed the bottle to Gail and then stood, arms awkwardly at his side, watching Gail feed her, his face screwed tight. When Maya finished, Jon took her into the nursery to change her without saying a word. Gail climbed under the covers and curled toward the window. She heard Jon lay Maya back into the bassinet, and he climbed into bed. He licked his lips, as if about to speak, but he spared her, spared himself her response. He tossed and turned for more than an hour, until he finally squirmed toward stillness. His breathing slowed and deepened. He would soon roll over onto his back, and the snoring would begin. Not obnoxious cartoon snoring, just a quiet rumble on the inhale with a delicate snort at the end of the exhale that Gail used to find cute. Gail knew that she wouldn't sleep. She wondered if she'd ever sleep again.

Gail couldn't stop thinking about the miscarriages. Until the phone call from Paige, the miscarriages were the worst thing that had ever happened to her. Every time, her lists had raced ahead of her body. Not just lists of things that they would have to do and buy over the next nine months, and the lists of the people they would tell and when they would tell them. Her mind raced beyond the birth, and she thought about names and toys and walking and talking. And she thought about siblings and how long to wait between each and how many and how to minimize the negative effects of birth order. She wondered about the difference between raising a boy and a girl. She tried not to hope for one or the other, because some things you just can't control.

What to Expect When You're Expecting doesn't tell you what to do when you stop. After each miscarriage, she worked hard not to think about it, not to dwell upon what might have been, what was supposed to be. She threw herself into her work, and she made lists about other things. Sometimes she would go into the shop on the weekend and repair a boxful of blades. The muscle memory would return, and the steady strokes back and forth across the stone would help her mind go blessedly blank. After her second miscarriage, she ground several knives from scratch, because if she couldn't make a baby, she felt like she had to make something. Back then, she did everything she could to keep her mind away from what had happened, but now, she was trying desperately to summon the memory of her miscarriages. Cindy bought her a book about grieving, and it told her to visualize her "safe and happy place," like a waterfall or a meadow. Her mind always raced right past those safe and happy places, barely pausing, finding the pain, circling it, sniffing at it. The miscarriages were hard, but nothing like this. Her miscarriages felt soft and warm compared to this.

Her miscarriages had become her safe and happy place. How messed up was that?

She smelled Maya in the bassinet at the foot of the bed, but she smelled her even when she wasn't in the same room. She smelled her on her shirt and on her hands and in the lining of her nose. That funky pear smell that was the way her baby smelled. Not just the way *a* baby smelled, but the way that *Maya* smelled. As she lay there, the fragrance became odor.

A stray thought about the adoption book distracted her from the smell and even the miscarriages—but not in a good way, more like a rock in her shoe. Two extra copies lurked in the file cabinet in the office and they tugged at her. She had changed the book, right before Paige gave one to Carli, and she still had two extra copies. She had kept them, in case it didn't work out with Carli, in case she needed them for the next situation. That's what Paige called them: *situations.* Mothers who can't raise their babies and barren couples marketing themselves to those mothers. Over the last four years, Gail had become increasingly obsessed with becoming a mother. But over the last few days something had shifted, and she didn't realize it until she thought of those extra books. She didn't need to be a mother, she needed to be *Maya's* mother. Before Maya, she had been confident that when they adopted, love would wrap them with its tendrils and, over time, they would harden into sturdy roots that would bind them all. But she hadn't grown to love her child, she'd fallen abruptly into love, like waking from a dream into a bright light. Or like a car crash. Another baby wouldn't fill the gaping hole that Maya would leave in their life. *Situations.* Even that word wouldn't be welcome in their home. It loomed too large, coopted forever by Maya. There would be no more fucking situations.

Jon had rolled to his back now, snoring as expected. Gail slipped out of bed and around the bassinet. She gave it a wide berth, refusing to look inside. She paused next to Jon, though. His face had relaxed into the softness of sleep. She wanted to touch him, to wake him, to say that she was sorry, but his face would just stiffen again, and he'd say words that she wasn't ready to hear. Instead, she padded down the hall to the office. She shut the door and knelt down next to the file cabinet. She opened the bottom drawer, her drawer, the adoption drawer, and she pulled out the last two books.

The covers were teal—Paige's advice—to make them stand out. Gail opened one and scanned the first page. *Dear Expectant Mother, Greetings from Gail and Jon.* She studied the picture of the two of them, posed in the backyard in front of the flower garden. Jon had shaved that day—Gail had insisted. They leaned toward each other, and they both smiled in that openmouthed way that suggested the beginning of a laugh. Gail remembered her anxiety that day as she tried to arrange the perfect photo, but Jon must have said something funny right before the shutter clicked, because they both looked utterly and totally happy. She tried to imagine how an expectant mother might view Gail and Jon, how Carli must have seen that picture. She tried to imagine the circumstances that would allow them to smile like that again, and she failed. She tore the first page out. She powered up the shredder and fed it. She tore out the page with her extended family. *What a nice grandmother that lady would make.* She shredded it. She tore out the page with Jon's extended family, complicated clusters of people forced into separate frames that the words in the book never really explained. She shredded it.

It took her an hour to shred every page of both books. She took the teal covers down to the kitchen trash can and slid them beneath some garbage so that Jon wouldn't find him, so that she wouldn't have to talk about that. She didn't go back upstairs, instead curling up under a blanket on the leather sofa in the den. At least she wouldn't have those damn books tugging at her anymore. There would be no more situations. Gail pressed her nose to the fragrant leather, trying to smother the smell of her baby, and she tried to shove her attention back to the relative comfort of her miscarriages.

Her mind, though, that wolf, wouldn't sit still. It loped right past the miscarriages and sniffed at the bassinet that would soon be empty. It nuzzled the emptiness that felt so vast it might swallow her. It sprawled on the wide-open middle of their too-big bed. But as night melted toward dawn, the shape of a terrible possibility began to emerge.

Jon

*

Jon woke with the opening note of Maya's first cry, and everything that happened the day before landed on him immediately. There was no blissful moment of ignorance, no confusion, no reprieve before reality returned. He woke with reality in the bassinet at the foot of his bed. Maya was howling by the time he plucked her from it. He held her to his shoulder and bounced her softly, shushing her. He'd slept poorly, but he was surprised to have slept at all. When his bleary eyes landed on Gail's empty edge of the bed, he felt no surprise at all.

Jon felt like he'd drift off if not for the weight of Maya in his arms. Even through his exhaustion, through the buzzing in his ears and the pounding headache, he knew that he wouldn't get used to the idea of letting Maya go. He tried again to imagine their house without her, but he failed. He rubbed Maya's fingers between his own. In seven short days, those fingers had kneaded his fear into expectation and then love. Those fingers had tricked him.

As he carried Maya into the nursery to the changing table, his muddled dreams drifted back to him, but all he could remember was the blackness and the searching. As he changed Maya's diaper, as he fitted her into a onesie, he felt again the terror of blindness, of not finding. As he picked up Maya and nuzzled the top of her head with his chin, it hit him. He hadn't been searching for Maya in his dreams. It was Gail that he couldn't find.

Don't touch me. Her voice was so cold when she said those words. Dead. The lifelessness of those words, more than the words themselves, had forced him back to his own edge of the bed without a word. All day yesterday, he'd been trying to sort through what it would mean to lose Maya. All day yesterday, he had grieved and prepared for the waves of grief to come. As he looked out the window at the redbud tree, he became certain in a way that made him cold all over again: he would lose Gail, too. He wasn't sure how it would happen or how long it would take, but their bed wasn't big enough. They would retreat again from the center, the house would go silent, and before too long he would look to her edge and find it permanently, terrifyingly empty.

"Hey," Gail said softly from the door of the nursery. "How is she?"

Jon looked at her for a long time before answering. "Where'd you go?"

"I couldn't sleep."

Gail walked across the room and slumped into the rocking chair. Jon took a long look at her, wondered how long she would stay after Maya was gone. Her shoulders sagged, and her eyes burned red from crying and lack of sleep. She held a full bottle, but when he brought Maya to her, she didn't hold her arms out to take her. Instead, she just handed him the bottle. He took it and walked with Maya across the room. He leaned against the wall and slid to the floor. He slipped the nipple between Maya's lips and she began to suckle. He stared at Maya's face, studying it, memorizing the features, storing them for later. For forever. Yesterday, no tears came, but now his eyes began to fill.

"When I talked to Paige last night—" Jon paused, but there was no delicate way to say the unsayable. "She said that she'd come at noon. She thought that it was best if we did this quickly."

The room was silent but for the slurp as Maya tugged at the bottle. Jon looked out the window at the roof of the McKenna house. He looked at the turtle rug. He looked at the crib. He didn't look at Gail. He held all the grief that he could hold in his arms. Later, after Maya was gone, he could begin to study Gail, memorize her. He could start preparing himself for that loss, too.

"What does she know about what's best?"

A much less profane version of what Jon had asked Paige. Jon leaned his head against the wall and closed his eyes. "She made it clear that she wasn't talking about us."

"What if we don't?" Gail asked.

"We have to, Gail."

"What if we go away?" Her voice came raw. "What if we take her?"

Jon's eyes clicked open. He stopped breathing. Holy shit. There it was. The wrinkle. The crease. From Gail. And she sounded serious.

"Where?"

"I have no idea."

"Just leave?"

"Yes."

Jon peered at her. Her jaw jutted like it did when she had made up her mind, and she stared right back at him. Holy shit. Jon's mind was clearing, and the shape of what came next began to form, and he found himself leaning toward it, back toward Gail.

"Could you really do that?" he asked.

"I know that I can't give her back. I try to imagine it, but I can't. I just can't."

"What about Carli?"

Gail was quiet for a long time, and Maya's breathing grew even louder. When Gail spoke, her words felt solid. "I can't think about Carli."

"What about your family?"

This time Gail didn't hesitate. "Maya is my family."

Marla

*

Marla checked the items on the order, closed the box, and sealed it with a shriek of packaging tape. She looked at the route and tossed the box onto the correct skid. She eyed the next order on the packing table, just binder clips and some pens, and started to build a smaller box. She fell into her rhythm, the rhythm that made the day pass quickly, a rhythm she'd found so long ago that she didn't think about it anymore. Build the box, pack, check, seal, toss. To stay in the rhythm, she avoided eye contact with Helen across the table. They had gotten along fine in the beginning, until an argument about overtime. After that, Marla didn't trust Helen, and working across a table from somebody that she didn't trust—all day, every day, for seven years—it was hard not to let the stupid little annoyances accumulate like hairs in a drain. After a while, they clumped into arguments and then congealed into grudges, until the whole damn thing spilled over into hatred. Marla and Helen had learned that a couple of wrong words, a wrong look even, could send the whole day sideways, so they both did their best to ignore each other from six feet away. Marla was leaving early, but even so, she wanted to maintain that rhythm. It allowed her mind to drift to the baby.

She could barely remember Carli and Wendy when they were babies, but the smell stuck with her. That same pudding smell that caught her off guard when she carried the baby down to the recovery room to make Carli look at it. She should have gotten up into Carli's grill right when Carli told her she was pregnant, when she started talking to Paige, before she chose the Durbins. But Marla was too pissed off. She should have gone into that diner with Carli. She could have wrecked the whole damn thing before it got started, but all she managed to do was yell at Carli.

As Carli got fat, Marla stopped looking at her. She kept her eyes glued to the TV when Carli walked by. The truth was, she had trouble enough sorting out how she felt about it herself. She was restless. Twitchy. She went for drives down by the river. She bought Wendy that sweater. That kind of shit. She even watched two episodes of *The Golden Girls* that one night before she snapped out of it. And she probably would have just yelled at Carli one more time when she got home from the hospital, and that would have been the end of it, if it wasn't for Durbin.

If that asshole didn't come over like he did, if he didn't say what he said, she probably wouldn't have made Carli look at the baby. And she wouldn't have smelled that pudding when she carried the baby back to the nurses' station. She wouldn't have remembered the wide-open space she'd felt inside of herself that first time she held Wendy, before she left Sean, before everything got all fucked up. She wouldn't have recognized her restlessness as hope.

The hope kept her awake that night after the baby was born, like a thunderstorm or a neighbor's dog that wouldn't stop barking. That nurse from the recovery room poisoned her with it, after

Marla brought the baby back to the nurses' station. When Marla finally stopped yelling, the nurse quietly took Marla aside and told her that Carli couldn't sign that last piece of paper until three days passed. When she found that folder on Carli's shelf the next day, she knew exactly what it held, and the hope felt like splinters wedged under her fingernails. The twisted confusion on Carli's face as she watched that paper burn made those splinters real.

Larry, one of the order pickers, delivered an armful of staplers to the packing table. He had that bounce in his step. Larry parted his hair down the middle and wore a mustache, which combined to make him look like a porn star from the seventies. He towered over Marla, and he carried fifty extra pounds of flab on his frame, mostly in his belly. But when he hadn't been drunk or stoned for a few days, when he was ready for action, he bounced on the balls of his feet like a little kid headed to the ice cream truck. Larry disappeared into the stacks.

A few minutes later, Kurt, another of the pickers, emerged from behind a set of shelves and dropped a case of copy paper on the table. Kurt and Larry were best friends and opposites. Kurt was short and coiled around an angry knot of muscle. Larry usually talked too much, but Kurt said little and hit hard.

Larry appeared with a case of pens. "Borrowed my cousin's car," he said to Kurt. "Gary."

Kurt cocked his head. Larry grinned, picked up his next order, and bounced off.

Marla watched Helen out of the corner of her eye to see how this would play out. Helen was skinny with a hatchet face and stringy hair. She glared at Kurt as he studied his next order, because Kurt and Helen were married, and Gary was Gary, Indiana, where most of the strip clubs had free lunch buffets. Helen and Marla both knew that after Kurt finished his free meal, he'd spend half his paycheck on lap dances, goaded by Larry and whoever else piled into Larry's cousin's car. He'd blow the whole wad if they found a trucker with coke to spare. Helen wouldn't be able to stop him, and if she tried, she'd return to work missing another tooth from running into a door.

Kurt looked up from the order, saw the look on Helen's face. "Fuck you lookin' at?" he demanded.

Helen held his gaze for just a second and then looked back down at the box she was building. The tape shrieked. Kurt skulked off. The silence between Marla and Helen thickened. The fluorescent light buzzed. Marla scowled at an order to keep from smiling. Helen built a box, squeezing the tape dispenser so tightly that it screamed.

The worse part about the whole damn thing was that Carli never once asked Marla to drive her to the doctor or help her get clothes that fit or ask her about what to expect next. Instead, that Durbin woman would show up at their house in her Subaru, and they'd go to the doctor appointments and then out to lunch and then to Nordstrom to buy her more clothes for fat ladies. And Carli, the dumb little bitch, seemed to be grateful for the ride and the clothes and for whatever they talked about at lunch, as if six lunches at Panera and a couple thousand dollars' worth of clothes was the going rate for a baby.

"I hear that Carli finally had that baby."

Marla looked up at Helen, said nothing, went back to packing. She wouldn't be goaded out of her rhythm.

"Shame she had to give it away," Helen said.

Marla dumped some file folders into the box. She wanted to tell Helen that it was handled, but it wasn't yet. And besides, it might give Helen the impression that Marla gave a shit what she thought.

"First grandchild and all."

Marla placed her hands flat on the table and leaned toward Helen. Helen glared defiantly back with bloodshot eyes. Just then, Kurt and Larry walked up to the packing table from opposite ends carrying their loads.

"Hey, Kurt," Marla said, still staring at Helen. It took some people longer than others to learn not to fuck with her. "Your old lady says you ain't allowed to go to Gary."

Larry snickered.

"Fuck you talkin' about?" Kurt said, glaring at Helen now, too.

Helen would definitely run into a door that weekend. Maybe even fall down the stairs.

"I do whatever the fuck I want."

Paige

*

Paige sat in her car in front of the Durbins' house for a long time, staring at the porch steps, trying to ignore the empty car seat behind her. She tried to visualize what was about to happen. When it got like this, she had to visualize. She tried to imagine the words she would say, how long she might linger. She hoped that Jon would answer the door. Jon would not want to hear words, and she'd get the baby quickly. She might not have to say anything at all. If they both answered the door, or if Gail answered, holding the baby by herself, there was no telling what would happen. She'd cry and probably scream. Paige would have to find the right time to hold her arms out for the baby, and she could imagine holding her arms out for a long time before Gail gave Maya up.

Paige was still pissed that she didn't come yesterday. She should have held firm when Jon asked for more time. Most of her eight failures came before the baby was introduced to the adoptive parents, but her fourth was a reclamation, too. She learned from that situation to pluck the baby as quickly as possible. She never should have agreed to ask Carli for more time.

She should have made the decision herself, instead of foisting it upon a confused, hormonal, eighteen-year-old girl.

Paige looked back at the porch steps. The last time she visited Elmhurst, she came for the home study, the report required by the state to certify couples as ready to be parents. Although nobody is ever really ready, almost nobody flunks, and Gail certainly didn't allow the Durbins to show poorly. All the electrical outlets had protective plastic plugs, and child gates stood guard at the top and the bottom of the stairs. She had mounted fire extinguishers every twenty feet, and all the upstairs bedrooms had a rope ladder stowed in the closet. Paige had never seen anything quite like it. Gail had even dressed Jon up in khakis and a turtleneck. Paige first inspected the house. Then they sat down at the kitchen table, and she inspected their life. She asked them how they met, how they argued, how they resolved those arguments. She drilled them about their finances, how much they had saved, who paid the bills, how much they had budgeted for a child. She interrogated them about who would care for the baby after Gail went back to work. She validated that they were on the same page about where they would send their child to school and how they would handle discipline. They weathered the storm of question better than most. Gail only had to say *I think what Jon really means* . . . three or four times. The home study pried into almost every nook and cranny of their relationship, but none of the questions touched upon how they would deal with a tragedy.

Paige finally gave up trying to imagine the unimaginable and forced herself out of the car and up the walk. She used the railing to pull herself up the stairs. She sucked a deep breath at the door before pushing the doorbell, announcing that time was up. Paige composed her features into the shape of compassion and kindness. She waited for a long time, tried to be respectful of what must be going on inside. They were saying goodbye. They were prying themselves away from everything that they had expected. They were dismantling a family.

Three or four minutes passed, though, and she started to shiver from the cold and the waiting. Her phone rang, but when she pulled it out of her pocket, it was Maggie, her daughter, so she sent the call to voice mail. She pressed the bell again, strained to listen for movement, but still she heard nothing. She waited. She pressed again and checked her watch—12:10. Shit. She walked across the porch to the front window, peered in. No lights. Nothing moved. She called Gail's cell phone. It went to voice mail on the first ring. She tried Jon's. Same. She thought about Gail's parents. They must be at Gail's parents, saying goodbye. But then a car pulled up, and Gail's parents got out. A knot began to form in Paige's stomach. She forced herself to wait for them on the porch.

Gail's parents seemed an even stranger match than Jon and Gail. Eleanor, her mom, brought to mind a lounge singer gone to seed, while Paul, her father, looked like a priest on casual Friday. Paul's stride hitched when he caught sight of Paige on the porch, but he didn't say anything to his wife, who was glaring at the ground. When he reached the top of the stairs, Paul nodded to Paige.

"Hi," Paige said.

At this, Eleanor, looked up, and her face hardened.

"Hello, Paige," Paul mumbled.

Eleanor said nothing, marched to the door, and rang the bell.

"They don't seem to be home," Paige said quietly.

"They're expecting us," Eleanor spat without turning from the door. "Where else would they be?"

"I was hoping that you might know," Paige said. There was that word again.

"You're like a goddamn vulture," Eleanor said to the door. "You just couldn't wait, could you?"

"I'm sorry?" Paige said.

"They told us you were coming at five o'clock," Paul said quietly. He looked at the empty driveway, out at the street. When he looked back at Paige, his eyes glistened. "We were planning to spend some time with Maya. Before we say goodbye."

The knot in Paige's stomach cinched tighter, and her mind churned questions. Why would they say five? Where were they? What the hell was going on? "We agreed that I would pick her up at noon."

Her words landed hard. Paul's face went slack.

Eleanor turned on Paige. "Bullshit. They said five."

Paige remembered the conversation with Jon only too clearly. It wasn't the kind of argument she'd forget.

She looked at Paul when she spoke. "Do you know anywhere that they might have gone?"

Eleanor pounded on the door.

Paul shook his head and sank into a wicker chair. He pulled his phone out, pressed a button, and held it to his ear. His voice cracked when he spoke. "Hey, Gail. This is Dad. Call me as soon as you get this. We're worried about you."

Paige lowered herself into the chair across from Paul. "Do you have a key to their house?" she asked.

"No," Paul mumbled.

Eleanor rang the doorbell again. She knocked and waited. Finally, she turned and marched over to where Paul and Paige sat. When she spoke, it wasn't clear who she was talking to. "Where in the hell are they?"

Carli

*

Carli wedged the crib between the bed and the window. She'd have to kneel on the bed to get at the baby, but she'd be so close when they slept. Right next to her, almost like they were sharing a bed. It was starting to feel real, and Carli allowed herself to picture the baby in the crib. She worked to remember that face, the face she'd turned from so quickly in the recovery room. She wondered how heavy the baby would feel in her arms. Every breath brought just a hint of vanilla cream soda.

She was stretching the sheets across the mattress when the smoke hit her. She tucked the sheet under the last corner and then sat on the edge of her bed, facing Marla. Marla took a drag on her cigarette, and they regarded each other. Plastic Goodwill bags hung from Marla's fingers. She didn't look angry for once, and Carli felt warm in a way that she seldom did.

"Food. Clothes. Diapers. Crib. Anything we forgot, we can send your sister." Marla tossed the bags on the bed. "You ready?"

While she was pregnant, the bulge in Carli's stomach that kicked and made her hungry and tired and numb belonged to

Gail. But now, that grainy, wriggling image on the ultrasound that she strained not to see, that blotchy, wrinkled face that Marla shoved at her in the recovery room, was going to be her baby. It was becoming real, and it was rushing at her fast, but Carli thought that maybe carrying a baby for nine months, catching all those stares and giggles at school, pushing eight pounds of person out into the world, went a long way toward making you ready. Carli nodded. "I'm ready."

Marla dumped the contents of the bags onto the bed. She put her cigarette on the windowsill, and for ten minutes, they sorted the clothes into piles without a word. They separated the onesies from the dresses from the socks from the pajamas. Marla had even bought a tiny pair of white leather shoes.

Marla took a drag from her cigarette. "What time's Paige bringin' her?"

"Two o'clock." Two hours. She had suffered nine uncomfortable months waiting to give her baby away. Now, in two hours, her baby would come home. Yes, Carli was ready.

Carli put a towel on the bed so that she'd have a place to change the baby. She straightened the stack of diapers and peeled the seal from a package of wipes. She reached to the top shelf of her closet and pulled out the blue stuffed frog that she'd hidden years ago to keep Marla from throwing it out. She propped it carefully in the crib. The vacuum growled in the front room.

In the kitchen, she pulled the can of formula from the shelf and studied it. Her nipples still leaked. That morning, she'd learned from the Internet that she'd still be able to nurse Maya, but Marla had bought formula just in case. She took a bottle from the shelf and dumped in two scoops of the chalky powder.

A half-eaten pizza lay on the table where Wendy and Randy had left it when Marla kicked them out. Carli's stomach was twitchy, so she folded the box closed and slid it on top of the fridge. The vacuum quit, and she wandered into the front room. She pulled the drapes back and peered out at the driveway, at the street.

"Twenty minutes," Marla said.

Carli settled into the couch while Marla wound the cord around the vacuum and shoved it into the closet. Marla sat down next to her and lit a cigarette. The smoke drifted toward the ceiling. Carli decided that now was the time to ask.

"Can you not do that when the baby gets here?"

"Do what?" Marla asked.

"Smoke."

Marla looked at her sideways. "You don't want me to smoke?"

"Around the baby."

Marla grunted a laugh. "In the same room? While I'm holding it? What're we talking here?"

"In the house."

She leaned back and cackled. "You think I'm gonna sit on the back porch all summer, sweating my ass off?"

"I don't want the baby to breathe the smoke."

"Do I gotta stay fifteen feet away from the door, or can I stand under the eaves when it's raining?"

Carli got up and pulled the curtain back. Nothing.

"You still got fifteen minutes," Marla said.

Carli sat back down, and for a while they were quiet. Marla's knee bounced, and she smoked, but when she stubbed the butt out in the ashtray, she didn't light another. Carli forced herself not to check the street again.

"What're you gonna name it?" Marla asked, breaking the silence.

"Her."

"Huh?"

"It's a her."

The corner of Marla's mouth twitched upward. "Right. What're you gonna name her?"

"Paige said they named her Maya."

"That don't mean shit. You can name her whatever you want."

"I kinda like Maya," Carli said.

Marla shifted on the couch but said nothing. Carli had carefully avoided thinking about Gail all day, about the promise that she had made, but the name that Gail chose brought Gail's endless lists, and her bottomless need for a baby back into sharp focus. They had spent so much time together in waiting rooms, and the need had leaked from Gail's pores. That need had comforted Carli back when they were visiting doctors—it helped her know that her baby would be fiercely loved—but now Carli knew that same need would wreck Gail.

"She's gonna be a mess."

Marla shrugged. "Kids that young don't remember shit. She'll be fine."

"No. I mean Gail."

"Gail Durbin?"

"Yes."

Marla's knee went still. "Fuck the Durbins."

Just then, a knock on the door. They both glanced at the clock on the cable box—1:50.

"She's early," Marla said.

Carli felt warm, and she shivered, and she felt her whole world begin to tilt. It would tilt forever, but now it was going to tilt the right way. She looked at Marla, and Marla almost smiled. Something passed between them that Carli couldn't wrap words around, something that didn't need any words. Carli followed her mom to the door. When Marla opened it, Paige came in carrying only her bag and a worried expression. Carli hugged herself, and she shivered harder. Where was the baby? Paige didn't have the baby. Marla peered outside to see if anyone was with her, and then turned on Paige, her face dark.

"Where the fuck is the baby?"

Paige looked around the front room as if searching for a place to hide. She licked her lips and swallowed twice before she spoke. "I don't know where the baby is."

Jon

*

They drove south toward St. Louis and littered their trail with credit card purchases. Best Buy for a computer and a half dozen burner phones. Gas in Romeoville. Clippers, bleach, and hair dye from Sally Beauty Supply. Jon withdrew nine thousand dollars from the Citibank in Joliet. The detour south would cost them some time, but when people came looking, it might send them in the wrong direction for a while. They were driving through Joliet, back toward the expressway, when Jon looked over at Gail. She'd been quiet since they left. She sat very still, staring through the windshield, blinking.

"You OK?" he asked.

She bit her lip and nodded.

Jon still couldn't believe those five words came out of her mouth. *What if we take her?* A question that he hadn't dared to consider, but as soon as she asked it, the shape of their future emerged whole from the fog of the present. Even before they had decided on Canada, his mind swirled with ideas and problems and solutions to those problems. By the time they settled

on Winnipeg, everything had locked into place, and he knew
what they had to do. Saying those five words seemed to cost Gail
everything she had. But she had done her part.

They stopped at a light, and he studied her again. He tried
to imagine how drastic this must be for her. She'd never lived
more than thirty minutes from where she was born. She still
talked to her dad every day. She was probably thinking about
Carli, but Jon knew that would lead nowhere. Carli had made
her decision to give up her baby. Maya was their daughter. For
him, the rest was just the messy business of the necessary.

"Listen, I don't want you to misunderstand what I'm about
to say," he said.

Gail finally looked at him.

"I'm all in," he said. "I want to do this, but I want you to be
sure. It's only two o'clock. If we turn back now, it's not too late."

Gail swallowed, but she said nothing.

"After this, there can't be second thoughts. I want you to be
sure." Jon searched for the right words. "I don't want you to
regret this."

Gail peered into the back seat. She stared at Maya for a long
moment. When she turned back to Jon, her jaw was set. "No
matter what we do, we'll have regrets," she said. "It's really just
a question of what we'll regret the least."

The car behind them honked. Jon looked up to find the
light green.

"We don't have a choice," Gail said. "Drive."

They came up empty in Channahon and Braceville and Eileen,
but when Jon saw WAYNE'S AUTOBODY AND CAR SALES carved
out of the cornfields a few miles west of Coal City, he knew

that he'd found the place. Half the lot was devoted to cars and trucks that ranged from dented to demolished. On the other half, a couple dozen older but hopeful used cars loitered in two ragged rows under a rope of fluttering plastic flags. An old service station lurked at the back of the lot. The counter and register had been ripped out, and a card table with three folding chairs took their place. CAR SALES. The single garage door stood open, and a dark-haired man with gray overalls and safety glasses sat on a milk crate buffing the rear fender of an old Monte Carlo. AUTOBODY.

Jon parked in front of the building and climbed out of the car. He walked the lot, surveying the choices. He kept coming back to a gray Camry. The tires weren't too worn. The white marker scrawled on the windshield demanded $7,999, a fraction of what their Subaru was worth. The man in the coveralls approached, wiping his hands on a rag. He smiled, revealing stained, crooked teeth. He thrust out his hand, and Jon shook it.

"I'm Wayne."

"Nice to meet you, Wayne," Jon said. A name. He needed a name. "Allen."

"She's a nice one," Wayne said, dipping his head toward the Camry. "Eleven years old, but only seventy thousand miles on her."

"Little old lady drove it?"

Wayne's smile widened. "That's right. But only to church on Sunday."

Wayne got the keys from the office, and Jon took it for a short drive. He tested the brakes, listened for noises. When he returned to the lot, he thought about popping the hood, but he had no idea what he'd be looking for. Wayne came back out to meet him.

"Whattaya think?"

"I'll take it."

Wayne's puzzled look told Jon that he was expecting complaints, excuses, delays, a tire-kicking negotiation at the very least.

"OK." Wayne looked at the time on this phone. "You can get a cashier's check over in Coal City. Bank's open till five."

"Actually, I'm gonna trade mine."

Wayne took a long look at the Subaru. "I don't usually do trades."

Jon knew that meant Wayne didn't have the cash to pay him the difference between the value of the Subaru and the Camry. "Even trade."

Wayne squinted at him. "Even trade?"

Jon nodded. Wayne turned back to the Subaru. He walked around it twice. "It run all right?" he asked.

"Yep," Jon said.

"Even trade?"

"Even trade."

Wayne asked Jon to start it up and pop the hood. He bent over the engine and listened to whatever Jon should have listened to on the Camry. Gail got out of the car and pulled Maya from the car seat so that Wayne could test-drive it.

Jon reached for Maya, and Gail handed her to him. She wrapped herself with her arms, stared into the corn, and shivered.

"You OK?" Jon asked.

She squeezed herself more tightly but kept her eyes fixed on the cornfield. "Just cold."

When Wayne pulled back into the lot, he climbed out of the car and looked back at it distrustfully. Finally, he turned to Jon and shrugged. "Bring your title and registration into the office and I'll get it writ up."

"See, that's the thing," Jon said. "I don't have any of the paperwork."

Wayne looked at the car again, at Gail, at Maya in Jon's arms. "No plates on it, neither."

Jon said nothing. He waited. He could see from the way that Wayne licked his teeth that the deal was done.

Wayne eyed Jon sideways. "Where you headed?"

"St. Louis."

"I don't guess you have your driver's license."

"Lost my wallet."

Wayne looked again at the Subaru, scratched his chin. "Reckon I'll have to do some additional paperwork. There'd have to be an administrative fee."

Jon remained silent, let Wayne calculate his risks.

"I figure about four grand'll cover it." Wayne kept his eyes on the Subaru.

"How 'bout a thousand? Cash."

"Two grand and you got yourself a deal, Allen. It's Allen, right?"

Just like that, like shedding a skin. Jon shifted Maya to his shoulder and held out his hand. Wayne shook it. "Right. My name's Allen."

Gail

*

Gail peered at the cornfields as they sped north and marveled at those five words that she had said. *What if we take her?* They had come to her while she lay on the couch that morning, before dawn, trying to imagine any other way. They started out murky, dark, unthinkable. They sat on her tongue for an hour as she lay there. They tasted metallic, sharp. By the time Maya woke, by the time Gail made it to the nursery where Jon held her, they felt inevitable and necessary. She could tell by the way that Jon clung to Maya, that the question only had one answer. When she opened her mouth, it was like someone else said those five words. She watched Jon's eyes widen and his mouth melt toward a smile, and just like that, those five words hardened into a blade that cut her, cut them, from everything, leaving her feeling weightless and unmoored.

Gail gripped a pen, but she had nothing to write on. Somehow, she had forgotten her notebook in their mad rush out the door. She tried to remember where she had left it. She had it when they decided and when they made lists of what they would take with them. And she had it when they chose Canada over Mexico and Winnipeg over Toronto. She had it while they packed. Maybe it was just as well that she didn't have it anymore. She would probably just write those five words over and over.

"You still doing OK?" Jon asked.

"Why do you keep asking me that?"

"Because your fingers are wrapped around that pen like it's saving your life," Jon said. "And I want you to be sure about this."

Gail dropped the pen in the console, forced her fingers limp. She leaned against the window and looked at a billboard for the Wisconsin Dells—a picture of a family splashing at a water park. She tried to find the words for how she felt. She shoved her mind away from Carli, because she couldn't think about Carli. "I've just never done anything like this."

Jon snorted. "Neither have I."

True that Jon never fled the country with a kidnapped baby, but it was different for him. He went to live with his aunt when he was eight, and from what Gail could tell, he practically raised himself before that. He packed off to a college five states away, and he landed in Chicago only because he knew a guy with a spare couch. After she said those five words, after they decided, she had managed only to pack Maya's clothes and write down the lists—Jon took care of everything else. In so many ways, he'd been preparing for this all his life. She said those five words, and he had sprung into action, as if he had been waiting, coiled.

The tires mumbled against the road, and the wind pried at the windows. As they sped past an empty rest area, Gail tried to pretend that this was just another long drive, just a road trip. They had driven to St. Louis too many times to count, but they had really only taken one honest-to-goodness road trip together. That first spring after they met, about six months before they moved in together, they drove seventeen hours to Austin for South by Southwest. They talked more that time. It came easy back then, and it felt necessary. They both held stories not yet told, questions not yet asked, answers worth listening to. They were still learning the other's preferences and opinions and pet peeves. And at night, in the tent, even after eight months together, they were still discovering each other's bodies. The disagreements were trivial. Waffle House (Jon) or Denny's (Gail). Beef jerky (Jon) or Skittles (Gail). Snow Patrol (Jon) or The B-52s (Gail). The level of commitment was negligible. A three-day pass. Half the gas money. Five nights in a tent. They both knew that at the end of those five days they could just walk away if things didn't feel right. But it was impossible for Gail to pretend. When they drove to Austin, they knew that they were coming back.

"You told him your name was Allen."

"Yeah," Jon said.

Allen. She was married to Allen now. "Why Allen?"

Jon shrugged. "First name that came to mind. It'll be the name that goes on the new passport."

"And he believed you?"

"Not a word of it."

"What if they trace the Subaru to us?"

"They probably will eventually, but without our name on anything it'll take a while. Long enough."

They drove in silence a bit longer, and she pushed her mind yet again away from Carli, toward Maya strapped in her car seat. They had no choice.

"What's my name?"

"Huh?"

"My new name."

"What do you want it to be?"

"I don't know," Gail said.

How do you choose a new name for the rest of your life? Allen didn't seem to have much trouble with it. Gail wondered how long it would take her to adjust to whatever she chose. When she gave up Tomassi for Durbin, she voided dozens of checks because she signed the wrong last name. For months she accidently said Tomassi when she answered the phone at work, and for much of that first year, when someone called her Mrs. Durbin, it took a moment to realize they were talking to her. She felt cut from her identity. She had always been a Tomassi. That name came from her dad and from the generations of Tomassis before him. She'd heard her family's story so many times that when they finally set up a website for the company, she wrote the copy in a single sitting. She could feel those five generations snaking back to the Val Rendena, that isolated valley in the Dolomites that gave the world its knife grinders.

Gail knew that her family's story differed only in the details from every other knife-grinding family in the country. Most knife grinders trace their roots back to that same valley. Gail watched the Cracker Barrels and truck stops drift past and felt the miles pile up behind her. She tried to center her thoughts on Giovanni Tomassi, her great-great-great-grandfather. He left Pinzolo with a new pair of shoes, two sets of clothes, and a stone fixed to a wheelbarrow. He walked halfway across Europe by himself, sharpening knives to earn his bread. He crossed an ocean in the dank hold of a ship and was dumped into a city where few spoke his language. He never stopped until he found a new place that he could call home and build a life. Gail's name was no longer Tomassi, but as she thought about those five words she had uttered at dawn, she tried to hear the whispers of Giovanni's blood in her own as it thudded in her ears.

Carli

*

As they drove to the Morris police station, Carli leaned her head against the window of the truck. Tears streaked her face and smeared the glass. In the waiting room, her grief churned with confusion as she tried to piece together where Jon and Gail and Maya might have gone. But it didn't matter where they'd gone; Maya was her baby, and they took her, and they had no right, and by five o'clock, she shivered with rage. But that kind of anger wears you out, and it was after seven before they saw a cop, and by then Carli just felt numb all over.

The cop who called her name probably wasn't even a real cop. She was tall and thick and wore wire-frame glasses. Her uniform looked like all the other cops, but her name tag read SERVICE OFFICER, which didn't sound like the real thing. She ushered them into a room off the waiting area. A round table and four chairs were crammed into a tiny space. Only a fist-size hole decorated the bare white walls. The service officer kept popping her gum against the roof of her mouth while she asked question after question, and each pop felt like an explosion.

Marla answered the questions, and the service officer slowly printed the answers onto a form. Even the pen scratched loudly. The woman didn't seem to care who answered the questions, which was good, because Carli wasn't sure that she could say anything without crying again. Instead, she concentrated on the hole in the wall and tried to ignore the pops from the gum and the scratch of the pen and the bored questions. Most of all she tried to ignore Marla's answers. When she finally reached the bottom of the form, the service officer flipped it over to see if there was anything on the back.

"So, let me make sure I have this right," she said to Marla. "You say that these people, the Durbins, they stole her baby."

"That's right," Marla said. That rumble lurked beneath the words.

"But they adopted the baby."

"But the adoption wasn't all done."

"So you changed your mind?" she asked.

It took a moment of heavy silence for Carli to realize that the service officer was talking to her. She tore her eyes away from the hole and tried to focus on the woman's nose.

"I did," Carli said.

"Why?" the cop asked.

How to answer that question? How to explain in a way that fit into a box on that form that she never intended to change her mind? How to tell about that vanilla cream soda she couldn't stop smelling since the recovery room? How to describe that face or that empty, ragged hole in her gut? Carli wondered whether the service officer had children of her own. How to tell this woman about love?

"Because she's my daughter," Carli whispered.

"But you gave her up, right?"

Carli's mind crackled and sizzled. She finally looked the woman in the eyes, but she saw only boredom. She wanted to scream at the woman, but no words came. Marla leaned into the silence. Her meaty hands gripped the edge of the table as if she meant to break it. Her upper lip curled, and her eyes narrowed like they always did just before she exploded.

"Is that on your fucking form?" Marla demanded.

The service officer cocked her head, studied Marla. "I'm sorry?"

Marla leaned further across the table. "I asked if that's on your fucking form."

"I was just trying to—"

"You was just trying to say my daughter don't deserve to raise her own baby."

The service officer stared blankly at Marla and then looked back down at the form. When she looked up again, a smile fluttered but disappeared. "It looks like I've got everything I need. Is your cell phone the best way to reach you?"

"Yes," Marla hissed.

The service officer stood. "Someone will contact you within the next week."

Carli made to stand, but Marla grabbed her arm, yanked her back into her chair.

"Why so long?"

The service officer looked to the door and then at her watch. "We'll assign a detective. He or she will need to coordinate with the Elmhurst jurisdiction and gather information from the adoption agency before they determine next steps."

"Next steps? What the hell does that mean?"

"It means the detective will determine what's appropriate based upon what he or she discovers," she said, her voice clipped.

"It means you ain't gonna do shit."

"We're busy. And to be honest, it's not real clear to me that a crime was even committed." She opened the door. "If you'll excuse me, there are other people waiting."

Marla glowered at the service officer as she stalked past. When they got to the truck, Carli climbed in and stared through the windshield. She waited for the onslaught, waited to hear how stupid she was for starting this whole fiasco, but Marla just glared at her for a long moment, before she pulled her phone from her pocket and punched out a number.

"Hey, Larry. It's Marla. It's payback time. I need you to do something. Tonight."

Jon

*

All the hotels in Tomah, Wisconsin, required identification and a credit card. So did the first two motels. Finally, out by EZE Storage, they found a motel that looked like a strong wind could bring it down. The man behind the desk was protected by bulletproof glass but took cash and asked no questions. The room's brown shag carpet and the bedspread with geese flying across a marsh looked like they were stolen from the set of a Nicolas Cage movie. Febreze tried but failed to mask the odor of mouse shit. Jon threw the bedspread into the corner and made a mental note to buy their own sheets the next time they saw a Walmart. He cranked the heater under the window, and it clattered to life. Spring hadn't quite arrived in Tomah.

The stink made Jon think about his mom. More precisely, it made him think of Aqua Bay. Those fourteen days in the Ozarks were the last that he'd ever spend with her, but it was a while before he'd realize that. A month after Aunt Carol rescued him from that crack between the bed and the wall, he asked her when he'd be going back to the trailer.

Aunt Carol said, "Let's just see how it goes."

After a while, the other kids at school began to talk to him, because it seemed like he might stick around. A few even played with him at recess. He got used to the idea of three meals a day, and he soon realized that he didn't have to cook any of them—much less walk to the 7-Eleven to buy groceries. He stopped wearing the same pants two days in a row, and he liked that he didn't have to wash them in the shower with dish soap, because at Aunt Carol's, the laundry was in the basement. Still, he continued to ask when he would go home.

It took a while to get used to the consistency. *Every* weekday, Uncle Mark went to work at the *same* time, and he went to the *same* job. Aunt Carol quit her job at the library so that she could be at the house *every* day when Jon got home, with snacks and questions about school. Aunt Carol helped him *every* night with his homework, and Uncle Mark helped him learn guitar *every* weekend. Nobody *ever* slept during the day. They ate dinner together *every* night. They hugged him before he went to bed and *always* said *I love you.* All of this disoriented him at first, but over time, he learned to expect it. As the months passed, he asked about his mom less often, and Aunt Carol's answers became more and more vague. He was expected to clean his room and load the dishwasher after dinner and say *please* and *thank you* and *I love you, too.* In short, Aunt Carol and Uncle Mark expected him to be a child and nothing more.

Jon never learned all the levers Aunt Carol had to pull in order to terminate his mom's parental rights and formally adopt him. His mom lived just three miles away, but she never visited. When he got his driver's license, he would drive toward the trailer park where she lived about once every month, but then veer in another direction before he got there. The summer after his senior year, he finally parked Aunt Carol's Saturn in the gravel next to the trailer. He didn't know what to expect when he knocked on the door, but he had learned a lot in the last decade. He had learned what it meant to be loved. He had learned what it meant to be part of a family. He had learned to recognize a parent, a mother. He had learned that the woman who shuffled around inside while the pit bull next door strained against its chain and barked, was not his mother anymore.

Gail fed Maya, read *Goodnight Moon*, and then settled her into the Pack 'n Play. Jon found the bag from Sally Beauty Supply in his duffel and pulled out the clippers.

"We need to take photos for the passports."

Gail touched her hair. "You want me to cut it?"

Jon smiled and tossed her the dye kit. "Clippers are for me."

They crowded into the tiny bathroom, and Jon sheared himself down to a military-grade bristle. His ears loomed enormous. Gail bleached and then colored her hair and eyebrows a dirty blond. After they snapped photos of each other against the white shower curtain, Jon settled into the chair to set up the new computer. He slotted his earbuds and played the Smashing Pumpkins loud so that he could focus. He configured the mobile data card so that the IP address couldn't be traced. He scanned the frantic emails from Paige. He moved their money from their checking account and savings account. He cashed out their 401(k). It took him just thirty minutes to convert their life savings to Bitcoin.

He checked his watch again. He might be able to figure out the rest himself, but it would take all night, and he didn't have the energy. Stuart could be trusted. Stuart could at least be trusted to be Stuart. He picked up one of the burners and dialed

Stuart's number. Almost one in the morning, but he would probably answer. He ran the security practice, so he did things that others didn't do. He knew things that others didn't know. He answered calls that came in late at night from numbers that he didn't recognize. Above all else, Stuart kept his mouth shut.

After six rings, Stuart finally answered. "Who is this?" he asked, no hostility in his voice, just curiosity, efficiency.

"Jon Durbin."

"Hey, Jon. How's the baby?"

"The baby's good. Real good. Listen. I need a favor."

"What's up?"

"I need to get on the darknet."

Stuart went quiet for a moment. "Let me call you back."

A few minutes later, Stuart rang from a different number. Jon could hear traffic in the background.

"This isn't your cell number," Stuart said.

"No. It isn't."

"Not that it's any of my business, but . . . why the darknet?"

"I've got an uncle in Missouri with colon cancer. No medical weed there. I told him that I'd set him up."

Another pause. Jon watched Gail. She sat on the bed against the wall, bent over blank pages that she had torn from the back of the Gideons Bible. Her hair hung wet against her face while she scribbled.

"We both know that there are easier solutions to that problem than the darknet," Stuart said. Jon let the silence settle. He knew that Stuart wouldn't believe him, but he didn't think it would matter. "So, I assume that you already downloaded TOR?"

"I did," Jon said.

"You need a VPN, too. I would use IPVanish."

"OK."

"DeepDotWeb has the best reviews of marketplaces. It depends on what you're really after, but I'd probably try Tochka. You can trust their suppliers as much as anyone's."

In about twenty minutes, Stuart helped Jon configure all the security protocols, got him logged in.

"Tochka's good," Stuart said. "But there's a lot of scammers up there."

"Yeah. I know."

Stuart was quiet again. Jon heard a siren in the background. "Whatever it is you're really after, be careful."

"Thank you," Jon said, and hung up. *Be careful.* It was too late for that.

It took another hour and several false starts to find someone who seemed legit and responded when Jon pinged them. The negotiation was brief, and Jon sent half the price in Bitcoin. He uploaded their photos and his new name, and a new name for Maya. He sent a Winnipeg address that he'd found on Zillow and the address for the UPS store in Grand Forks, North Dakota.

"I need your name," he said.

Gail looked up from her lists and blinked. She looked different, and it wasn't just the new shade of hair. It was the tentative way she moved, the look of uncertainty on her face. She had been so quiet all day. After she had said those five words, after she asked that question, she hadn't said much else, as if she was still unsure of the answer herself. In the long moment before she replied, he felt certain that she would suggest that they go home. He wondered what he would do if she did.

"Kimberly," she finally said.

"Kimberly. I like that."

* * *

Jon took a long shower, trying to clear his head. The lights were off when he came out of the bathroom. He climbed into bed, rolled toward the center, and found Gail there. He wrapped his arms around her and squeezed her tight. Gail's breath slowed toward sleep, and her head grew heavy on Jon's arm. He closed his eyes and tried to fall asleep himself. He tried to convince himself that Gail was ready for this, that she knew what she was headed toward. *What if we take her?* Jon had never felt more certain about an answer. The same memories that terrified him a week ago now drove that certainty. Carli would struggle—maybe not in the same way that his mom had—but she would struggle, and Maya would be the one to suffer. As Jon drifted toward sleep, the smell of Milk Duds mingled with the smell of mouse shit, and his certainty hardened into something else altogether.

Marla

*

Marla and Helen packed without speaking. They pointedly avoided eye contact. The towering shelves of product seemed to push inward, pressurizing their silence. The bruises on Helen's chin and next to her eye were already beginning to yellow around the edges. Kurt had gone easy on her.

The morning moved slowly. Only three pickers. Marla kept one eye on the time clock over by the receiving dock. She figured that Larry would be late, but she knew that he would come. And she knew that he'd do what she asked him. She had lent him bail money when he had that scrape with those Albanians up in Lockport a while back. For all his faults, Larry paid his debts.

At half past nine, Larry clocked in carrying a plastic Jewel bag. He wore a cutoff Budweiser T-shirt that showed the rash of tattoos on his arms. He headed to the break room to get his morning Mountain Dew, and he returned a few minutes later without the bag. He grabbed an order, and after studying it, he handed a wadded Post-it to Marla as he walked off into the maze of shelves. Marla glanced at Helen, but she didn't seem to have noticed. When Helen carried a box to a skid, Marla opened the note and read it. *Meet me at the paper in five minutes.*

Marla packed one more order and then headed around the shelves toward the bathroom. When she neared the binder aisle, though, she turned left instead of right and walked to the far end of the warehouse, to the paper aisle. Copy paper, printer paper, legal pads, fax paper, wide-ruled, yellow, recycled—all of it stacked on skids and perched on shelves. Larry sat on a case of all-purpose bright white copy paper smoking a cigarette, the Jewel bag at his feet. His beer gut strained against the Budweiser logo.

"You were right," he said. "They gone."

"How you know for sure?"

"Baby's room was tore up. All the drawers on the floor. Their bedroom was a shitshow, like they packed real fast. I checked the trash cans like you said. Nothing but Kleenex and junk mail."

"What's in the bag?"

He pulled a laptop computer out of the bag and laid it on the top of a skid of paper. "They left this sitting right on the desk. Seems like a weird thing to leave behind. I tried to start it up, but you need a password. Not sure what the hell you'll do with that."

Marla had no idea about computers. "What else?"

Larry pulled a leather notebook from the bag—the one Gail Durbin was scribbling on at the hospital. Marla plucked it from his hands, paged through it, and found list after list in neat print. *Ointments and Creams, Summer Clothes, Children's Books About Diversity, Schedule for Fire Alarm Testing.* Most of the items on each list had a single straight line through them. Marla chuckled when she saw the list *Perfectly Good Reasons Why Carli Hasn't Called Back.* What a nutjob.

"Check out the last page she wrote in."

Marla flipped from the back of the notebook. The last list wasn't titled. The writing was by the same person, but it was messy, written in a hurry. Nothing was crossed out. *Hair clippers, cash, laptop, hair dye, Grand Forks, cell phones, 401K, Winnipeg.*

Gail

*

Gail watched the trees slide by, the exits, the mile markers. North of Minneapolis, the maples and the oaks gave way to tall, straight pines. She felt the cold through the glass. Spring was another month away this far north. They would need heavier coats. They would need an apartment and a pediatrician for Maya and a job for Jon, and she had to learn to sign her new name. Kimberly. Or Kim. While Jon worked at the computer the night before, Gail had made lists on the pages she tore out of the motel Bible. She ached for her notebook, but she knew that scribbling on stolen Bible pages wouldn't be the biggest adjustment she'd have to make. She tried to organize her mind around everything that they would need when they got to Winnipeg. Lists of clothes and toiletries and furniture and cleaning supplies. Thinking about those lists helped to settle her, center her. They helped her lean into their future. They kept her mind away from Carli.

Gail looked at the clock on the dash—10:45. She wondered if her dad was at work. The rasp of metal on stone bothered some people, but it calmed her dad. Did he hear that soothing racket right now, or was he at home, dealing with her mom, worrying? Would he guess what had happened, that they had run with the baby, or would his mind slip to something worse?

Jon was quiet. She wondered what he was thinking, wondered how he could stay so calm. After she had said those five words, everything seemed to shift in him, and he started to move with a settled certainty. He seemed to be slipping from their old life so easily, like he was changing a sweater or switching the channel. And he didn't seem to give Carli a second thought.

Gail's mind drifted to the thick calluses on her dad's hands and to the calluses that she had earned each of those three summers that she spent in the shop. During the winter, her hands would go soft, and the first week was always bad. The inevitable contact with the stone sent her home with raw fingers, and she'd take Tylenol every four hours. That first summer, she coated her hands with moisturizer, until her dad told her to put the lotion away. He said that softness wasn't the answer, that she had to trust that the hardness would come. And it did. The second week, the calluses began to form, the result of the abrasion, but a shield against it, too. By the end of the summer, when her hands brushed the spinning stone, she didn't even feel it.

Maya's nose already looked so much like Carli's that thoughts of Carli would be impossible to avoid. And as Maya grew, there was no telling how much she would come to resemble her birth mother. Maybe it was best to let her mind drift toward Carli, let it chafe against what they had done to her. Maybe Gail should trust that if she let it tear at her a little bit at a time, that calluses would form, to shield her from that nose.

So she leaned her head against the window and used the mile markers to find her rhythm. As they passed each green sign, she thought about a doctor's visit, or a lunch at Panera, or that terrifying first meeting in the diner. When they passed an exit, she let herself think about the pain and confusion and rage that Carli must have been feeling even as they sped north. It hurt, but she had to trust that the pain would prove worth it in the end.

Two hours north of Minneapolis, the engine belched and then resumed its hum.

"You have gas?" Gail asked.

Jon checked the gauge. "Almost half a tank."

The engine spluttered again, a buzzer blared from the dashboard, and then the motor stopped altogether. Jon forced the car onto the shoulder, gravel pelted the wheel wells, and Maya woke, her cries competing with the buzzing. Jon put the car in park, turned the key off and back on. The buzzer blared. He turned it off and leaned back against the headrest.

"What's wrong?"

"It's broken," he said.

"No shit."

He turned the key again. The buzzer wailed. He turned it off. Gail's dad would get the bag of tools from the trunk, lift the hood, take a few things apart, and as likely as not get it running again. But Jon could only troubleshoot computers—Gail knew there would be no hood lifting. He turned on the hazards and reached into the back seat for his backpack. Gail had forgotten that Maya was crying, had tuned it out, until Jon said, "Why don't you try holding her?"

Gail climbed out and into the back seat. A semi rushed by, and the wind pulled at the door as she struggled to close it.

Maya's face bloomed red, her eyes squeezed shut, and her mouth stretched wide with the crying. Gail took Maya from the car seat and hugged her tiny body to her chest and whispered in her ear, but she only cried louder. Gail fumbled to fill a bottle with water from the thermos. She fed Maya as Jon called for a tow truck. Maya sucked, only surrendering the nipple to breathe and to cry a bit more. As the bottle emptied, Maya stilled, and Gail focused on her nose, let it tear at her a little. But she also smelled those pears that told her that she was holding her baby. Maya's eyes creased open just a tiny bit. The gray of her pupils distracted Gail from the blue and red of the lights, until Jon cursed. Gail finally tore her eyes away from Maya's and looked out the back window at the squad car.

Carli

*

Carli lay on her side, staring through the slats of the empty crib and out the window. As the morning wore on, a shaft of sunlight crept across her room. Dust motes fell through it to the floor. Soon, the sun would reach her face and she'd either have to get up and close the curtains or let go of the crib, roll over, and face the other way.

Her sleep the night before had been choppy and sloppy with half-awake dreams of Andy sweating and grunting over her and her own sweating and grunting in the delivery room. She felt like she was pushing all over again. She felt split open. And then she was pulling back, trying to suck the baby back inside her. She kept seeing the baby's face, half hidden by that pink blanket, with those slits for eyes, and that tongue poking from between thin blue lips. And the service officer kept asking the same question: *Why did you change your mind? Why did you change your mind? Why did you change your mind?* Around dawn, she went to the refrigerator to get one of Marla's Mountain Dews and brought it back to her room—not because she wanted to stay awake, really, but because she could no longer bear what came with sleep.

Carli wanted to blame Gail and Jon for disappearing with Maya. She wanted to blame Paige for telling her that the baby was coming and then screwing it up somehow. She wanted to blame Marla for forcing her to look at that wrinkled face and smell that vanilla cream soda. But she knew who to blame. As that baby grew, she had carefully built a wall around it and she didn't touch that wall, didn't even look at it, and she didn't allow herself to become attached to what was on the other side. That wall protected her from the empty place after she gave eight pounds of herself away, and she counted on the idea that the empty place would have grown smaller and smaller until she would only feel it when she wanted to. But then she let Marla kick the wall down, and she found that space behind the wall wasn't empty at all. It took Carli a while to recognize love for what it was, but then love was all she could feel, and it hurt. And after she talked to Paige, and Paige told her she'd bring the baby back, and they bought the diapers, and they set up the crib, she allowed herself to wedge hope alongside it. And while she waited with Marla in the front room, she was stupid enough to pack that space that wasn't empty with new ideas—ideas about having a daughter and being a mother and building a family, and that space beneath her ribs grew full and stretched tight. But then, of course, everything had melted into a bloody mess and she was afraid to move, because everything fucking hurt.

The front door opened, and Carli heard the familiar sound of keys dropping into the mason jar next to the TV. She closed her eyes and pretended to be asleep, breathing heavily and slowly. She heard her bedroom door open, but she kept breathing steady, hoping that Marla would go away, knowing that she wouldn't.

"Get up," Marla said.

Carli opened her eyes but didn't roll over. "Why aren't you at work?"

"I took the rest of the day off. Get up."

Marla tugged the blanket off, but Carli clung to the sheet. "Why?" she asked.

"I need help with the computer."

"Why?"

Marla smacked her on the back of the head, and Carli realized that she'd been bracing for the blow.

"Because I fucking said so." Marla's voice rumbled. "It's time to tell your side of the story to someone who will listen."

Jon

*

Jon gripped the wheel, eyes on the rearview mirror. A bead of sweat rolled down the center of his back and slipped into the crack of his ass.

"What's he doing?" Gail asked.

"I don't know," Jon said. The cop had been sitting in his car with the lights flashing for almost fifteen minutes. "Running the plates, maybe?"

"Why's he running the plates?"

"I don't know, Gail," Jon snapped. And then, more gently, "It's probably standard procedure."

Jon hoped it was standard procedure. Surely the cops hadn't been notified yet. Surely there was no APB, no nationwide alert, no manhunt. Not yet. He was expecting a week of confusion and inaction. Counting on it, really. Finally, the cop got out of the car and put on his trooper hat. He walked to the driver's side, his hand on his gun. Also, standard procedure, Jon hoped. He rolled down the window.

"Hello, Officer."

The cop bent warily. His hair was cropped tight. His eyes were hidden behind mirrored sunglasses that reflected Jon's own nervous face. "Mr. Hendricks?"

Hendricks? "No. No, sir. Reynolds. Allen Reynolds."

The trooper peered into the back of the car at Gail and Maya. "Registration for your plates says Wayne Hendricks."

"Really?" Jon said. "We just bought the car yesterday. Guy who owned the lot was named Wayne."

"Usually doesn't work that way."

"I wouldn't think so," Jon said. "Why would he put the plates in his own name?"

The cop looked to the back seat again, and then back at Jon. "Beats me." A smile finally flickered. "Illinois is a strange place."

Jon laughed, but it sounded false even to him. "Car died just before you pulled up. Maybe Wayne can keep it in his name."

The cop's smile broadened. "There's a couple of shops up in Fergus Falls."

"I already called one of them. They're sending a tow truck."

The cop checked his watch. "I'll give you folks a ride into town."

Jon looked up at the sunglasses but found only his own reflection. "Thank you, but that's really not necessary. They should be here shortly."

Maya started to cry again.

"They won't have room for all three of you. I'm headed that way anyway."

"We should be fine." Jon didn't care if he had to ride on the back of the tow truck, in the trunk of the Camry if necessary. "Thank you, though."

The cop cocked his head and looked into the back again. "How old's that baby?"

Why was *that* relevant? Jon considered adding a week or two, but the truth came out instead. "Seven days."

Another pause as the cop looked through the back window. "I can't leave a newborn on the side of the road. My wife would kill me."

Jon studied the glasses, looking for a seam, a way to wriggle free, but there was none. He nodded and climbed out of the car. They loaded the car seat and the diaper bag into the back seat of the patrol car. Gail, stone-faced, got into the back with Maya and strapped her in. Jon climbed into the front with his backpack.

"I'm Lathan," the cop said after he settled into his seat and radioed his plans to the dispatcher. "Lathan Jennings."

"I really appreciate this, Officer."

"Not a problem." After he pulled onto the highway and gained speed, he glanced in the rearview mirror at Gail. "Mrs. Reynolds, what's your name?"

Gail didn't respond at first. Jon looked back through the metal grate at Gail, who was staring out the window. He wasn't sure whether she didn't hear the question or couldn't remember her new name. He considered answering for her, but Lathan repeated his question more loudly.

"Kim," Gail finally said.

"And the baby?"

"Emma," Jon blurted at the same time that Gail said, "Maya." Shit. He hadn't yet told Gail Maya's new name.

"Whoa." Lathan looked in the mirror again. "There two babies back there?"

"Emma's her first name, and Maya's her middle name," Jon said quickly. "We're still arguing about which to use."

Lathan nodded, looking unconvinced. "I been married for

fourteen years and have two kids." He cast a look at Jon, smiled a tight smile. "I highly recommend you lose that argument."

They drove in silence. Jon hugged his backpack, tried to think of something to say, but Lathan beat him to it. "Where you folks headed?"

"Grand Forks," Jon said quickly, before Gail had a chance to say Winnipeg.

"Grandparents?"

"Huh?"

"You visiting the grandparents?"

"Oh. Yeah. Right."

"Where in Grand Forks?"

Jon squeezed the backpack. "Northwest side," he murmured.

"Really? I grew up near there. What neighborhood?"

Shit. "I'm not sure," he said, and looked out the window. "I left the address in the car."

Long pause. "Your parents or Kim's?" Jennings's voice had changed, the friendliness had fallen away. He now sounded a bit like a cop interrogating a suspect.

"Mine," Jon said. He guessed at the next question. "They just moved there."

"North Dakota instead of Florida?"

"My dad took a new job."

"Who's he work for?" Lathan asked immediately.

Jon's mind scrambled for an answer specific enough that it wouldn't spawn more questions, but vague enough that he wouldn't be caught in a lie. "State Farm."

They drove the next several miles in silence. Jennings alternated his attention between the road and Jon and Gail in the mirror. Jon couldn't help but get the feeling that he was tallying up the inconsistencies in the story, memorizing their faces, crafting his next question. If Jennings asked for his license, Jon would tell him he lost his wallet. If he asked for Jon's parents' names, he'd say Carol and Mark Reynolds. If he asked for their phone number, he'd give him one of the burner numbers that he'd memorized. The trooper opened his mouth to start in again when Gail spoke.

"How old are your children?" she asked.

"Ten and twelve."

"Those are fun ages. Boys? Girls?"

"One of each."

"They play sports?"

For the next twenty minutes, Gail interrogated Jennings, who dutifully answered her questions about wrestling and soccer and braces and ballet. By the time they arrived at Advanced Repair, he and Gail had agreed that the offside rule was incomprehensible, dance recital costumes cost too much, and orthodontics was a racket. After they unloaded the baby gear into the shop's dingy waiting room, Gail took Maya to the bathroom to change her diaper. Jon shook Jennings's hand and thanked him again. Jennings took his sunglasses off and appraised Jon with cold gray eyes. "Allen Hendricks, right?"

Jon shook his head. "Reynolds."

"Right." He took out his notebook. "Why don't you give me your phone number, Mr. Reynolds? I'd like to check in with you later. Make sure everything turns out all right." He nodded to the restroom. "You know. With the baby and all."

Paige

*

Paige hung up the phone and crossed Allison Markham off the list. Allison didn't know anything more than the rest of Jon and Gail's friends. It seemed that they didn't even tell anyone but Gail's parents that Carli wanted to reclaim. It was as if they had known from the very beginning what they were going to do.

Paige had arrived at the agency at seven in the morning. She made herself coffee—tea wouldn't cut it—and then she shut her office door so that nobody would bother her. She spent the first hour paging through Jon and Gail's home study, highlighting names and looking up phone numbers. For the last four hours she'd been making calls, asking questions, listening for the hesitation, the strained response that would tell her someone was hiding something. Usually, home studies are useless—just paperwork to cover the state's ass. But Jon and Gail's served as a nice directory of all the important people in their life. A list of informants. Potential witnesses. Soon the home study would be collected as evidence in a criminal investigation. Paige knew before she drove to Morris to tell Carli, even before she left the Durbins' porch, that she was dealing with a crime.

She didn't find the right word for it at first. After she left Carli's house—after she was thrown out by Marla, really—Paige drove directly to the Elmhurst police station. When she asked to see a detective, she called it a disappearance. She cooled her heels in the waiting room for almost two hours. *Disappearance* wasn't quite right, but that other word felt so overly dramatic, extreme, harsh on her tongue. Finally, she walked back up to the desk and told the clerk that it was more than just a disappearance—it was a kidnapping.

She talked to the detective for more than an hour. She had all the documentation—the birth certificate, the adoption statute, the reclamation filing. The detective kept asking why Carli had changed her mind, and Paige kept asking him why that was relevant. It might help him *gain context*, he said. By the end of the hour, the complaint was filed, but Paige felt certain that it would fall to the bottom of his pile. Something in the way that the detective closed the folder, the way that he avoided eye contact with Paige, told her that he had already chosen sides.

On the way home from the police station, she called Henry, the agency's lawyer, to see if he could connect her with someone. He said that he had a friend from law school, a federal prosecutor, who undoubtedly knew agents in the local FBI field office, and he promised to call. She checked her watch. If she didn't hear from somebody soon, she'd call the FBI directly. As she dialed the number for Jon's aunt, she tried to push her own culpability from her mind.

"Hello. This is Carol."

"Hi, Carol. This is Paige Wellington, the social worker for Jon and Gail's adoption."

"Yes?"

No hesitation, just curiosity cut with confusion. Before Paige even asked the question, she knew the answer. "I'm wondering if you've heard from Jon or Gail in the last couple of days?"

"Jon called on Saturday. Why? Is something wrong?"

Everyone who Paige called asked the same question. She made the mistake of telling the first few what was going on. She spent thirty minutes answering questions, and most of those questions centered around why Carli changed her mind. They had, of course, chosen their side.

"No. I'm just trying to tie up some paperwork. Can you give me a call if you hear from them?"

Paige gave her phone number and then hung up as quickly as possible. She had learned long ago not to take sides. Adoptions, even the successes, can get complicated. She learned during the first dozen, that with so much emotion involved, with so much at stake, there wasn't room for favorites. Everyone talked about the best interest of the child. Until the shit hit the fan. Then everyone screamed about the best interest of the child. There were laws and processes and procedures, though, and when people started yelling at her, Paige would purr in her smooth-jazz social-worker voice and take them through the process. She tried to be empathetic to everyone, but she never steered the outcome. She never took sides.

Last on the list: Jon's mother. Even during the home study—a process designed to hash through every detail of a couple's life—Jon's mom remained a mystery. Whenever Paige asked a question about her, Jon would look down at the table, and then Gail would say something vague before changing the subject. Before she could pick up the handset, though, the phone rang. A downtown number.

"This is Paige."

"Hi, Paige. This is Agent Bradford from the FBI. I was asked to call you."

Finally. Finally, it would begin. It had been almost twenty-four hours since Paige went to the Durbins to pick up Maya. She would use the right word this time. And she had chosen sides. "Thank you for calling, Agent Bradford. I'd like to report a kidnapping."

Gail

*

Gail emerged from the cramped, fetid bathroom and found the car seat on a chair in the car repair shop's lobby. She settled Maya into it and sat down next to her. Jon was discussing their situation with a man behind the counter who wore greasy coveralls and a blank expression. It did not seem to be going well.

"What do you mean you haven't sent the truck yet?"

The man—he was really no more than a chubby boy—spoke slowly and loudly, as if Jon were hard of hearing or from a foreign country. "We haven't. Sent. The Truck. Yet."

"When? When will you send the truck?"

The boy shrugged. "By end of the day."

"Are you kidding me? I called more than an hour ago."

The boy arranged some papers on the counter. Gail had seen this particular movie too many times, and she knew how it ended. Jon always lost his mind with people who reminded him of his time in the trailer, reminded him of where he might have ended up if his aunt hadn't plucked him from that life.

Gail thought about standing up, stepping in, but she worried that might only make things worse.

"Maybe I should go to the other shop."

The boy's lips flickered. "Roy's?"

"Yeah. Roy's."

The boy chuckled. "Good luck with that."

Jon turned and looked at Gail and Maya. He pulled out his wallet, leaned against the counter. "How much?" he muttered.

"Huh?"

"How much? To get it towed now?"

The boy shrugged again. "Hundred bucks might expedite things."

"What the fuck does *might* mean?"

The boy said nothing, straightened the papers again. Jon counted out a stack of twenties and pushed them across the counter. The boy swept up the bills and crumpled them into the pocket of his coveralls.

"We'll call you soon as it gets in."

Jon glared at him as he hefted the car seat. Gail grabbed the diaper bag and waited until the door closed behind Jon.

"Thank you," she said quietly.

He looked at her for a moment and then nodded ever so slightly. Gail pushed through the door and hurried to catch up to Jon.

A few blocks down the main street they found the Viking Cafe, a brick box with round windows like portholes and a Coca-Cola sign. A bell rang when they pushed through the door. Wooden broadswords decorated the walls, and a model of a Nordic long-boat dangled from the ceiling. A short, fat waitress stood at a booth at the front, gabbing with four old men talking loudly about fish. Jon and Gail walked the long aisle to the back and slid into the last booth. Jon pulled out his laptop and pounded the keyboard. Gail unbuckled Maya from the car seat without a word and started to feed her. She knew to give Jon a few minutes to regain his equilibrium.

Although it was nearly empty and looked completely different from the diner where they first met her, something about the place tugged Gail's mind back toward Carli. It was probably the ribbed-glass saltshaker on the table. Gail remembered Carli fidgeting with the salt that first time they met. She had also played with the salt the first time Gail took her to lunch after a checkup. And that time after the twelve-week ultrasound, when Gail couldn't stop thinking about her miscarriages, Carli had made a mess with it. She had grabbed the salt, poured a pile of it onto the table, and pushed it into lines and squares and circles while she talked to fill the silence. She told Gail that giving up the baby made it so important that she do something with her life. She wanted to do something that she could be proud of but something that would give her some flexibility. *For when I have kids of my own*, she had said, drawing a smiley face in the pile of salt. Somehow Carli managed to say those words unselfconsciously, without irony, as she sat there, three months pregnant, across the table from the woman who would take her baby. *Kids of my own.*

"That's a little cutie."

Gail looked up to find the waitress, her stomach brushing the table, her sausage-like fingers gripping a pen. "Thank you."

"Whatcha havin'?"

After the waitress took their order and drifted away, Gail said, "I've never been in the back of a police car."

239

This coaxed a slice of a smile from Jon. His college years had been a bit more volatile than Gail's, and she knew that he couldn't say the same.

"What did you think?"

"There were no handles on the inside of the back doors. And that cage."

"Nice work, by the way."

"Huh?"

"With that cop. Distracting him. I was running out of answers."

"Ballet costumes *are* a scam." Gail poured a tiny pile of salt onto the table. "What were you doing just now?"

"Checking emails. And messages from that guy. The passports were sent. Birth certificates and driver's licenses, too. It should all be in Grand Forks by tomorrow at ten."

"What else?"

"What do you mean?"

"Any other messages?"

Jon straightened the silverware in front of him. "Paige is looking for us. Confused and alarmed. So far no mention of the cops." He glanced at the laptop and then back at Gail. "And your dad. Wondering where we are."

At the mention of her dad, Gail brushed the salt onto the floor, dusted the grains from her palms.

"Can I check my email?"

"Sure. I'll log you on." He clicked and typed and spun the laptop her way. "Don't respond to anything."

Eighteen emails crowded her in-box. Nine were spam. Paige sent six, Cindy two, her dad sent just one. None from her mom, which made her angry and relieved at the same time. Paige's all read pretty much the same: *Where the hell are you?* Cindy didn't seem to know that they were gone. Her dad's was short, but Gail read it three times.

> Gail,
> I'm really worried about you. Call me as soon as you can.
> I love you.
> Dad

Gail closed the browser and then folded the lid of the laptop. She pushed it back across the table. "I need one of those phones," she said.

"What for?"

"I need to call my dad."

For a moment Jon said nothing. He looked from Gail to his backpack and then back at Gail. Finally, he said, "Should we wait until we get across the border?"

"I need to tell him we're safe. That we're OK."

"You sure you're ready?"

Gail nodded. She needed to hear his voice.

Jon reached into his backpack and pulled out a phone. He hesitated before handing it to her, and she could see him decide not to argue.

"Please don't say where we are or where we're headed."

Gail found a bench on the sidewalk and sat. She dialed quickly, before she could change her mind. Her dad answered after the first ring.

"Hello?" He sounded bewildered. Lost.

"Hey, Dad. It's me."

"Gail," he said, her name a sigh. It sounded like a please and a thank-you and a prayer. "Are you OK?"

"I am." She stared across the street at the barbershop. "We are."

"Where are you?"

"I—I promised Jon that I wouldn't say."

"But—but you're safe?"

"Yes. We're safe."

Another long breath released. "I guess it's probably best that I don't know."

"It is," she whispered.

"A cop is coming by in a few minutes. To ask some questions. He said it was about a kidnapping."

A kidnapping. That word had been nagging at Gail, fluttering into her thoughts like a moth toward light, but hearing it from her father felt like a slap in the face. "It's not like that, Dad."

The long silence before he spoke again told Gail that her dad thought it was exactly like that.

"So you're just going to run? That's your plan?"

"We're leaving the country. Jon is getting us fake passports."

"Jesus, Mary, and Joseph."

A Fergus Falls policeman drove by, and Gail had to remind herself that she was still just another woman sitting outside a diner on a cell phone, that she looked as innocent as anyone else.

"Gail. Are you sure this is the right thing to do?"

"Dad. Don't."

"This is killing me, Gail."

No mention of her mom. Her dad had learned long ago not to speak for her mom.

"I know."

"When can I see you again?"

"I don't know."

"Family is family, Gail. This makes my chest hurt."

"Maya's our daughter," Gail said. "She's part of our family now, too."

A long silence. Gail leaned forward on the bench, tried to decide how to end the call, wondered if she could.

"What about Carli?" he finally asked.

"Dad—"

"I talked to Paige this morning. She said that Carli's torn up by all of this."

"Don't do this, Dad."

"She's the baby's mother, Gail. I've always taught you to do what's right no matter how hard it might be."

Gail shivered. *Do what's right,* her dad's mantra. But this wasn't an invoice dispute or lost knives or a wrecked van.

"She promised."

"Gail—"

"No. She promised that I would be Maya's mother, and then she broke that promise. Tell me what's right about that."

Gail could hear her dad's ragged breath. Although she'd never seen him cry, she thought that he might be crying now.

"I know this is hard," he whispered. "But you're going to live with this the rest of your life." He coughed, cleared his throat. "Feel the balance of it, Gail."

Gail gripped the phone, her eyes squeezed shut. *Feel the balance of it.* Her dad always said that you can never tell a good knife just by looking at it. If you're not careful, the fancy flourishes might fool you—the choil, the fuller, the granton scallops. Good steel is most important. And a full tang—when the blade extends all the way through the handle—provides strength and contributes to the balance. Balance. Above all else, a good knife feels right in your hand. *Pick it up*, he would always say. *Hold it and feel the balance of it.*

"I have to go, Dad."

"I love you, Gail. More than you'll ever know."

Gail's throat burned, and a sob escaped with her reply. "I love you, too."

After she hung up, she sat on the bench and looked across the street at the barbershop for a long time. Her mind tried to shrink from the truth—that she'd never return home, that she might never see her dad again—but she forced herself to lean into it. It hurt, but she had to trust the pain. She had to trust that the hardness would come.

Jon

*

The bell above the door rang when Jon entered the shop. From the garage, he could hear men talking and the muffled clunk of metal tools dropping on concrete. He knew he'd been too aggressive earlier about the tow truck, so he forced himself to sit down and wait.

Gail had talked a long time with her dad. Afterward, her eyes were bloodshot, and she wiped at her nose like a coke addict, but all she would say while they ate was that her dad was worried. When she asked for the phone, Jon had thought about pressing her to wait, but he knew that look on her face too well. He checked his watch. Ten minutes had passed and there was a bell right there on the counter, so he stood up and rang it.

"Give me a goddamn minute," someone barked from the garage. Jon sat back down. Five minutes more until the same grease monkey from earlier limped into the waiting area, wiping his hands on a rag. He was in his early twenties with sparse whiskers on a wide, round, scowling face. He walked behind the counter but just stared at Jon with his mouth open a little so that he could breathe.

"Listen. I'm sorry about earlier," Jon said. "I lost my temper."

Will—if the stitching on his coveralls was to be believed—waited.

"You called and said my car is here."

"Which one's yours?"

Jon tried to figure out if he was stupid or just still pissed off. He reminded Jon of the guy in the trailer next to his mom's. The guy who owned that pit bull. "The Camry? You just towed it in?"

"The one from Illinois." Will looked up at the clock. "Tomorrow."

"You'll have it fixed tomorrow?"

"No. We'll look at it tomorrow."

Jon glanced at the clock. Quarter after one. He did his best to stay calm. "There's no way you can look at it today?"

"Nope." Will stood impassively, still wiping his hands with the rag. "Probably won't get to it till tomorrow afternoon."

Jon reached into his pocket for his wallet, opened it, and looked for the right bill. "Can I pay you another expediting fee?"

"Nah. Keep your fucking money."

Will walked back into the garage, still wiping his hands on the rag. Jon stood at the counter, his wallet open, his head pounding, trying to decide whether to ring that bell again. If they looked at the car tomorrow afternoon, there wasn't a chance they would fix it until the day after. Which was the day after their passports would arrive in Grand Forks, the day after he planned to cross into Canada. But the grease monkey held all the power, and the grease monkey hated his guts.

*   *   *

The bell on the door of the Viking rang too loudly when Jon pushed through. A group of blue-haired women looked up from their coffee. Gail looked up. Maya started crying. Jon slid into the booth, working the angles, searching for the seam. His fingers ached for his guitar or his banjo.

"What's wrong?"

"They're not even gonna look at it until tomorrow."

"Is there another—"

"Just Roy's. I called on the walk back. Number's disconnected. I think there's a shop in Carlisle, but that's thirty miles up the interstate."

Gail looked down at Maya. "So they fix it tomorrow."

"Maybe. But I doubt it." Jon rubbed his face, looked out the window. "My buddy Will does not seem to like my attitude."

"So. What do we do?"

"We can't rent a car—not without a license. Not that there's a Hertz in this shithole. We can buy another car, but that'll take a big chunk out of the cash we have. We can try to get our car to Carlisle, but in the time it would take to work all that out, that wanker would probably have it fixed."

Jon wondered if there was a bus to Grand Forks. And then he thought about high school. He thought about what his friend Eric had taught him that night they took his neighbor's Firebird for a joyride. "Or we could wait until dark and lift one."

Gail looked at him sharply. "You mean steal one?"

Jon shrugged. "Borrow it for a while."

Gail's lips disappeared, and she looked down at Maya. "That's the dumbest idea I've heard in a long, long, time."

Jon bristled. "So, what? Should we wait four days for that douchebag to fix our car?"

"Should we rob a liquor store? Maybe cook some meth?"

"You have a better idea?"

Gail looked toward the front of the diner and then down at Maya. She stood, put on her jacket, and lifted Maya from the car seat.

"What're you doing?"

"We're going to see about the car."

Marla

*

Marla left the house—she had to leave the house. She couldn't just sit there and wait for somebody to call her, pacing the living room like a caged animal. She couldn't go back to the warehouse and clock back in—she had told her boss that she was sick—so she just drove. She drove down by the river and then up through Minooka and found herself in Shorewood. She wasn't planning to stop at Holy Family, but the car seemed to pull itself over to the curb in front of the church, so she put it in park and got out. And she didn't expect the enormous wooden doors to pull open, but when they did, she stepped into the dusty, cool dimness. She walked past the holy water without dipping her fingers and slipped into the last pew. Three old ladies were scattered throughout the church, kneeling, heads bent. They fingered the well-worn beads of their rosaries, pestering a God who didn't give a shit, for favors he wouldn't deliver.

Marla flipped her lighter through her knuckles. She wouldn't be praying today. If God existed, she had concluded long ago that he was a mean son of a bitch—careless at a minimum. She hadn't seen the inside of a church for almost twenty years, since before she finally left Sean. But churches had always calmed her, allowed her to clear her head and think.

The woman in the first pew stood up, genuflected, and shuffled down the center aisle. She smiled and nodded at Marla. Marla did not smile back. Her gaze drifted from the woman to the windows. It was the windows that did it for Marla. The way the light filtered through the stained glass and littered the pews with blues and reds and greens that glowed in the gloom. That and the candles with their milky stink allowed Marla's breathing to slow, her fists to unclench. They allowed her to push past the Durbins; past that fucking cop; past the sleepy, stupid look on Carli's face, to feel the gentle weight of that baby again. Those eight pounds reminded Marla of what she had missed. She had missed it while she was cleaning up Sean's puke and icing her bruises. She missed it while she was working three jobs to pay for their apartment and food after she left him. By the time she got her shit together, Wendy and Carli were more or less grown and had started calling her Marla instead of Mom. She'd missed everything, and she wasn't going to miss it again. And she wouldn't let Carli.

She thought about calling the cop to tell her about what she'd found in Gail's notebook, but she would want to know how Marla found it, and they still wouldn't do anything. Cops worked for people like the Durbins, not for people like her. She was considering a backup plan, for when Fox News didn't call. She was thinking about Larry again, when her phone rang loudly into the quiet of the church. A downtown number.

"This is Marla."

The two remaining pope lovers turned in their pews to scowl at her.

"I'm sorry. I was looking for Carli Brennan."

"I'm Carli's mom."

"Oh. This is Dean Thompson from Fox News Chicago. Can I speak to Carli?"

"She's sleeping right now. She's awful upset. I could probably answer your questions."

For a moment, Marla thought that she lost him, but finally he spoke. "So this email says a baby was stolen?"

"Right. Carli put her baby up for adoption, but she changed her mind."

"After the Durbins had the baby?"

"But she didn't sign the final consent."

"The final consent?"

"Right. Nothing was final, and when my daughter changed her mind, the Durbins took the baby and ran."

"Ran? What do you mean ran?"

"They were supposed to give the baby back yesterday, but instead they disappeared." Marla flicked the lighter, let the flame burn briefly in the gloom. "They're headin' to Canada right now. With my daughter's baby."

"I saw that in the email. How do you know that? About Canada?"

"They told me. I called 'em when the adoption agency said they disappeared. They said there wasn't nothin' we could do about it 'cause we can't afford the lawyers."

"Did they say that?"

Time to make it simple for him. Time to write the headline. "They think they can just take my daughter's baby because they're rich and we got nothin'."

"They said all that?"

"Pretty much."

"Have you talked to the police about this?"

Marla laughed bitterly. "Yeah. Told us that they'd call us in a week. Maybe. But they won't do shit. Cops don't listen to people like us."

The line fell silent again. The worn wood of the pew in front of Marla glowed purple and red. "I can't promise anything," he finally said. "But I'll make a few calls. Give me the names and phone numbers for the adoption agency and the policeman."

Bingo. "It was a lady."

"I'm sorry?"

"I'm not even sure she was a real cop."

Gail

*

Gail stood at the counter for a moment, almost tapped the bell, but thought better of it. Instead, she pushed through the door to the garage. The front tires of a black Trans Am perched on yellow ramps. "Proud Mary" wailed from a transistor radio hanging on the wall. A pair of scuffed black boots poked from beneath the car, the toes gently tapping to the music. In the second bay, the boy Jon bribed earlier leaned into the engine of a Corolla with a flashlight in one hand. Gail carried Maya around the Trans Am and the boots. This was nothing but a sales call.

When she first started selling, just out of college, she always talked too much. She'd launch into her spiel about Tomassi Grinding, eyes would glaze, and a few minutes later she'd find herself on the sidewalk with nothing to show for it. She finally learned to ask more questions, to listen, so that when she spoke, her words might prove relevant.

As she approached, the boy saw her and straightened. He pulled a rag from the pocket of his coveralls and wiped his hands. He looked at Gail, at Maya. Gail glimpsed a wedding band. She looked him in the eye, and alongside his irritation she saw an intelligence that told her that lies would get her nowhere.

"Hey," Gail said. "I'm Kim. Allen's wife."

The boy didn't say anything, just nodded. The stitching on his coveralls said his name was Will.

"But you know that my name isn't really Kim, and you know that my husband's name isn't really Allen."

He said nothing, but he stopped rubbing his hands with the rag. His irritation faded toward curiosity.

"I want to apologize for the way my husband acted earlier."

Will nodded. "He was a real prick."

Gail shifted Maya to her other shoulder. "He can be. He's under a lot of stress."

"Ain't we all."

"Yes," Gail said quietly. She kissed Maya on the top of the head. "We all are."

Will glanced at the Corolla and back. "That all?"

"You married, Will?"

He nodded. "Three years."

"Kids?"

"No." Will's eyes flicked to Maya. Gail felt his hesitation. She recognized his need. "Not yet."

"She's our first, after trying for a really long time."

Will's eyes lingered on Maya.

"You ever do anything that you weren't supposed to do?" Gail asked.

Will became very still, but he said nothing.

"Did you ever do something that everyone else thinks is wrong, but you know in your heart it's the rightest thing you've ever done?"

The radio blared its tinny beat, and a wrench clanked to the concrete floor under the Trans Am, but a silence had settled between them. Gail waited for him to respond, to admit what her gut told her was true. Finally, his head dipped in the slightest of nods.

"Me, too," Gail said.

Will took a deep breath, glanced at the boots poking from the Trans Am, and then back at Maya. When he spoke, the suspicion and defensiveness had dropped away. His words came softly. "What's her name?"

Gail didn't have to fake the tears that welled in her eyes, and when she spoke, the hitch in her voice came naturally. "We lied to you about our names, but her name is really Maya. It means *love* in Nepalese. It means *generous* in Old Persian."

Maya squirmed and gurgled.

"She's my baby."

When Gail pushed through the door of the Viking, Jon's head snapped up from his laptop at the sound of the bell. His face held a question as she made her way down the aisle. She settled Maya into the car seat and then slid into the booth herself.

"What happened?"

Gail allowed herself a smile. "He said to call around five. He'll get to it by then."

Jon's eyes narrowed. "What'd you say? How'd you get him to change his mind?"

"I didn't." Gail kissed Maya's head. She inhaled her scent. "Maya did."

Carli

*

Carli lay on her bed, on top of the covers, with her clothes on. She lay on her side, her fingers curled around the smooth wooden slat of the empty crib. She tried to imagine where Gail was, what she was thinking, what she was feeling. She got to know Gail pretty well during the pregnancy, during the doctor visits. It took no effort from Carli. Gail didn't like silence, couldn't let the silence sit like Carli could, and she'd talk about anything to fill it. Mostly she talked about things she was buying for the baby, the theme for the nursery, the children's books she liked the most. At first, all the talk about the baby annoyed the crap out of Carli, but then she let it sand some of the edges off her guilt.

After the twelve-week ultrasound, they went to lunch. When they sat down, though, Carli was forced to settle into the silence, because Gail didn't fill it. Carli tried to figure out if she had done something, said something, but she had said little that day while they put jelly on her belly and waved the wand. Mostly she had tried to keep her eyes fixed on a point on the wall that wasn't near the monitor.

And when Carli asked what was wrong, Gail had talked about her miscarriages. She talked about her emptiness. She talked about her expectations. Carli gripped the wooden slat and felt a tear trickle onto the pillow. That was the problem, really, wasn't it? Carli tried to think about what *she* would do, if she was standing at the Canadian border carrying a lifetime of expectations and someone else's baby. Expectations. That was the problem for both of them.

"Carli!" Marla shouted from the front room. "The FBI's here!"

Carli forced herself up and wiped her face dry. She made her way to the front room, where a bald man with a lean face sat on the edge of the couch, elbows on his knees. He stood and tightened his tie.

"Ms. Brennan. I'm Agent Bradford." He offered his hand and she shook it. His voice was clipped, formal. The handshake was sweaty, but firm.

"It's nice to meet you."

Carli sat in a folding chair, and Bradford perched again on the edge of the couch. His crisp suit made Carli self-conscious about her sweatpants, the folding chairs, the half-full ashtrays. Marla leaned back, arms folded across her chest, legs crossed at the ankles in front of her.

"It's nice to finally talk to a real cop," Marla said.

At that, Bradford allowed a tiny smile. "You'll have to forgive the Morris police. You're in a bit of a legal gray area."

"Nothing gray 'bout it," Marla blurted. "They stole my grandbaby."

"I understand how you feel, but it's not quite that simple. Most of the time when the birth mother reclaims, adoptive parents return the baby without issue. It doesn't happen often, but when the adoptive parents don't cooperate, a court order is required. The agency's lawyer is working on that right now. They should be able to get in front of a judge later today."

"So, you ain't gonna do anything till then?"

"I didn't say that. Certain—" He looked down at his hands, back up at Marla. "We don't want to be seen as dragging our heels."

Marla leaned back further, coughed a laugh. "I love Fox News."

Bradford shifted his weight. "Anyway—I'm mainly here to provide status on the investigation. We reached out to the Durbins by phone and email, but they've gone dark. We searched their house and found evidence of a hurried departure. We interviewed Mrs. Durbin's parents, and they haven't heard from her. That, or they're really good liars. Same with Mr. Durbin's aunt and uncle. We haven't been able to reach his mother. We've issued an all-points bulletin with their picture and a description of their car, and we've been in direct contact with the Wisconsin, Minnesota, and North Dakota state police. Our liaison at Homeland Security has put a hold on their passports and notified Canadian Immigration."

"It's about fucking time," Marla said.

Carli slouched lower on the chair, tried to pretend that Marla wasn't in the room. "Thank you," she said. She forced herself to look Bradford directly in the eye. "I just want my baby back."

"I know," he said. The formality softened. "We're doing our best, ma'am. Do either of you have any questions?"

"Yeah," Marla said. "What about that thing that makes your cell phone chirp?"

Bradford looked puzzled for a moment. "You mean the Amber Alert?"

"Yeah. That's it. Why don't you do one of those?"

"I'm not sure that it's really appropriate in this situation."

"Why's that? Only *appropriate* for rich people's babies?"

He paused, swallowed. "I'm not the one who makes that decision."

"Who does? Maybe *they* need a call from Fox News."

The room went still, and Carli resisted the urge to apologize, to make excuses for Marla. Bradford opened his mouth several times before he finally spoke. "I have a question for *you*." He paused and eyed Marla. "I've been trying to sort out the Canada angle. How did you find out about that?"

Marla tucked her feet under her chair, met Bradford's eye, and thrust her chin forward. "I already told the Morris cop."

"Why don't you tell me?"

Marla leaned forward now, elbows on her knees. "I called them. I talked to them on the phone."

Bradford watched her intently. He didn't blink. "Thing is, we checked their cell phone records. After Tuesday morning, nothing. No calls made. None received. So. I'm wondering how that can be."

Marla leaned back again, crossed her arms, squinted.

"When we searched their house, a window in the sunroom was broken. Looked like a forced entry."

"What're you sayin'?" Marla demanded.

Bradford shifted his gaze to Carli. "I'm saying that if you want us to find your baby, you need to tell us everything."

Carli looked at Marla, and Marla scowled back. Carli thought about that empty crib crammed between her bed and the wall, and she forced herself to stand. She walked into the kitchen and found the notebook in the drawer under the Yellow Pages where she knew it would be. She opened it to the last page that Gail had written on and carried it back to Bradford. She felt the heat from Marla's glare on the side of her face.

"This was Gail's notebook," she said.

Bradford studied the last few pages slowly. "Do they have family in Grand Forks?"

Carli shrugged. "I don't think so. There was nothing in their home study about that. And Gail never talked about anybody from there."

"Thank you. This will help." He stood, and he turned to Marla, waved the notebook at her. "I won't ask how you got this, because I really don't think I want to know. I bet Fox News would, though."

"What the hell is wrong with you?"

Carli knew the shouting would start as soon as she closed the door behind Bradford. And she knew better than to argue with Marla, so she walked back to the kitchen. She might as well make herself something to eat while Marla screamed.

"You think you're smart?" Marla filled the kitchen doorway. "You're a dumbass is what you are."

Carli put a pan on the stovetop, turned on the burner. She pulled the butter and cheese from the fridge, the bread from the pantry.

"I told you to keep your fucking mouth shut! I thought you were starting to grow up a little bit. I thought I could trust you."

Carli buttered the bread. This was how it would go. Marla would spend the next twenty minutes telling her she was a worthless piece of shit, and Carli didn't care anymore. She just wanted her baby back.

"You think Bradford gives a shit about us? He thinks we're trash. He's rooting for the Durbins to make it to Canada. He'd probably give them a ride if it was up to him."

Carli put the cheese on the bread and set the sandwich, sizzling, into the pan. She felt Marla move closer.

"What the fuck were you thinking?" Marla rumbled from behind her.

Carli plucked a spatula from the sink and nudged the sandwich, to keep it from sticking to the pan.

"I asked you a question," Marla growled. "What the fuck were you thinking?"

She knew there was no answer to the question that would satisfy Marla, so she said nothing. And then Marla's meaty hand landed on the side of her head just below the ear. Carli reached out to keep herself from falling, but her own hand found the edge of the frying pan, and it clattered to the floor with her.

Carli slumped against the cabinet, stunned, holding her burnt hand with the other. She looked up at Marla, who glared at her, and then down at her hand, which was blooming a scarlet smile from the rim of the pan. She squeezed it tightly and held back the tears. She wouldn't let Marla see her cry anymore.

"I asked you a fucking question."

"I just want Maya back," Carli said.

Marla's three chins quivered, and her faint mustache beaded with sweat. Her fists opened and closed as if she couldn't decide whether to lash out again. "You think laying in your bed is gonna get you your baby back? Do you think the Durbins are just gonna turn around and bring your fucking baby back? Your friends, Kelly and what's-her-name—are they fucking helping you?" Marla poked herself hard in the chest. "I'm the one that's doin' everything while you whine and sniffle about getting your baby back. If you really want your baby back, you gotta do something about it."

Carli stood, picked up the pan by the handle and set it in the sink. She ran cool water over her hand and managed to not make a sound. She turned to her mom, stood straight, and looked her square in the eyes. "You're right," she said.

Marla opened her mouth but then closed it. She expected an argument, not agreement. She wanted a fight. Carli stepped around her and grabbed her keys, her wallet, and her phone from the table. She was halfway through the front room when Marla yelled, "Where the hell you goin'?"

"Out," Carli shouted back.

Marla said something else, screamed it really, but Carli didn't hear it, because she slammed the door on the noise.

Gail

*

In a lot of ways, the room reminded Gail of the one in Tomah, but it boasted cheap prints of Monet's *Water Lilies* instead of geese, bleach battled the mouse shit instead of Febreze, and a patch of carpet the size of a body had been cut out and replaced with a slightly darker shade of brown.

Gail called the shop right at five. Fuel pump, they told her. It would be fixed by eleven in the morning. She and Jon were both exhausted. They lay on the sagging bed and stared at the ceiling as the sunlight faded. Maya must have been tired, too, because she lay between them and didn't stir. They would need dinner, but Gail's stomach wasn't ready yet. Jon's breathing drifted toward sleep, but her own mind refused to give in to her body's exhaustion. Dealing with the car, finding a motel with bulletproof glass, and trying not to gloat had distracted her from those words her dad had forced upon her. Staring at the ceiling, though, they flooded back.

Feel the balance of it. That was exactly what Gail had spent the last two days avoiding. Yes, she had thought about Carli and her pain and her loss, but that was to protect herself, to build those calluses. She had pointedly refused to weigh Carli's need against her own, Carli's broken promise against their crime. She had refused the urge to find the fulcrum of it all, the tipping point between right and wrong, and she refused again. It was impossible, and she'd only hurt herself trying. The weight of Maya on the bed next to her was enormous. And there was only one baby. There was no way to balance that.

"What're you thinking about?" Jon murmured.

Gail hesitated. She knew she shouldn't say anything—Jon didn't really want to know what she was thinking, and she didn't want him to get the wrong idea. She wasn't having second thoughts, but the word fell from her mouth before she could close it. "Carli."

Jon groaned. "What did he say?"

"What're you talking about?"

"Your dad. You talk to your dad, and now all of sudden you're worried about Carli."

When would she learn to keep her mouth shut? "He didn't say anything."

"Really? Then what changed?"

"Nothing," Gail said. "Nothing changed."

"It's a little late for second thoughts, Gail."

"I know," she said quietly.

Jon propped himself up on his elbow. "Forget about us and forget about Carli. Think of Maya. Think about the life she'd have in that house."

She knew that she should just agree. She should just roll over and try to nap for a while, but the contempt in Jon's voice demanded an argument.

"What makes you so sure it would be bad?"

"Are you fucking kidding me?" Jon said, his voice rising. "You saw Marla. You spent enough time with Carli. They're white trash. I grew up in that shitshow, Gail. I know how that movie ends."

"That's not the same, and you know it."

"Bullshit! It's exactly—"

Jon's backpack trilled. It lay on the floor on Gail's side of the bed, so she jumped up and scrabbled through it until she found which phone was making the awful noise.

"Don't answer it," Jon said.

No shit. Gail looked at the number. A 612 area code. The phone finally stopped ringing. They waited, tense, until it chirped again, signaling a voice mail. Gail pressed the button and listened to the familiar voice.

> Mr. Reynolds, this is Officer Lathan Jennings. Call me as soon as you get this. We need to clear a few things up.

Gail turned the phone off and stared at it.

"Who was it?" Jon asked.

"The cop from earlier. He wants you to call him."

Jon pushed up from the bed and yanked the computer from his bag. He sat and opened it on his lap. He rubbed his face with both hands as he waited for it to boot. Gail watched over his shoulder as he logged on and opened his email. The subject line of Paige's latest message blared *FBI*.

> Jon and Gail,
> Please contact me as soon as possible. A reporter from Fox News called asking me a lot of questions. He said that you're taking Maya to Canada. An FBI agent called shortly afterward, asking

the same questions. I think that you're running out of time to do
the right thing.
Paige

How could they know about Canada? Jon gripped the sides of
the computer as if to steady himself. Maya stretched and began
to whimper, so Gail dropped the phone back into the backpack
and plucked her from the bed.

"What did you tell your dad?" Jon asked through his teeth.

"Nothing. I told him we were OK."

"Then how the hell do they know about Canada?"

Gail looked down at Maya, adjusted the baby in her arms. "I
told him we were leaving the country," she said quietly. "But I
didn't tell him where."

"Goddamn it, Gail!"

Her own anger surged. "I didn't say anything about Canada."

"Did you tell him where we are?"

"No. I didn't tell him anything else."

"Then how the hell did they figure out where we're headed?"

His eyes were red and wild. His whole body quivered. He
thought she was lying. After everything, he didn't believe her.
"It didn't come from my dad, Jon. Because I didn't tell him
anything else."

Jon glared down at the screen. The heater near the window
clattered. Maya started to cry.

"Emails from the reporter and the FBI. Damn it, Gail."

"You think I'm lying."

Jon stared at the computer for a long time. He didn't look
up when he spoke, and his words were clipped short. "How else
could they have found out?"

Gail went still and stared at Jon, her mouth open. They didn't fight often, but when they fought, they fought hard. They had yelled and screamed and cried and gone silent, but never, in the heat of their worst arguments, had Jon ever called her a liar.

Marla

*

Marla stood in the laundry room behind Wendy, peering over her shoulder, feeling itchy and impatient. It took twenty minutes of shouting to get Wendy's lazy ass off the couch and another half hour for Wendy to figure out how to connect Carli's printer and get it working. The printer now grumbled on top of the dryer, spitting out sheet after sheet, and Wendy pecked at the keyboard. She knew how to work a computer better than Marla, of course, but not as good as Carli. She was able to find what Marla needed, but it was slow going. She typed with two fingers and didn't seem to know where to click.

Wendy hit print again and then looked at her watch. "I gotta go."

"Is that all of 'em?" Marla demanded.

"Yeah," Wendy muttered. "That's all of 'em." She stood, pushing the chair back into Marla's knees. She brushed past Marla on the way to the door.

"You sure?"

Wendy stopped, turned, and leaned against the doorframe. She crossed her arms and glared at Marla, chewing her gum furiously. "Why Grand Forks?"

Marla wanted to tell her to mind her own fucking business but decided that Wendy had earned a true answer. "It was in that notebook. The Durbin lady wrote it down."

Wendy stopped chewing, narrowed her eyes. "Are you fucking kidding me? She writes down the name of a town and you waste an hour and half of my life?"

Marla grabbed the stack of paper off the printer and thumbed through it. Her lower back prickled. She squinted up at Wendy. She tried to think of something to shut her up, to get her out of the doorway, but instead the truth slipped out again. "It's all I got."

Wendy's eyes drilled Marla. She blew a bubble. It popped, and she gathered the gum back into her mouth with her tongue. "Why?"

Marla felt the heat creep up her spine. "Whattaya mean *why*?"

"I mean, why do you give a shit about that baby? Why you wanna find it so bad?"

Marla set the papers down on the washer. "It's Carli's baby."

"Bullshit. It's like you want that baby more than Carli does."

The heat found Marla's neck. She didn't have to explain shit to this spoiled little bitch. She didn't have to tell her about what it was like to get beat up by Sean, or to work fourteen hours a day, or to drag herself from one shit job to the next. She didn't have to tell Wendy about the cockroach-infested apartment that she was probably too young to remember, or about that one and only boyfriend who treated Marla more like a whore than a girlfriend, or about how she used to come home from work every night and watch her two young daughters sleep for just a few minutes before she fell, exhausted, into her own bed. And she could tell by the look on Wendy's face that she wouldn't listen to any of it anyway, so Marla said nothing.

Wendy's lip curled and her eyes narrowed. "It's like you want that kid more than you wanted your own."

And then Marla felt nothing but the heat, and her vision went black around the edges, and her fists hardened. She closed her eyes and took a deep breath before stepping forward, but when she opened them, Wendy had disappeared from the doorway. Marla somehow stopped herself from chasing her into the front room. Which was good, because she didn't have time for all that. Besides, she had already punched one of her daughters that day.

Paige

*

Paige pulled into the Denny's parking lot and turned off the engine. She could see Carli, sitting still and alone at a booth by the window. Framed by the big sheet of glass, she looked tiny. She stared straight ahead in a way that spoke of exhaustion and sadness. Carli sipped from her mug and turned to the window, but because it was dark, she was probably just staring at a reflection of herself. Paige wondered what Carli saw reflected in the glass. And she couldn't help wondering whether she had looked so alone sitting in that Steak 'n Shake so many years ago, fresh off the bus from Des Moines, pregnant, waiting for her aunt to pick her up.

Paige heaved herself out of the car and went into the restaurant. Carli spotted her as soon as she came through the door. She pushed her hair out of her face and tried to smile. Paige wedged herself into the other side of the booth and reached for Carli's hand. She gave it a little squeeze.

"How are you?" she asked, because she really wanted to know.

"I've been better."

"I'm glad that you called."

Carli looked down at her coffee. "I'm so sorry about all this."

Christ. She was blaming herself. "Stop. I should be the one apologizing to you."

"This isn't what I meant to happen."

"You had every right to do what you did."

"But if I didn't—"

"Carli," Paige said, louder than she intended. With an effort she softened her voice. "Maya's your baby."

Carli fell silent. Her eyes flickered up at Paige, out the window, and then settled back on the mug. "If you knew where they were, you'd tell me, wouldn't you?"

"Of course. And I'd tell the police. I'll do anything I can to help." Paige shook her head, tried to swallow all the anger she'd been chewing. "I still can't believe that Gail would do this."

"I can," Carli said.

"Why do you say that?"

"She wants that baby as bad as I do."

Paige took in a big breath, held it, let it out. She hated Gail and Jon for what they had done to this girl. She hated herself for letting it happen. "I talked to Agent Bradford again on the way here. It sounds like they're doing everything they can."

"But they haven't found them."

"No. They haven't found them."

Carli swallowed. "Do you think they will?"

Paige looked at the table and then back at Carli. If she could give the girl nothing else, she could at least give her the truth. "He said that if they make it across the border, the odds go way down. He just doesn't think that the Canadians will make it a priority."

"What about her parents?"

Paige shrugged. "I keep calling them, but they're hard to read. I don't think her mom knows anything. It's harder to tell with her dad."

Carli put her hands flat on the table, swallowed, and then looked Paige right in the eye. "Will you help me?"

"Any way that I can."

"Will you lend me some money?"

"For what?"

"Gas. Food. Hotels."

"To go where?"

"Winnipeg."

Oh shit. Paige reached to squeeze Carli's hand again, but she pulled it away. "Carli—"

"I'll pay you back."

"It's not that, honey. I'd give you the money. But Winnipeg's such a big place. And we don't even know for sure that's where they'll end up. You'll be looking for a needle in a hayfield."

"I need to do something. I can't just sit here and wait for the FBI to tell me my baby is gone forever." She rubbed her eyes with the heels of her palms. "I have to see her again. I *have* to go."

Paige picked up the saltshaker, rolled it between her fingers. A tiny kernel of a thought had sprouted sometime in the last twenty-four hours, but Paige had refused to acknowledge it, burying it away. She imagined Carli wandering the streets of Winnipeg, alone, searching in vain for a glimpse of her baby. She thought about going to Canada with Carli, but she knew that was a fool's errand, her guilt getting the best of her. Finally, she let the seedling struggle through the soil. It just might work, but saying it aloud felt like a betrayal of the side that she had chosen. "I have one idea."

Carli looked up, her eyes hungry.

"I hesitate to even bring it up."

Carli leaned forward. "I'll do anything," she said.

"It's a long shot."

"I said I'll do anything."

"And it if works, it will only give you part of what you really want."

Marla

*

Marla climbed the stairs to Larry's apartment, clutching an envelope, her shoulders still tight, her mind still chewing Wendy's words. When she reached Larry's door, the smell of weed leaked from it. Kurt must already be there. She walked in without knocking—they wouldn't get up if she knocked anyway. Kurt and Larry sat next to each other on the couch, tiny plastic steering wheels in their hands, their glazed eyes fixed on the TV. *Mario Kart* music mumbled from the television and their cars bounced off the walls and careened over cliffs. Larry leaned into every turn. Kurt's hands barely moved.

"Hey," Larry managed.

Marla knew better than to interrupt the race, so she sat on an aluminum lawn chair next to the couch. Empty Pabst cans and full ashtrays crowded the milk crates that served as coffee tables. Dirty clothes and candy wrappers lay scattered on the scarred hardwood. Marla lit a cigarette and waited. Finally, Princess Peach (Larry) won.

"You suck," Larry said in his flat, stoned voice.

"Fuck you," Kurt mumbled. He dropped his controller onto the couch and reached for the one-hitter and lighter.

"You said it was important," Larry said.

"I need you to go to Grand Forks."

"Where the fuck is that?" Kurt asked.

"North Dakota," Marla said.

Kurt held his hit and then blew it out with a giggle and a cough. "North Dakota? Fuck that."

"Carli's baby might be there."

That shut him up. The two men looked at each other for a long moment.

"How you know that?" Kurt asked.

"Grand Forks was in that notebook Larry found. Right above Winnipeg."

Larry's eyes narrowed. "They write the name of a town, so you want us to drive to North Dakota?"

Ever since Bradford left, she'd been trying to figure why Grand Forks, what it meant, but she couldn't figure it. The name of that town was all she had, though. If they made it across that border, the baby was gone for good. She looked from one of them to the other, tried to act more convinced than she felt. "That's right. My gut says they're gonna stop there on the way."

"Your gut." Larry looked at her skeptically.

Marla shifted her weight on the lawn chair, tugged at the sleeve of her sweatshirt, and then fixed Larry with a stare that he couldn't ignore. "Five grand," she said.

"Huh?"

"You get me my grandbaby back, I give you each five grand."

"Where the hell you gonna get ten grand?"

Marla had been doing the math in her head since shortly after she knocked Carli to the kitchen floor. She had squirreled away almost five thousand dollars over the last decade—for when something went wrong—because something always goes wrong. She might be able to borrow the rest against the house. If not, then she'd have to sell the truck. "You let me worry about that."

They both leaned forward, now, perched on the edge of the couch. Marla could see the gears in their foggy brains reengage. Five grand.

"How we gonna find 'em?" Kurt asked.

Marla pulled the sheaf of papers from the envelope. "I got a list of all the hotels in Grand Forks and a map of the city." She thumbed to the stack of pictures of Jon and Gail. It took half an hour to find the adoption book in Carli's room and a trip to the UPS Store to make copies. "And photos of 'em."

Larry and Kurt considered, glanced at each other. Kurt shrugged. "How we gonna get there?" Larry asked.

"You drop me off at home and take my truck. I got a thousand bucks in my pocket. Five hundred for gas and food. 'Nother five hundred to wave at the hotel clerks." She could see that they were in. "It'll take you eleven hours to get there."

Larry tried to focus on the picture of the Durbins and then on Marla's face. "Why you payin' us? Why don't you just go yourself?"

"I gotta stay here and make sure my dumbass daughter doesn't do anything else stupid. Besides, you two can be a little bit more . . . persuasive."

Carli

*

Carli didn't sleep until about four in the morning. It made sense what Paige suggested—a terrible, brutal sense—and it just might work. What Gail and Jon did wasn't right, and that's what made it hard to decide, but right had nothing to do with it anymore. Being right didn't fix anything. Gail was working to fix things. Marla was working to fix things. Carli's mind kept settling on a sentence from the chapter on grief in her psych book. *Some things you can't fix*, it read; *some things you just have to carry.* That made sense, a gentle kind of sense, and that helped her to decide.

After she decided, she fell into a deep, dreamless sleep and didn't wake until nine thirty the next morning. She felt the sun on her face, and she opened her eyes to the glare. It came through the window and through the slats of the crib. The shadows striped her bed like prison bars. She reached out and rubbed the smooth wood with her fingertips, and she almost began to second-guess herself, but instead, she pushed herself out of bed and forced herself to dress. She opened the bedroom door and listened for

Marla, sniffed the air for smoke. But all she heard was Randy killing people, and all she smelled was microwave popcorn.

She ate a breakfast of peanut butter toast and then grabbed her things and headed through the front room. Randy was slumped in his regular spot, working the controller. Wendy curled into the other corner of the couch, thumbing her phone.

"Marla took your car," Wendy said without looking up.

"What? Why?"

Wendy shrugged. "Dunno. She asked me where you keep the spare keys."

"Where's her truck?"

"I said. I. Don't. Know."

Shit. Carli pulled back the curtain, and sure enough, only Randy's orange pickup sat in the driveway. "Randy. Can I borrow your truck?"

"Hell no," Wendy answered for him. "What if we need to go somewhere?"

"I'll be back in two hours."

"I said no."

"It's a thing I need to do for the baby."

Wendy looked up from her phone. Randy put the game on pause and looked up, too. This was the first time that Carli had mentioned the baby to Wendy since she came home from the hospital. Ever, maybe.

Randy looked from Carli to Wendy, and when his eyes rested back on Carli, they held a curiosity she'd never noticed before. "What about the baby?"

"I need to do something," Carli said. "I can't really say, but it's important."

Randy didn't look at Wendy as he shoved his hand into his pocket. He ignored Wendy's glare as he tossed Carli his keys.

"Get me a Red Bull on the way back," he said, and picked up the game controller.

Wendy glared at the side of his face for a long moment, but eventually bent back to her phone. "And a pack of smokes," she mumbled.

With traffic, it took Carli forty minutes to drive to Paige's office. She waited in the conference room for ten more minutes while Paige finished a call. When Paige entered, she carried a laptop and a small stack of papers, looking grim. "You sure you want to do this?"

Carli nodded.

"It's real important to me that you don't feel like I'm pressuring you into this."

She didn't want to do this, of course. She wanted to reclaim Maya like the law said she could. She wanted to hold Maya and feed her and sleep next to her and find a way to care for her. She didn't want Maya to grow up thinking of her as that woman who gave her away. She wanted Maya to call her Mom. But none of that was possible. She didn't blame Paige for any of it. She blamed Gail and Jon. But blame didn't fix anything. Blame wouldn't help her to see her baby again. Paige wasn't forcing her to do this. She was forcing herself.

"I want to do this," she lied.

Paige used the phone on the conference table to call in the notary, a short, wrinkled woman who said nothing and refused to look at Carli or Paige. Carli's hand didn't shake when she signed the final consent. She looked out the window while Paige witnessed it. No tears came when the notary stamped and signed.

"I'll go scan this in," Paige said. She pushed the laptop over to Carli. "You can use this."

Carli logged into her email and hit Compose. The words came quickly. She'd been writing the email in her head all morning.

> Gail,
> The final consent is attached. Maya is yours now. You can bring her home. Please let me see her. That's all I ask. Just let me see her.
> Carli

Paige returned and helped Carli attach the scanned document to the email. She laid her palm on Carli's forearm. "Carli, are you sure—"

Carli shrugged off Paige's hand and hit Send. She stared at the screen for a long moment. She wanted to unclick that button. She wanted to pull that email back through the wire. But the moment passed, and she willed it to reach Gail's in-box, to find Gail, to find Maya.

"You have to call Bradford."

Carli looked up at Paige, blinking. "Huh?"

"Agent Bradford. From the FBI. You need to call him and tell him about this."

With that, what she had done became real, and although she expected to feel empty, she felt hopeful. She wasn't quite sure which was worse.

Jon

*

It took Jon fifteen minutes to walk to the shop, and he timed it to arrive just before eleven o'clock. Gail was still being a bitch about the night before. Her eyes were glazed over, and she only let him hold Maya when she had to pee. After they fought, she had locked herself in the bathroom for more than an hour, which was probably best, because it gave Jon time to calm himself, to point his anger where it belonged: Gail's father. There was no telling what she told him about Canada. Even if Gail didn't say anything directly, he must have been able to piece together their plan from bits of what she said. Jon tried to come up with another explanation, but there wasn't one. Gail had decided that she could live without her parents, but Paul couldn't live without his daughter. That son of a bitch would rather have her in jail than gone. But, of course, Gail wouldn't be able to hear any of that. As far as she was concerned, her dad's feet didn't even get wet when he walked on water.

Jon knew only too well the shape of what would happen next. Gail would stay mute. Jon would apologize again, and then again, even though she should be the one saying sorry. Eventually, her resentment would wear itself out, and she would set it aside, like kindling, handy for the next time an argument flared.

The bell jangled when he entered the shop. The same guy from yesterday, Will, stood at the counter, studying the same stack of paper. A big, bearded bear stood next to him.

"I'm here to pick up my car."

Neither looked up. "Don't turn around," Will said. "There's a cop in the alley across the street."

Jon's whole body went stiff, and he fought the urge to turn. It was starting.

"Same guy that dropped you off yesterday. He came in earlier and asked a bunch of questions about you, your wife, and the baby."

Shit. Shit. Shit. "What kind of questions?"

Will ignored him. "First you're gonna pay me seven hundred dollars for the tow and fuel pump. I assume you're paying cash."

Jon pulled out his wallet. "Yeah. I've got the cash."

"And then Kevin's gonna drive off with your car. Cop'll figure it's you in the car, since he just saw you walk in here. I'm betting he'll follow Kevin and pull him over."

Jon counted out the bills. "But what about—"

"Kevin'll tell the cop he's test-driving it. The cop'll come back here looking for you. I'll take you to the hotel, and Kevin will meet us there. Where you stayin'?"

Jon handed him the stack of cash. "But how do I know that—"

Will finally looked up at Jon. "You either trust us or come up with a different plan real fucking fast."

Jon again fought the urge to turn around to see the cop for himself, but the hi-hat that was clattering in his brain told him that the squad car would be parked right where Will said. He looked from Will to Kevin and then back at Will. He had no choice. "Rodeway Inn."

"Let's go," Will said, and Kevin led them down a hallway to the back door. Will grabbed Jon's arm as Kevin went outside. "Wait here."

They watched through the smoked glass as Kevin got in the car, drove it down the alley, and disappeared.

"Now what?" Jon asked.

"Wait for it."

Sure enough. Ten seconds later the trooper's car sped through the alley after the Camry. As soon as it was out of sight, Will said, "Let's go."

They hustled out to an old, rusted Malibu. Will popped the trunk. "Get in."

Jon looked from Will to the trunk and then back at Will. "Not a chance."

"I'm willin' to help, but I ain't getting arrested on account of you. Get in, or go sit in the office and wait for the cop."

Jon looked at the trunk, then back at Will.

"Decide fast. You got about two minutes before he's back."

Jon's mind scrambled for options, but he found none. He climbed in, and the lid slammed. Everything went dark. Jon smelled raw meat, and he knew he'd made a terrible mistake. He was locked in a trunk, his wallet packed with fifties, Gail a sitting duck at the motel. The motor started, and the car lurched. Every time they hit a bump, Jon's head slammed into the lid, and when Will took a turn at speed, Jon crumpled into the side of the trunk hard. It took fifteen minutes to walk from the motel, but in the bouncing blackness it seemed to take much longer to get back. Jon started to imagine the deserted country road they were driving down when Will slammed on the brakes and

Jon crashed forward, cutting his shoulder on something sharp. When Will opened the trunk, Jon blinked into the sunlight, working to gain his bearings. No country road, just the parking lot of the motel.

"You need to get the hell outta town fast," Will said, as Jon climbed out. The Camry swerved around the corner of the motel and screeched to a stop next to Will's car. "I don't know what y'all did, but I got a hunch they're gonna be looking for that car. I'd maybe find myself a different one. If you know what I mean."

Jon nodded. "Thank you."

"Don't thank me," Will said. "Thank your wife."

Kevin heaved his bulk out of the Camry. "And next time, don't be such a prick."

Gail

*

Maya slept on the center of the bed while Gail packed. Gail's eyes were twitchy from exhaustion, her shoulders sore from the clenching. When she managed to drift off the night before, Maya soon woke her with that crackling cry. They fed and changed her, but sometimes she wasn't hungry or wet. She seemed to wake because she, too, felt edgy, as if the tension between Jon and Gail clouded *her* dreams.

When Gail had everything packed and stacked by the door, she thought about lying down on the bed next to Maya. She wanted to breathe in those pears, maybe close her eyes for just a while. But she might wake Maya, and Jon would be back soon, and she'd probably just lay there and brood. So she pulled the laptop out of Jon's bag. She sat on the chair in the corner, booted it up, and connected to the motel's Wi-Fi. She clicked through to her email. If there was more bad news coming, she might as know about it.

Fifteen unread emails filled her in-box, and she scanned them from the bottom up. Mostly Pottery Barn Kids and Pinterest and the messages from the reporter and the FBI and Paige that she had read over Jon's shoulder. She scanned to the top and her tired, itchy eyes locked on the most recent message. Carli Brennan. Gail stared for a long moment at that name and the subject line: *Please Bring Maya Home.* Her finger rested on the Delete button. She knew that she wasn't ready for what the email said, that the hardness hadn't come to her yet. But she knew she couldn't just delete it, that she had to read it. She could leave it for later, but then it would just be sitting there in her in-box, and that would be all she could think of, and that would be no good, either. Finally, she clicked it open.

The message was short, but she had to read it twice to digest it, and then a third time to believe it. Her feet tickled, and her stomach twitched as she clicked open the attachment. She scanned the familiar document and then paged down to the signatures. Carli's scrawl perched on the correct line, Paige had witnessed it, and the notary had stamped it. Gail melted into the chair, her clenched muscles relaxing. Her eyes landed on Maya in the center of the bed, and she seemed to see her with a sharpness and clarity that had been missing. The key rattled in the lock. Tears leaked into the corner of her smile. But then Jon stumbled in with his sleeve torn and bloody, his eyes wild.

"We need to pack," he barked.

Gail's smile faltered. "What happened—"

"We need to pack now!"

"We're packed."

"Put Maya in the car seat. We need to load the car."

"Jon. What's—"

"The cops are after us, and we need to leave now!"

Gail didn't move. "Jon. It's over."

Jon's eyes widened and darted around the room. "What do you mean?" he demanded.

"The final consent. Carli emailed it to me." She spun the computer around on her lap so that he could see for himself. "We can go home."

Jon stared at her for a moment, his eyes still wild. Finally, he walked to where she sat, knelt down on one knee, and read the email. Maya started to whimper. He, too, clicked open the attachment, and Gail watched his face, waiting for that smile. But it didn't come. And when he looked up from the screen, his eyes had hardened.

"Are you really that stupid?" he asked.

Gail's shoulders clenched again. Maya started to cry. "What are you talking about?" she snapped.

"You really think this is legit? The cops were waiting for me at the garage. The FBI is involved, Gail. It's a trick."

"But—"

"Gail! Snap out of it. Home is Winnipeg now." He lifted the computer from her lap and sat on the bed. He pounded the keys and peered at the screen. "Pack the goddamn car."

Larry

*

Larry walked into the lobby of the Budget Inn Express in Grand Forks. Stop number eight out of twenty-five. The gray tile floors were riddled with cracks, and water stains decorated the ceiling. A rack of candy stood guard on one side of the reception desk, a round cooler marked SANDWICHES on the other. An old man sat behind the desk reading a newspaper. His powder-blue T-shirt was several sizes too large for him, as if he had shrunk. His chin bristled with gray whiskers, and his lips worked a toothpick. Larry leaned against the counter, and the clerk glanced up. Nothing but his eyes and the toothpick moved.

"Help you?"

"I'm looking for some friends." Larry held up the picture of Jon and Gail. "They'd be traveling with a baby."

"We don't usually—"

Larry spread five one-hundred-dollar bills on the counter. "I really want to see my old friends."

The clerk took the paper from Larry and studied it for a long time. He glanced at the cash fanned across the counter.

"Nope," he said with reluctance. He made to hand the picture back to Larry.

"Keep it. That's my cell number on the bottom." Larry scooped up the cash and straightened it like a deck of cards against the counter. "Just call me if they show."

Larry climbed into the truck. Kurt put it into drive, and he pulled out onto the frontage road. "Nothin'?"

"Nothin'."

"We ain't gonna find 'em," Kurt grumbled.

"Probably not."

"Waste of fucking time."

"But worth five large if we do."

Kurt grunted and then turned into the parking lot of the Ramada.

Marla

*

Marla moved without thinking. The boxes packed themselves. The orders went unchecked, and if a box of pens or some binder clips got missed, she didn't really give a shit. She didn't notice the rattle of the fan forcing cool air in from the street, or the insistent beep of the forklift. She didn't even hear the shriek of the tape sealing the boxes. Ten forty-five. Larry and Kurt should have called by now. She should have sent them earlier. She should have sent them right away. Marla made a special effort to avoid eye contact with Helen. She had no idea how much Helen knew or didn't know, but Kurt probably told her something. Marla wasn't sure what she'd do if Helen said the wrong thing.

Marla checked her phone for a missed call, even though she had the ringer all the way up. She could feel the heavy weight of Helen's gaze. She shoved the phone back into her pocket and built another box. She should have known better than to count on anyone. She called Dean from Fox four times before he finally called her back. Said that thing with the missiles in North

Korea was sucking up all the airtime. They wouldn't be able to devote resources to Carli's story. Because to them, that's all it was—a story. He wished her luck, whatever the hell that meant. Bradford answered on the second ring when she called him on the way into work, but he said that he didn't have anything new to report. The way he said it, though, that tiny hitch in his voice and the long pause after, told her that he was holding something back. She called Larry during her nine-thirty smoke break, but he still hadn't returned her call.

"Ten grand's a lotta cash," Helen said.

Marla said nothing, kept building the box, and all the noises of the warehouse rushed in to fill the silence.

"You must really want that baby back."

Marla put down the box and tape and settled into stillness. The rattle of the fan competed with the buzzing in her head. She didn't look up because she knew that the look on Helen's face would force her to do something that she didn't have time for, something that would make everything more complicated.

"Don't get me wrong. I'd love the cash," Helen said. She let the words hang in the air along with the rumble of a truck at the dock. "But if you ask me, Canada'd be the best thing to ever happen to *that* baby."

Marla sighed and started to walk around the table. Blood pounded in her ears, blocking out all other sounds. She eyed Helen's greasy hair and yellowing bruises, and she knew that she didn't have time for what was about to happen, she knew she should walk away, but she was past choice and was left with just movement and rage. And she could see that Helen knew this, too, the way she took a step back, the way her hand gripped her tape dispenser with its jagged metal edge. Her beady eyes darted from the table to the shelf to the floor for a more useful weapon, but she mostly held her ground. Marla was almost on her when her cell phone rang.

Marla glared at Helen as she pulled out the phone. She looked down—Wendy's number. "What?"

"Carli left a little while ago."

"So what?"

"She said she had to go do something about the baby."

Helen grabbed a stapler in her other hand, and she stood, feet apart, waiting.

"Where was she going?"

"I dunno. But I thought you might want to know it."

"Yeah. Yeah, I do."

Marla slipped the phone back into her pocket. "Best if you ain't here when I get back," she growled at Helen, and then she stalked off to the time clock.

Jon

*

While Gail packed the car, Jon had charted a backroads route through Erhard and Pelican Rapids. It would add an hour to the drive, but Jon knew they had to stay off the interstate. And he knew that Will was right about the car. As he drove Route 59 toward Dunvilla, they passed lake after lake, and every lake had a boat ramp. Despite the chill, most of the boat ramps had at least one car or truck parked next to it with an empty trailer.

Jon glanced at Gail, who was staring out the window at the pines. He still couldn't believe that she could be so naive. Like Carli would just give them the baby. After all of this. It didn't make any sense. He shouldn't have called her stupid, though, and she'd make him pay for that with her silence. He knew from long experience the easiest way to break that silence, whether he meant it or not.

"Listen. I'm sorry about what I said back there."

Nothing.

"I shouldn't have called you stupid. I'd just climbed out of the trunk of that redneck's car. I saw the cop." He glanced at Gail again and then back at the road. "I was scared."

Gail didn't turn from the window, and she didn't make a sound. It was going to be a quiet ride. It would be a short one, though, if they kept driving the Camry.

"Listen. I know that you're mad. And I know that you're not gonna like what I'm about to say next."

Gail finally turned from the window. Her stillness, the sag of her mouth, told him that she wasn't going to like much of anything.

"We need to dump this car for a different one."

Jon braced himself for an argument, ready to remind her that this was all her idea, that she knew the risks, but she didn't say anything. She just looked at him for a long moment and then turned back to the window.

"I'm gonna find an unlocked car at one of these boat ramps, and when I do, you're gonna drive to Detroit Lakes. It's about fifteen minutes down this road. Find a big parking lot, a Walmart or something, and wait for me there."

Nothing.

"Hello? Are you with me here?"

Gail turned to him again, and suddenly her eyes were alive like she was ready to fight and bite and spit, and she leaned toward him as if about to say something. But instead, she turned back to the window. "Detroit Lakes," she finally mumbled. "I heard you."

Jon took two of the phones from his backpack and called one with the other. He gave Gail the phone that he called. "Call that number when you get there. Let me know where you're parked."

Jon stopped at two boat ramps, but every car was locked. At the third, the door of an old Country Squire station opened when he tugged the handle. The part of the lake he could see was empty of boats. He came back to the Camry and got his pocketknife from the backpack. "This is it."

Gail got out of the car wordlessly, walked around to the driver's side, and got in. Jon leaned against the open door. "I love you."

Gail stared straight through the windshield and took a long time to respond. And when she did, just before pulling the door closed, all she said was "Me, too."

Jon watched her drive off. *Me, too?* What was it going to take this time? Two more apologies? Three? A bouquet of flowers and a fucking poem? He shook his head and turned back to the wagon.

He opened the driver-side door and knelt in the gravel. He pried the plastic covering off the steering column and sorted through the wires until he found the ignition. He cut apart the wiring harness, and Eric's words from high school echoed in his head: *red to brown.* He wrapped the wires, and the radio turned on, flooding the car with country music. *Yes.* He sparked the yellow against the red, and the starter kicked and kicked, until finally the engine rumbled to life. Jon smiled—his teenage years hadn't been entirely misspent.

He darted to the back of the car to remove the trailer. He knelt to unclasp the chains and unlatch the hitch. Maybe it was the rumble of the exhaust in his ear, or maybe he just wasn't paying attention, but he didn't hear the boat's motor.

"Hey!"

Jon looked up. Two large men in flannel shirts drove an aluminum johnboat right up onto the muddy bank.

"Hey, motherfucker!"

Jon jumped to his feet and yanked the trailer from the hitch. Boots pounded the gravel as he scrambled into the driver's seat. He slammed the door closed and locked it. An angry, bearded face appeared at the window, yelling and pounding. Jon shoved the car into drive just as the passenger door swung open. The other man dove and grabbed Jon's arm. Jon slammed the accelerator and yanked the wheel to the left. Gravel slapped against the wheel wells as the wagon careened out of the parking lot. The momentum of the turn proved stronger than the man's grip on Jon's sleeve, and he flew from the open door, rolling across the asphalt. Jon swerved into the northbound lane, and the passenger door slammed shut.

Jon peered into the rearview mirror as he sped off. The man lay in the middle of the road, his friend bent over him. The man on the blacktop didn't stir. Jon slowed, urging the man to move, but he didn't. Jon's scalp prickled, and his eyes flicked from the mirror to the road ahead and back again. As he approached a curve, he slowed even more, his eyes fixed on the mirror, but the man wouldn't move. They finally disappeared behind the trees, and Jon gunned it.

Gail

*

Gail sat in the Walmart parking lot with the cell phone on her lap. Of course there was a Walmart. There was always a Walmart.

Although Gail sat still, and Maya slept soundly in the back seat, Gail vibrated internally, with exhaustion and confusion and rage. So, she wasn't just a liar, she was a stupid liar. And this from the man with whom she was racing toward the border, toward a new life, risking—and trusting—everything. She knew that she wasn't a liar, but as she sat in the Walmart parking lot with the phone in her lap, she couldn't help wondering whether she was stupid.

When she first saw the final consent, she was instantly wrapped in a warm blanket of relief. They could go home. That email told her exactly what she wanted to hear, and she didn't stop for even a moment to consider whether it was real. But what if Jon was right? What if they drove back to Elmhurst and walked right into a trap? What if they took her baby?

She looked down at the phone and thumbed the familiar number, even though she knew that she shouldn't. She pressed the dial button before she could change her mind. She held the phone to her ear, and as it rang, she formulated the questions, because she knew that she could hear the truth most clearly during those first few seconds of surprise.

"This is Paige."

"Is it real?"

"Gail?"

"The final consent. Is it real?"

"Yes." Paige sounded confused. "Of course it is."

"Were the cops involved?"

"What? What are you talking about?"

Gail closed her eyes and leaned against the headrest. It was real. It was true. She was right. "So, she's ours?" she managed.

"Yes, Gail," Paige said. But she seemed to have regained her bearings, and her voice hardened. "Maya is yours. You got what you wanted. I hope that you're happy."

Gail blinked at the pickup truck parked in front of her.

"Is that it?" Paige demanded. "No other questions?"

"What do you mean?"

"You take Carli's baby, you tear her life to shreds, and you don't have the common decency to ask how she's doing?"

Gail stopped breathing for a moment as she took in what Paige said. She felt the urge to shout at Paige, to explain herself, to make excuses. But as she digested the words, she tasted their truth, and instead she just said, "How is she?"

"How is she?" Paige asked, her voice rising. "How is she? She just gave her baby away to the people who stole her. And you know why she did it, Gail? Do you know why?"

Gail said nothing, squeezed the phone.

"Because she wants to see Maya again." Paige let that hang in the air. "She gave away her baby so that she can see just a tiny sliver of that baby's life."

In the silence, Gail could hear Maya stir in the back seat. She tried to form words, to say something, to defend herself, but no words came.

"I wrote your home study," Paige said. Anger crackled through the phone. "I know all about you and Jon and your families and Marla." Paige paused, and Gail could hear her breathe. "In this whole fucking fiasco, Carli might be the only mother worthy of the name."

Shame flooded Gail as Maya started to cry. The phone beeped. Jon. "I have to go," Gail said quietly. She hung up on Paige and answered Jon's call.

"Where are you?" Jon demanded.

She heard the question through Maya's scream, but at first, she couldn't answer. For a long moment she didn't know where she was or who she was or how she got there.

"I'm in the Walmart parking lot," she finally said. "By the garden center."

Carli

*

Carli went to the cellar and sorted through the piles of boxes until she found one filled with videos from when they used to have a VCR. She dumped them on the floor. She found another box filled with Randy's wrestling trophies. She stacked them along the wall behind the water heater and brought both boxes upstairs.

She started in the kitchen, carefully packing the bottles and formula into the first box. Then she went into her bedroom and neatly folded each of the outfits that Marla had bought at Goodwill and stacked them into the other box. She put the diapers on top of the clothes and the creams and ointments on top of the diapers, and she put both boxes next to the crib. She checked her email on her phone, but Gail hadn't replied to her message. She wondered where they were, whether they were still in the country, what Gail would think when she read it. And she wondered how long she would continue to wonder. Carli went to the kitchen and found a screwdriver and pliers in the shoebox on top of the fridge. On the way to her bedroom, she checked her email again. Still nothing.

They brought the crib in from Marla's truck assembled, but the cellar door was narrower than the front door. If she was going to get it down there, she'd have to take it apart. But the crib was old, and the screws were stripped. She struggled to loosen them.

"What the fuck are you doing?"

Carli looked up to find Marla at the door, her hands on her hips. "Taking it apart."

"Why?"

"I'm putting it down the cellar. I can't look at it."

"You'll get the damn baby back."

Carli met Marla's glare, forced her voice steady. "No. I won't."

"The cops might still find them. Anything can happen."

"It won't matter if they do."

Marla's eyes slowly narrowed. "Why?" she demanded. "What did you do?"

If they came back, Marla would find out what she had done. Besides, Carli was past caring what Marla thought. "I signed it."

"Signed what?"

"The final consent."

"Why the fuck would you do that?"

"Paige said they might come back." Saying it to Marla, watching Marla's face contort with disgust, made it seem less likely, less true, but she'd already made her decision. "Once they have the final consent, they won't have a reason to run."

Marla grew still in that dangerous way of hers. "You still don't get it, you dumbass. She. Works. For. Them."

"I just want to see my baby again."

"You are one stupid little bitch."

Carli turned back to the crib with the screwdriver. She couldn't look at Marla anymore. She had made her decision.

"You can leave the crib where it is," Marla said. "But start packing your own shit. I want you out of my house before dark."

Carli didn't wait until dark, and it didn't take long for her to pack her things. She packed her clothes and her shoes and her computer and her textbook. She packed her yearbooks and her makeup and deodorant and a bottle of shampoo and a bottle of conditioner. Five garbage bags in all. Eighteen years. Just five bags and a computer.

When she carried the first bag from her room, the TV in the den was turned up loud. It sounded like *Here Comes Honey Boo Boo*. In the front room, Randy was driving a Lamborghini through Miami with the cops on his tail, while Wendy chewed gum and paged through a *Cosmo*. Wendy looked up and squinted at the bag.

"What're you doin'?"

"Marla kicked me out."

Randy paused his high-speed chase. Wendy snorted. "She's kicked me out a dozen times. Just ignore her. It'll pass."

Honey Boo Boo's mom cackled from the den. Carli knew that Wendy was right, but she had to get out. It wasn't just the slaps in the head and the threats and the insults and the cigarette smoke in her face. She'd gotten used to Marla's bitterness, her hatred. *That* was the problem—she'd gotten used to it all. She had stopped thinking for herself. She was turning into Marla.

"I wanna leave."

Wendy's eyebrows squirmed in confusion. Randy cocked his head. He regarded her for a long moment, then nodded and stood. He reached for the bag in her hands.

"Let me carry that for you."

With Randy helping, it took just three trips to the car. Carli came back to her room and scanned it for anything she was forgetting. The volume of the TV in the den increased.

"What about those?" Randy pointed to the two boxes at the foot of the crib.

Carli checked her phone but found nothing from Gail. She was probably in Canada already. She had probably become a new person. She would probably never check that email address again.

"No," she said. She forced herself to look away from the crib. "I won't need those."

Jon

*

S omething rattled under the hood of the station wagon, and the muffler rumbled. The steering swung loose, bordering on nonresponsive. Halfway to Detroit Lakes, Jon found the keys nestled in the console, rendering his high school skills irrelevant. He fiddled with the radio, trying to find music that would soothe, that would settle, but it was mostly country or Christian rock. The best he could manage was Journey.

None of this distracted Jon from that man lying in the road. He didn't move. He might have just been gathering himself from the fall. At worst, it was probably no more than a concussion, a broken arm, maybe. But Jon didn't see him move, and he couldn't shake the idea that he might have killed somebody. He fought the urge to turn back. That was nonsense, of course—he couldn't drive a stolen car back to check on the man he stole it from. And his wife and his baby were waiting. They had to get over that border. He didn't see the man move, but he had to wall it off. He wouldn't tell Gail. He wouldn't search the Internet for a carjacking just north of Dunvilla. Jon

Durbin stole that car. If the man in the flannel shirt was hurt, Jon Durbin had hurt him. Allen Reynolds had nothing to do with it.

He found Gail just where she said she'd be. Maya was screaming when Jon opened the door of the Camry, but Gail was just sitting very still in the front seat, ignoring the noise. Still pissed off. They loaded everything from the Camry into the station wagon without a word. Gail climbed into the back with Maya and mixed a bottle. Maya pulled at the formula, and eventually the car fell quiet.

The lakes and pines gave way to fields, the earth freshly turned, and they passed through sad little towns like Bejou and Winger and Plummer. Maya fell asleep after she was fed, and Gail slumped against the window. Rush was playing on the radio, but Gail's silence seemed to drown out the music. Jon looked at her in the rearview mirror. He couldn't do anything about that man on the blacktop just north of Dunvilla, but he'd better do something about Gail.

"Listen," he said. "I'm sorry about this morning."

Gail didn't turn from the window. When she spoke, her voice sounded dead. Rotten. "Maybe you're right," she said.

Jon knew that he was right, but he also knew to keep quiet.

"Maybe I *am* stupid."

Shit. She had her teeth into this one.

"I was scared, Gail. And tired. I don't think you're stupid."

"And a liar. Don't forget about my lies."

This was going to take until Winnipeg. Maybe longer. "Gail. We're both under stress. I haven't slept in three days. I'm just worried about Maya."

"But what if it's true?" she said. "What if Carli really signed the final consent?"

It wasn't. Jon knew it in his bones, but he could play along. "We'll hire a lawyer to contact Paige when we get to Winnipeg. We'll do it from the other side of the border."

Gail finally turned from the window and locked eyes with him in the mirror. "That's not what I mean. If it's true, what would that say about Carli?"

It would say that she was a confused teenager who couldn't make an important decision, and once she did, she couldn't stick with it. It would say that if she somehow ended up with Maya, she would get confused and distracted and their lives would devolve into the kind of shitshow that Jon knew only too well. It would tell him that he was doing exactly the right thing, that every mile they drove north was a mile toward safety. Instead, Jon just said, "The only thing that matters is that the three of us stay together."

Gail turned back to the window and mumbled her next question. "And what does that say about us?"

What the hell was she talking about now? He tried to find her eyes in the rearview mirror again, but she was staring out the window at the stubbled fields.

"What do you mean by that?"

Gail said nothing.

"Gail. What do you mean by that?"

She wouldn't look at him. She didn't move. She said nothing. She just stared out the window.

Marla

*

Marla lit her next cigarette from the last and drank from a can of Cherry Coke. She turned off *Honey Boo Boo* after Carli left—that was mainly for Carli—and was watching *Ice Road Truckers*. She still couldn't believe that stupid bitch signed the final consent. Free pass for the Durbins after all they did. And she was surprised when Carli left. Marla didn't think she had it in her. She thought for sure that Carli would come into the den with apologies and excuses, begging for another chance. She'd be back, though. She thought that being pregnant taught something about real life. She didn't yet know that was the easy part.

Marla finally turned off the TV and drank another gulp of soda. The only sounds in the house were Randy's war and the occasional murmur from Wendy. She checked her phone to make sure that she hadn't missed a call from Larry. She thought about calling him again but couldn't gather the energy for it, couldn't find the hope that she had felt just the day before. He and Kurt had probably already given up. They were probably already driving back.

She thought about calling Bradford, but might know what Carli had done, that she had signed the final consent. When he first showed up with his fancy suit, his talk about all-points bulletins and state police and Canadian Immigration had felt solid and real and hopeful. But then Carli gave him that notebook, and that hope got buried by rage.

What a dumb little bitch. Marla didn't mean to hit her, but when Carli gave him the notebook, Marla's blood started pounding like it did sometimes, and her vision narrowed to a small dark tunnel, and she couldn't think anymore. She couldn't even remember Bradford leaving, just the heavy weight of anger that forced her hand into the side of her daughter's head.

It bothered her that she couldn't stop that hand, but there was something else that was bothering her, something tugging at her. Right before that smug son of a bitch started to interrogate her, right before Carli went for the notebook, two stray thoughts had collided and were forming themselves into a question. Marla tried to sort through the conversation before the blackness, to see if she could piece it back together, but she failed. It probably didn't matter anymore. The Durbins were probably across the border, looking for apartments in Winnipeg. Seven hundred thousand people in Winnipeg. They were gone.

Marla grew still in her chair. The border. Canadian Immigration. Homeland Security. Passports. The Durbins would be stopped at the border when they tried to use their passports. They'd be locked in a tiny room, and Carli's baby would be taken from them and sent south. That was too easy, though. Durbin would have thought through all that. He would know how to get fake passports, and that would probably take a day or two. And he would get them on the Internet the way that Wendy got her fake ID when she was seventeen. They would have to be sent somewhere. Grand Forks was just south of the border. Passports and Grand Forks—that was the connection that the blackness had erased yesterday. Marla sat very still for a long time and sorted through the possibilities and probabilities until they hardened into certainties. She thought about calling Bradford, but all she could see was that bastard's self-righteous smile. When she picked up the phone, she dialed Larry's number instead.

Gail

*

The soybean fields gave way to the occasional warehouse and then a strip mall. When they crossed the bridge into North Dakota and Grand Forks, the Red River swirled beneath them, brown and muddy. Gail said nothing more to Jon as they drove, and he said nothing to her. She wanted to tell him that she called Paige, but that would just make him explode again. And she wanted to tell him what Paige said about Carli, but he wouldn't be able to hear any of that. So, she said nothing. Jon bounced the wagon across the railroad tracks, made two turns, and then eased into a parking lot. She couldn't avoid the smell pouring from the car seat next to her, and she couldn't avoid the reality that her silence, her withholding, made her a liar.

"This is it," Jon said.

It looked like every other UPS Store, but it wasn't, of course. This UPS Store held the future. Maya started to cry as soon as the car stopped moving.

"It's been a while since you fed her," Jon said in a careful voice.

Gail reached wordlessly into the diaper bag at her feet for a bottle and the thermos. She could feel Jon's eyes in the mirror as she scooped the formula into the bottle. Gail poured the water from the thermos and put the cap back on. She shook the bottle. She rolled it between her palms. Maya screamed. Jon turned, and his once-familiar face, unshaven, sagging with exhaustion, looked like a stranger's. His eyes asked her what she was thinking, and she wanted badly to tell him, but she knew that the stranger wouldn't listen.

"Go get the package," Gail said.

She unbuckled Maya from her car seat, held her on her lap, and started to feed her. Jon turned forward and slumped in his seat. Gail willed him to stay silent, didn't trust what she'd say if he spoke. Finally, he climbed out of the car and went into the shop. Gail studied Maya's features as she slurped, searched her face for answers. Maya's eyes squeezed shut, and her lips worked the nipple. Her ears wriggled with the effort. And then her nose demanded Gail's attention. Its gentle, familiar slope, the way her nostrils squirmed. Carli's nose. In time, she suspected, freckles would appear. All at once, Gail knew that no callus, no matter how thick, would ever protect her from that nose.

The door to the shop opened, and Jon came out scowling, hands empty. He climbed into the car and braced his hands against the steering wheel. "It's not here yet."

"What?"

"The package. It's not here yet. They said four o'clock."

"I thought you said ten?"

"That's what the guy told me. They're saying four now."

"What time is it?"

Jon looked at his watch. "Almost two."

Two hours. It didn't seem like enough time, even as it felt like forever.

Larry

*

Larry climbed back into the truck, and this time Kurt didn't ask him how it went. Larry checked the TownHouse Hotel off the list. Number twenty-one out of twenty-five. They had tried all the hotels and motels along the interstate first, and then the few along the river. The last four were scattered across the center of town. The seedier places had staff with hungry eyes and greedy hands that took the photo from him and folded it into their pockets. The clerks at the chains gave Larry the hairy eyeball as soon as he stepped foot into their lobby. They stood behind the counters wearing their pressed oxfords and peering over their glasses at him while he spoke. They never reached for the photo. They talked about policy and privacy, and they ignored the cash that he fanned across the counter. It probably didn't matter. The Durbins were probably already in Canada drinking Molson. Kurt was right. The whole fucking thing was a waste of time.

Larry's cell phone rang. Marla again. She'd been calling him over and over for the last thirty minutes, but he had nothing to tell her, so he had let it roll to voice mail. The last thing he needed was Marla crawling down his goddamn throat.

"How many more?" Kurt asked.

"Four," Larry muttered.

"It's a waste of fucking time."

Larry didn't say anything, because Kurt was right. Four more hotels would just mean thirty more minutes of bullshit. Time to turn the truck south. His phone rang again. Marla, of course. He answered.

"We're done," he said.

"Passports," Marla said in a rush. "They need fake passports."

"We're headed back," Larry said.

"There's a FedEx store and a UPS Store. They're both on Columbus. Six blocks apart."

"Waste of fucking time," Larry said.

"Wendy's gonna text you the addresses. Go into the stores and tell them you're Durbin. Tell them you're looking for your package," Marla said. "See what happens."

"Screw you."

"Five grand, Larry. Don't be a dumbass."

"Waste of fucking time," Larry said, and he disconnected the call.

"What did she say?" Kurt asked.

"Some bullshit about passports."

"Waste of fucking time."

Eleven hours. If they left right now, they'd get back a little bit after midnight. Larry's entire skull ached from lack of sleep. His eyes burned. Like buying a fucking lottery ticket. Stupid. Kurt stopped at a light, and Larry tried to figure out how much of Marla's money they had left. They'd only spent two hundred on gas and food. They could probably get back with another two hundred. That would leave three hundred each. Of course, Kurt wasn't keeping track, so Larry could probably keep four hundred and give Kurt two hundred. If he needed a bit for rent, he could always hit up Marla. She owed him that at least. And then he looked up and saw the street sign. Columbus. His cell phone chirped with the text from Wendy. He knew they should just keep right on driving to the expressway. But he was fucking stupid.

"Hang a right," he said.

He bought a lottery ticket every week. He was that fucking stupid.

The FedEx store was just three blocks down, but when the guy behind the counter searched the computer for a package from Durbin, he came up blank. The UPS Store was four more blocks and it was on the way to the expressway anyway.

When Larry opened the door, the bell jangled. The skinny, zit-faced kid behind the counter was pouring foam peanuts into a box and didn't look up. "How can I help you?" he murmured.

"My name's Jon Durbin. I'm expecting a package."

The kid pulled tape across the seam of the box. He still didn't look up. "I already told you. Your package won't be here till four."

Larry smiled for the first time all day. Jackpot.

Jon

*

When Jon came out of the bathroom, Gail was still sitting in the armchair next to the window, bent over Maya, watching her sleep. Ever since they checked into the Wyndham, ever since they left the parking lot of the UPS Store really, she'd clung to Maya and said nothing. When he asked if she wanted to check her email, she just shook her head.

The Wyndham was two blocks from the UPS Store. Jon knew that they had to stay out of sight, but he had to try to keep Gail on the rails, so he didn't want to drive around looking for a motel with bulletproof glass. And the Wyndham had a parking garage, so they could keep the station wagon off the street. Jon had shit himself three times since they checked in. Not that they really checked in. Jon tried to pay the clerk five hundred dollars to overlook the fact that he had lost his credit card and driver's license. The clerk wouldn't acknowledge the cash on the counter and started to ramble about corporate policy. Jon pulled out five more hundred-dollar bills and laid them on top of the stack.

The clerk stopped talking midsentence, glanced around the empty lobby, and then swept the bills off the counter. He clacked his keyboard, swiped a key, and handed it across without looking up. "Room 323."

Jon sat back down at the desk and refreshed the UPS website. The status still read *In Transit.* The package left the Grand Forks distribution center at 2:03. Jon checked his watch. 3:17. He tried to distract himself with sample images of Canadian passports. He clicked back to the UPS website. Still nothing. How far away could the distribution center possibly be?

Jon looked at Gail. Her face was tight, and her hands were still in a way that was new and strange. This wasn't just because he called her stupid or accused her of lying. She was pissed, but that didn't explain the special brand of silence, thick like gravy, that had filled the car for the last two hours of the drive. He had to get those passports. He had to get them over the border. The border meant a certain measure of safety, but it meant more than that. It was more than a line on a map they'd be crossing. Once they crossed that border, he knew in his gut that they'd never come back.

He refreshed again. *In Transit.* He looked again at Gail. The way that she stared at Maya unsettled him further. It was almost as if she were memorizing Maya's face.

He refreshed the site again. *Delivered to Store!*

"It arrived," he said.

Gail finally looked up. He grabbed the key and his license from the desk, and then went to where she sat. He bent to kiss the top of her head. "I love you," he murmured into her hair. She said nothing and kept her eyes fixed on Maya. It wasn't until he grabbed the door handle that she spoke.

"Jon," Gail said, her voice hoarse. "I love you, too."

Carli

*

Carli pulled into the truck stop near the interstate, to gather herself and to formulate a plan. She parked in the gravel where the rigs idled, so that she'd be sure to see nobody that she knew. She turned off the car and pulled out her phone. She refreshed her email but still found nothing from Gail. She thought about calling Kelly or Madison or Andrea. She pulled up their Instagram feeds and scrolled through images of boyfriends and tattoos and selfies and beer bongs. She tried to find her way back to a picture that included her, but so many images, so many moments had stacked up since then. She couldn't find herself, and her friends' faces had taken on the sterile look of strangers. Her hands shook as she dialed Paige's number. Paige answered on the first ring.

"Carli?"

Paige's voice came familiar, warm, worried.

"Can I ask a favor?" Carli said.

"Anything."

Carli swallowed, built the courage to ask, braced for rejection. "Can I stay with you for a little while? A few days. Maybe a week?"

Paige only hesitated for a split second. "Of course you can," she said, and a wave of relief washed over Carli. "You can stay for as long as you need. What happened?"

"I told Marla about the final consent."

A longer pause. "I see."

Paige gave her the address, and after Carli hung up, she leaned her head against the headrest and closed her eyes. The diesel engine next to her rumbled like her stomach. The hiss of airbrakes sighed. She had a place to stay that night, and she could stay at Paige's for a week or two, but she couldn't stay there forever. Her baby was gone, her in-box was empty, and her car was crammed with all her worldly possessions. She had a maxed-out credit card in her purse, three hundred bucks in the bank, and a half tank of gas. Even if Paige let her stay longer, Carli knew that she wouldn't, that she would land on somebody's couch or in the back seat of her car.

Homeless. That word had always seemed so remote. A word that belonged to other people. *Home.* She had left home just thirty minutes ago, but that word already seemed less familiar than the first. She sat quietly and tried to concentrate on the rumble of the engine. After several minutes, her breathing finally slowed, and her stomach grew quiet. Carli opened her eyes and forced herself to focus. She was typing Paige's home address into her phone to get directions, when it vibrated with a call. She didn't recognize the number. For a moment she thought about letting it roll to voice mail, but it might be Gail, so she answered it.

"Ms. Brennan?"

A man's voice. "Yes?" she said warily.

"This is Officer Bradford. From the FBI."

Hope fluttered. "Did you find them?"

A pause. "Not exactly. But there have been developments."

Developments. "What kind of developments?"

"A Minnesota state trooper came across a couple with a baby. We believe it may be the Durbins."

Carli pressed the phone to her ear. "Where are they?"

"Unfortunately, he didn't receive the APB until after his encounter."

"Wait. So, they're—are they gone?"

"We're not sure where they are. The good news is that we were able to get a sketch of what they look like now."

Good news. "What does that mean?"

"Haircuts. Hair dye. That sort of thing. Anyway, we're focusing our efforts on Grand Forks based upon that notebook you shared with us. They told the state trooper that they were headed there, too. We're still not sure why Grand Forks, but we've given the sketch to the police up there, and we've asked them to send it to all the hotels. To be honest, it's still a long shot, but I thought you should know."

Another long shot. "There's something that you should know, too."

"What's that?"

Carli took a deep breath and let it out. "I signed it." Telling Bradford made it real to Carli in a way that she hadn't expected.

"Signed what?"

"The final consent."

For a moment Bradford said nothing, and that tiny bit of silence felt like an accusation. "So that means—"

"—the baby belongs to them now." Carli couldn't let him say it. "I emailed it to Gail a few hours ago."

More silence. "Well. That adds a wrinkle. To say the least. Why now?"

Why now? Because she could feel her baby slip farther north every moment. Because with every hour that passed it became less likely that she'd ever see Maya again. Because she didn't have a choice.

"I want them to be able to come back," Carli said. Tears spilled down her cheeks and her breath snagged. "So that I can see my baby again."

"Have you heard from them?"

Carli swallowed the sob building in her throat. She gripped the phone tightly, worked to steady her voice. She managed to force the next words out in a rush. "I'm not sure she's even still checking that email account."

Another long pause, and Carli squeezed her eyes shut against the tears, against the silence. "Well," Bradford said quietly. "In that case, I guess we better keep after them."

Jon

*

Jon stepped out of the UPS Store and glanced at the label on the envelope to see where it shipped from. Ottawa. He tore off the seal and fished out one of the passports. He flipped it open to the main page, and Gail's unsmiling face stared back at him. He studied the fonts and the maple leaf watermark. He counted the digits in the passport number. He tilted the page, and the hologram glinted in the sunlight. The paper felt thick. Everything looked legit. His trembling hands began to settle. The reviews on Tochka were right—whoever took his eight thousand dollars was likely an insider. He quickly thumbed through the other two passports, and they were just as good. He didn't bother with the birth certificates and the driver's licenses at the bottom of the envelope. All that mattered right now was getting across that border.

Jon shoved everything back into the envelope and tucked it under his arm. He walked quickly back toward the hotel, although he wanted to run. Adrenaline pulsed through his system, and for the first time in days, his mind leaped to the next step and the step after that. It felt like they had been slogging through mud, but suddenly everything was moving quickly again. Seeing the passports, holding them, helped him feel the force of the current that would sweep them across the border, to Winnipeg, to their new life.

Jon smiled at the desk clerk when he walked past, but the man just looked down at his computer. Jon held the elevator door for two maintenance workers carrying tool bags, and he smiled at them, too. He couldn't help but smile. The momentum had shifted, and he thought that Gail might feel it, too. Maybe, when she saw their new passports with their new names and their new pictures, she might feel the tug of that current, too. In an hour they'd cross into Canada. The arguments that had wrinkled the last several days would fall away. They would seem like just that, wrinkles, part of their former life. By the time they reached Winnipeg, those arguments would be forgotten.

Jon forced himself not to run down the hall. He found 323, licked his lips, and swiped himself into the room. And then he froze. Gail's chair—empty. The door to the bathroom—open. The bathroom light—off. The silence—total. Jon let the door close behind him. He drifted to the center of the room. He resisted the urge to peer under the beds. A buzzing sound grew loud in his ears and drowned out the silence as he took inventory. The diaper bag—gone. The car keys—he'd left them on the desk next to the computer—gone. Gail and Maya—gone.

And then she knocked. Jon let out a breath that he hadn't known he was holding. Relief washed across him, and his smile returned as he opened the door.

Jon was on the floor before the pain registered, fists battering him. He covered himself the best he could, curling into the fetal position. Before he could cry out, tape covered his mouth.

The punches stopped, and Jon was forced roughly onto his back. A man sat on Jon's chest and pinned Jon's shoulders with his knees. Jon tried to knee him in the back, but someone else dropped onto his legs. Jon heard the screech of the duct tape as it wrapped his ankles. He finally took a good look at the man on top of him, but all he saw was a black ski mask and a grin gleaming through the mouth hole.

The weight lifted from his legs, and another man, big as a tree, walked past. He also wore a ski mask, and a nightstick dangled from his hand. He stepped around Jon and went to turn on the TV. The room filled with the applause of a game show, and the man turned it up loud. He came back to where Jon lay and turned on the bathroom light. He turned it off. Finally, he looked down at Jon.

"Mr. Durbin. My friend's gonna take that tape off, and you're gonna tell us where the baby is."

The other man ripped off the tape, and Jon gulped air. "My name's not Durbin," he said.

"Put the tape back on," the big man said. He picked up the UPS envelope from the floor and studied the label. "Your mail here says your name's Durbin."

The big man knelt and handed the nightstick to the man on Jon's chest. He grabbed hold of Jon's arms. "Start with the knees."

The man on Jon's chest turned around and sat back down. Jon saw the club flash through the air, and he heard his kneecap shatter, even before the pain exploded into his brain. Jon squeezed his eyes tight against the bright lights and sharp colors. He screamed into the tape. His back arched beneath the weight of the man. The pain was so complete that he only vaguely felt the club land on his other knee.

The big man said, "Stop."

More applause from the studio audience. Jon screamed into the tape.

The two men waited. They may have waited an hour, but it might have been just a few minutes. The pain from Jon's knees made it hard to measure time or even think. Slowly, his screams became moans and then whimpers.

The host on the game show shouted, "COME ON DOWN!"

"Mr. Durbin."

Jon opened his eyes and found the big man's face looming over his. The man's eyes were bloodshot. His breath stank like tuna. "I'm gonna take that tape off again, and you're gonna tell me where the baby is. If you don't, my friend's gonna shove that nightstick up your ass."

Jon's eyes grew wide. The big man grinned through the mask. When the tape was peeled away, Jon thought about screaming, but nobody would hear him, and that nightstick would shut him up quick. The pain surged. The nightstick tapped the carpet next to Jon's shoulder. Jon's mind crackled and fizzed, and he couldn't manufacture a lie or even a reason to hold back the truth.

"I don't know where they went," he rasped. "They were gone when I came back."

The man looked at his partner for a long moment and then back down at Jon. He put the tape back over Jon's mouth. "Let's tape his wrists," he said wearily. "I kinda hoped we were going to do this the easy way."

Carli

*

Paige's town house wasn't at all like Carli expected. She thought it would be cluttered with afghans and throw pillows and framed needlepoint of inspirational quotes. Instead, she found sharp angles and clean surfaces and stainless steel. All the furniture sat low, made of metal frames and black leather. All the pictures on the wall were black-and-white photos, mostly of Paige's daughter.

Paige cooked potpies for dinner, and they ate together perched on stools at the black granite island. Carli could only manage the crusts and a few chunks of turkey. And she couldn't take her eyes off the pictures. They were scattered throughout the kitchen. Pictures of the girl as a baby and as a child and as a teenager and as a young woman. Carli struggled to connect that girl with the heavy, gray-haired woman hunched over her potpie. The girl was tall and skinny, and her hair fell dark and long. But her eyes shone in that same way as Paige's, and her lips rested in the same soft, gentle curve.

"Her name's Maggie," Paige said. "She's away at school. You'll be sleeping in her room."

"She's your daughter?" Carli asked.

Paige looked at the picture that Carli had been studying—Maggie at a beach as a toddler, sitting in a bucket. The corner of Paige's mouth curled. "She is. I don't usually tell clients, because that conversation can get a little bit complicated."

"How's that?"

Paige looked back at Carli. "Well, first off, I never married."

"Is she adopted?"

For a moment Paige said nothing, and Carli could see her struggling with how much to tell. "She was supposed to be adopted." Paige said. "I was just a little bit older than you when I got pregnant. My mom wasn't much like yours. She didn't say many words after I told her. She bought me a bus ticket from Des Moines to Chicago so that I could stay with my aunt while I was pregnant. So that nobody would know."

"You don't have to—"

Paige shook her head. "I don't mind. It's my story. My mom had it all arranged with my aunt and the agency and even bought me a return bus ticket for after."

"But you kept her."

Paige nodded. "I did."

Carli pushed the potpie around on her plate with her fork. She could feel Paige's eyes on her. "How did you decide?"

Paige didn't answer for a long time, and Carli started to wonder if she would.

"I don't know," Paige finally said, her voice a whisper. "It just felt right to me. It was hard those first years. My aunt helped us some, but she didn't have much herself. I never talked to my mom again. She died when Maggie was nine. It was really, really hard."

"But it turned out OK," Carli said.

Paige nodded. She looked back up at the bucket. "It turned out wonderful. But it could have all gone to shit. I've seen things go really bad for girls who made the same choice that I did."

Paige stood and scraped what was left of her dinner into the sink. "I guess that's why I do what I do," she said, her back to Carli. "So that girls like us have a choice."

Larry

*

"He doesn't fucking know," Kurt said.

He stood over Durbin, his mask on, his fists opening and closing, his shoulders slumped. Durbin lay on the floor next to the bed, his hands still duct-taped, one of his legs bent in a way that legs aren't supposed to bend, his eyes swollen almost shut. His moans leaked through the tape across his mouth but were only audible when *Family Feud* cut to a commercial break. Kurt was right, of course. Larry had come to the same conclusion half an hour ago. The dude totally expected his wife and the kid to be waiting for him when he got back from the UPS Store. If he'd known where they were, he would have told them after thirty minutes with Kurt, much less an hour. The last half hour of pain was pure payment. Marla wouldn't pay them without finding the baby, so they charged Durbin for their time and trouble.

"Let's clean up," Larry said.

He went into the bathroom and soaked two rags with warm water. He handed one to Kurt. "Wipe down anything you might have touched."

341

They cleaned the doorknobs, the TV, the light switches, the table. They wiped the FedEx envelope and the duct tape around Durbin's wrists and across his mouth. Larry even rubbed down the flush handle on the toilet, because Kurt took a piss while he rested between beatings. When they finished, Larry tucked the rags into his bag, and then stood over Durbin. He had stopped moaning, and his eyes had rolled back in his head. Larry pulled out his phone and took a picture of him, making sure to include the broken leg. He sent the picture to Marla.

fucker doesn't know where the baby is

"What're you doing?" Kurt asked.

"Letting her know we did this right. I don't wanna listen to her shit when we get back."

Larry surveyed the room one last time to make sure that they hadn't left anything. Just before he opened the door, he heard somebody in the hallway. He waited until the noise settled. He put his ear to the door to be sure. He heard wood splinter just before the door exploded into the side of his skull.

When Larry came to, he was facedown on the floor, his hands cuffed behind his back. They had pulled the mask from his head. A knee pressed between his shoulder blades.

"Where's the baby?" the cop on top of him demanded.

Great fucking question. Larry answered with a question of his own. "What baby?"

Carli

*

After dinner, Paige settled into a low-slung chair in the den and opened a book on her lap. Carli went into Maggie's room and dropped the first of her garbage bags on the bed. She tried to avoid looking at the posters of New Edition and the photos of Maggie and her friends tacked up on the bulletin boards. She opened the closet and found it filled mostly with empty hangers, but there were still a few outfits. She wandered back into the den. She turned on the TV and sat down on the sofa. She turned down the volume so that she didn't bother Paige and clicked through channel after channel of baseball games and cooking shows and Kardashians and news anchors and countless other things that didn't have anything to do with her. She turned off the TV and wandered back into the bedroom. She pulled her jeans from the bag, folded them, and started to stack them into the top drawer of the dresser. But halfway through, she decided she should hang them instead. She threw them onto the bed and wandered back into the den. She sat on the couch and turned the TV back on. Paige closed

343

her book, and Carli could feel Paige's eyes on her as she clicked through channel after channel.

"What are you thinking about?" Paige asked gently.

Carli clicked past cartoons and *Spider-Man* and an old *Seinfeld* episode. What was she thinking about? She was thinking about school and about work and about where she would sleep in a week or two. Weather forecast, soccer game, *Law & Order*. She was wondering how many miles to Winnipeg and what Jon looked like without hair and how Gail could do this. Music video, car chase, stock market charts. She was thinking about the creases in Agent Bradford's suit pants and the wrinkles around Marla's mouth and the folds in that pink blanket that she'd glimpsed for too little time. Geiko commercial, *The Sound of Music*, bowling-alley scene from *The Big Lebowski*. She was thinking about that little girl in the bucket and Maya's nose and Paige on a bus from Des Moines. She was thinking about everything. The past and the future and what might have been and what was inevitable were all sliced up and mixed together like a kaleidoscope. She was thinking about everything at once, but she could only smell vanilla cream soda.

"Nothing, really," Carli finally said.

Her phone vibrated on the coffee table, and she leaned forward to look at it. Same number as earlier. Bradford.

"Hello?"

"Hello, Ms. Brennan. There have been some developments."

More developments. "Did you find her?"

A breath of silence. "No. We found Jon, but not Gail or the baby."

Carli leaned forward, stared at the carpet, squeezed the empty place closed. "Did he say where they went?"

"He's not saying much of anything right now. Seems he was beaten pretty badly."

Beaten? "What? By who?"

A long pause this time. "We're still trying to sort that out."

"Did he . . . was it Gail?"

Bradford coughed into the phone, but it might have been a laugh. "No. The police have two men in custody. It wasn't Mrs. Durbin."

"But . . . Maya?"

"We still don't know where she is. When I learn more, I'll call you right away."

Carli hung up the phone. She turned off the TV and stared at the blank screen. Somebody beat Jon. Gail was gone. Maya was gone. What the hell was going on?

"Who was that?" Paige asked from the corner.

"Agent Bradford."

"What did he say?"

Carli tried to piece together everything that Bradford said and what he didn't say, but only one fact loomed large enough to settle into words. "They haven't found Maya yet."

Gail

*

G ail drove the speed limit, because if she got pulled over,
and they ran the plates, things would get even more complicated than they already were. Once it got dark, the tears made
it harder to see the road. Gail cried without making a sound,
just tears trickling down her cheeks, over her chin, down her
throat, to her chest. They smeared the bloody taillights in front
of her, and they splintered the headlights in the mirror.

Maya had slept for most of the ride so far, opening space for
Gail to think about Jon. She didn't leave a note. She didn't risk
the time it would take, and she wasn't sure what she would have
written, anyway. He must be out of his mind by now. She'd send
him an email when she got home. She'd have most of the night
to compose it in her head, while she drove and cried. She would
ask him to forgive her. She wasn't sure that he'd be able. Hell,
she wasn't sure that she could forgive herself.

The tears were for Jon and for Maya and for Carli, but she
also mourned what was supposed to be. She'd known since that
first pregnancy what her life would look like. She thought that

if she planned well enough and made the right lists and completed the items on those lists, that she could grind her life into the shape that she had grown to expect. She had let those expectations harden until there was no bend left in them. Brittle blades break so easily.

Maya started to cry, and the stink from the back seat told Gail the reason, so she took the next exit and pulled into a truck stop. She wiped her face dry and forced a pause to the tears even as Maya took up the slack with her own. When she walked from the car to the truck stop, the wind was cold but lacked the bite from earlier in the day. While she changed Maya, she didn't let her eyes land on Maya's face, and she didn't allow herself to tickle Maya's feet or make funny faces. Gail just let her cry. When she carried her back to the car, she held her low across her belly so that her nose wouldn't brush against that hair, so that she wouldn't be assaulted by the pears.

As she slipped back into the driver's seat and settled Maya onto her lap, the tears returned. She mixed a bottle and fed Maya while watching the headlights swim past on the interstate. She had finally decided in the hotel room, while Jon sat glued to his laptop, waiting for the package to arrive. She finally let herself feel the balance of it, and Maya felt lighter and lighter as Gail decided. She almost said something before he left the hotel room, but she knew that he wouldn't be able to hear it, that he was past the point of reason. He wouldn't be able to accept the truth that had become obvious to Gail: Maya wasn't their baby.

When Maya finished the bottle, Gail strapped her back into the car seat, careful to keep her nose clear, careful to keep her eyes on the buckles, away from that face. Back behind the wheel, she closed her eyes and breathed long and slow. She tested her voice, to make sure it still worked, and then she dialed Carli's number.

"Hello?" Carli's voice grated rough, as if she'd been crying herself.

"This is Gail."

"Gail?"

Gail gripped the phone hard, squeezed her eyes tight and forced the words out. "I'm bringing Maya back."

Gail heard what sounded like choking and then a long silence. Only Carli's heavy breathing told Gail she was still on the line. "You got my email?" Carli finally asked.

"Yes," Gail said, forcing her voice steady. "I got your email. We'll be there around three in the morning. I'll come by your house."

"I'm at Paige's."

Gail thought to ask why, but it didn't matter, and the tears were returning, so she pulled a scrap of paper and pen from her purse and wrote down the address.

"Carli?" Gail whispered.

"Yeah?"

Gail wanted to tell her why and give reasons and make excuses, but those words wouldn't come to her, and even if they did, she wouldn't be able to get them out. "I'm sorry."

And then Gail broke down, sobbing into the phone. She cried so loud that Maya woke and joined her. She cried so hard that she almost didn't hear Carli's tiny voice just before she disconnected the call.

"Me, too."

Gail put the phone down on the bench seat, closed her eyes, and leaned back into the headrest. She wasn't sure how long she sat there, but Maya's crying subsided before her own chest

349

stopped heaving, before her own tears slowed to a trickle. All she could hear were the cars on the expressway rushing to wherever they were going and the quiet whistle of the baby's breathing. Gail wiped the streaks from her cheeks, and then started the car. Mercifully, the rumble of the muffler made it impossible to hear Carli's baby sleep.

Carli

*

Paige brought two mugs of tea into the den and sat down next to Carli in front of the TV. Carli's head felt too large, and her stomach twitched. Paige set the mug on the coffee table in front of her. Carli cycled through the channels. QVC. Bravo. Lifetime.

"What time did she say?" Paige asked.

"Three in the morning," Carli said. "Why would she bring her here in the middle of the night? Why not just wait until tomorrow?"

"I don't know," Paige said. "I really don't."

Who Wants to Be a Millionaire? Survivor. Lost.

"Waiting can be hard," Paige said.

Carli smiled despite herself. "No shit."

"That's my job, really."

"What's that?"

"Helping people learn how to wait."

"And what do you tell them?"

"I tell them to live their lives. If they focus all their energy on the waiting, they get all twisted up."

"Does it work?"

Paige shrugged. "Often. For those who listen."

"Did Gail listen?"

Paige choked on her tea. "Sorry. I should have known that you'd ask me that." She shook her head. "No. Gail did not listen."

Carli tried to focus on *Sesame Street*. Big Bird was yakking to Mr. Snuffleupagus. A make-believe bird talking soundlessly to his make-believe friend. She tried to digest what Paige was suggesting. *Live your life*. What did that even mean for her anymore?

"It worked," Carli finally said. "The final consent."

Paige nodded. "It did." She took a sip of tea. "How do you feel about it?"

Always the social worker. Fact was, she felt confused. The call with Gail was so strange. Gail's sobbing didn't make any sense. Maybe she was crying about Jon, but it didn't seem like it. Why was she coming without him? And why visit in the middle of the night? "I'll get to see Maya again," she said, to reassure herself, as much as anything.

Paige studied her. "Open adoptions can get complicated. Especially with someone like Gail."

"What do you mean?"

"Everybody goes into it with different opinions about how it should work. Different expectations. You should expect some bumps."

Carli shook her head. "I'm not going to expect anything. That's how we got into this mess."

Carli couldn't sleep, of course, and she grew tired of flipping through channels, so she sat on the couch with Paige's laptop, searching for apartments she could maybe afford and second jobs she might land. But after a while all the jobs and apartments started to look the same, and Carli's eyes began to itch. Around midnight she closed the laptop and pulled out her psych text-book. She would reenroll in the fall, and even though she'd have to reread everything come September, she knew that reading things twice always helped her figure it out better.

She picked up where she left off. She reread those last two sec-tions. Kohlberg's stages of moral development. Gilligan's ethics of care. She still had trouble sorting through both, but she couldn't help noticing that Kohlberg's stages, based upon men, were lit-tered with words like *contract* and *authority* and *conformity* and *order*. Gilligan's levels, based upon the way women think, talked about nothing but avoiding harm. *Do no harm to yourself, and do no harm to others.* Carli still got twisted up by that. She struggled through a dense section about classical and operant conditioning, and her eyes grew heavy while reading about memory and forgetting. She finally put down the book when she came to Charles Snyder's hope theory, because she just couldn't read about that.

Carli looked at the clock. Two more hours. She asked Paige for some paper, and Paige gave her a spiral-bound notebook and a pen. Carli opened the laptop again, and she made careful lists in the notebook of the cheapest apartments and the jobs she was most likely to get. She typed *homeless grundy county* into Google and made another list of nonprofit organizations that might help her. She made a list of things that she still needed to get from the house—her high school transcript, her birth certificate, the blue frog. She was squinting at the Waubonsee Community College website and making a list of all the classes she'd take to become a nurse's aide, when the knock finally came.

Paige leaned against the kitchen doorframe, drying her hands on a towel. She didn't move toward the door, so there was nothing else for Carli to do but to get up and open it herself. Gail stood on the steps holding a bundle of pink. Her hair was dyed a greasy blond. Her eyes burned red. Her face looked creased as if it had been folded and refolded too many times.

Carli's eyes fell to the baby. Gail held Maya away from her body. Not so much offering the baby to Carli—more like she was trying to touch Maya as little as possible. Carli couldn't see the baby's face—just a tiny clenched fist protruded from the blanket. Carli tried to smell the baby, but a cold April wind blew the scent away. She looked at Gail's face again, and it was beginning to collapse, so Carli held out her own arms, and Gail placed the baby into them. Maya felt lighter than Carli expected, but warm, even through the blanket. She squirmed as she settled in against Carli. She peeled back the corner of the blanket and found that same face from the recovery room, but the lips glowed pink now instead of blue, and her eyes squinted shut as if she were counting to fifty while everyone hid. Something that must have been joy churned in that space below Carli's ribs. She pulled the blanket back further and studied Maya, drank in every feature, memorizing them, because she didn't know how long they would stay, or when she would see Maya next. She brushed Maya's cheek with her fingertips and marveled at its feel, like rose petals or suede.

Paige said in a clipped voice, "Gail, why don't you come in."

"No."

Carli looked up to find tears streaming down Gail's face. It was the first word Gail had spoken since Carli answered the door, and it rasped like a hacksaw on rusty steel. No? Why the rush? And why the hell was *she* crying?

"When your email turned up in my in-box," Gail said. "I felt nothing but relief." Gail's voice faltered. "But someone helped me understand what that email must have cost you."

Carli gaped at Gail. As if she knew the first fucking thing about cost. Carli took a deep breath and was about to lay into her, when Gail spoke again.

"So I brought her back. To you."

Maya squirmed against Carli's ribs. "What do you mean?"

Gail looked directly at Carli. Her whole body seemed to vibrate with the effort. "I mean that you're Maya's mother."

Holy shit. Carli searched Gail's face for answers to the questions she couldn't quite form, and the tears that streamed down Gail's cheeks spoke more directly than any words ever could. Those tears explained the strangeness of that call. They explained why Gail came in the middle of the night. They explained her stiffness, her sadness. They explained the sudden weight in Carli's arms, and the trembly feeling that bubbled in her throat. Gail wasn't just bringing the baby back. Gail was bringing Maya back to *her*.

"But I signed the final consent," Carli managed.

"I know," Gail whispered. "That doesn't matter. She's your child."

Carli fixed her eyes on Maya, and for a long moment held her breath, afraid that Gail might change her mind. When she felt Gail move toward the street, Carli forced herself to look up. "Gail," she said.

Gail turned back to Carli. Her empty arms hung awkwardly at her side, and her shoulders sagged.

"I just want you to know that—"

Gail held up her hand. "Carli—" she said. "I can't. Not now." And then she turned again and walked quickly to the old station wagon idling at the curb.

Carli bent to pick up the diaper bag that was sitting on the porch, and she went back inside. Paige closed the door. Carli sat with her baby on the couch. Her baby. She peeled back the folds of the blanket and looked at Maya's face, the face that Marla had thrust at her in the hospital. It was suddenly all so real and familiar. Not so much in the details—that moment in the hospital was so short. She hadn't noticed how thin Maya's eyelashes were, like new grass, and the way that her ears seemed pinned to the side of her head, and how her nostrils flared and wriggled when she breathed. But the essence was unmistakable—the curve, the color, the Maya-ness of that face was just as she remembered. And that smell, like vanilla cream soda. Maya was hers.

Another knock startled Carli, and she looked up at Paige, who seemed rattled, too. Carli couldn't move, paralyzed by the thought that Gail, after all that, had come back for the baby. Paige draped the dish towel over her shoulder, ambled back to the door, and opened it. Carli heard Gail's voice, dry and raw and cracked.

"Can you give this to Carli? Maya seemed to like it."

Paige closed the door and brought a book to Carli. She set it on the coffee table. The cover showed a green wall, a window, and a fireplace. The title read, *Goodnight Moon*.

Gail

*

Gail lay on her bed for an hour before the fiery dawn arrived. Jon had probably filled her in-box with worried emails. She composed and recomposed in her mind the email that she'd send him from her dad's phone. She made it longer, packed with reasons and logical arguments and apologies. And then she made it shorter, terse and to the point, until the reasons and explanations and apologies drifted back into it. Finally, she got out of bed and went to search for the cordless to call her dad. On the way to the stairs, though, she found the door to the nursery ajar, and she stopped in front of it. She stared at the sea turtle rug for a long time, before she finally went to the attic to get boxes and to the office to get packaging tape.

She packed the books and the stuffed animals and the clothes that they hadn't taken when they left. She packed the creams and the ointments with the diapers and the wipes. She stripped the sheets from the mattress and packed those, too. She taped the sea turtle rug into a roll. She carried it all to the mudroom, and as the nursery emptied, so did Gail. After she carried the last box, she went back to make sure that she hadn't missed anything. Only the furniture remained—the crib, the changing table, the dresser, the rocker. She'd need help moving those. And that border. That border with the animals shaped like letters wrapped around the top of the room, declaring it still a nursery.

Gail went to the basement and returned with a stepladder, a bucket, a sponge, and a scraper. She filled the bucket with water in the bathroom, sponged wet a section of the border, and started to scrape. The progress was slow. The shellac she had brushed across it to make it shiny didn't help. After an hour, she had removed just two letters—the snake angled like a Z and the frog contorted into a Y.

Gail climbed down the ladder and stared for a very long time at the X, a giraffe with its back legs spread and holding its front legs up in the air. She considered sharpening the scraper, but the reality was, it was the wrong tool for the job. She went to the basement again and returned with a hammer. She closed the door and climbed the ladder and, without hesitation, slammed the head of the hammer through the giraffe's torso. Plaster clattered from the lathe to the floor, and dust rose in a cloud. It settled on her hair and her skin as she hammered and hammered. She tore at the stubborn pieces with the claw of the hammer, and she only stopped to move the ladder and to wipe the dust from her eyes. Sweat beaded on her arms, dimpling the powder. It streaked down her face and her neck. Sweat, but no tears. She didn't seem to have any tears left.

It took her an hour, and when she was done, the whole room was covered by a snowfall of white dust. She dropped the hammer into the rubble and left what used to be the nursery and closed the door behind her. She trailed white footprints to the bathroom, where she climbed into the shower with all her clothes on and washed off the dust that used to be the walls of the room that used to be the nursery.

Gail sat in the front room and waited for her dad. He didn't ask why when she told him to come alone, without her mom, because he knew why. She picked up a notebook and a pen but then put them back down and just waited. When the phone rang, Gail thought that it might be Jon, but it was a nurse from a Grand Forks hospital. She used a lot of words that Gail didn't comprehend. The words made it clear that Jon was hurt badly, but Gail didn't ask any questions before she hung up, so she had no idea what to expect. She would ask her dad to drive her to Grand Forks when he arrived. She climbed the stairs, confused, exhausted, and numb. She packed enough clothes for a long stay. She packed clothes for Jon.

She did not pack a notebook.

Marla

*

Marla woke up in her recliner a little bit before dawn. The TV droned. *The Bachelorette* was on, so she switched it to *Duck Dynasty*. She wouldn't go to work. Not after yesterday. Before Larry had sent that picture of Durbin sprawled on the floor, she had paced the house and checked her phone for what seemed like forever. Her forearms burned where she held that baby in the hospital. And she kept smelling pudding. She didn't like hoping. Hope gnaws at you, until you get what you want. Or until you kill it for good. That picture from Larry told her everything that she needed to know. No way that a pussy like Durbin could keep a secret through a beating like that. He didn't know where they went—Gail and the baby were gone. She could stop hoping. She never should have started. Hope could be so fucking exhausting.

She spent the morning clicking from channel to channel, expecting to hear from Larry and Kurt asking for money they didn't earn, or from Carli, begging to be taken back. She watched *Chop Shop* for a while—the sound of the saws and blowtorches calmed her nerves. By late morning, she was watching one of the *Real Housewives* shows, trying to figure out if they lived in Miami or LA. The housewife was ripping into her cook for fucking up a dinner party when the doorbell rang.

Marla pushed out of the recliner and walked to the door feeling tired and stiff, but she walked quickly. Whether she found Carli or Larry and Kurt, she would get to tell them to fuck off, and that would make the rest of the morning pass better. But when she opened the door, she found a suit, and in that suit, she found Bradford.

"Morning, Ms. Brennan."

"What do you want?" she growled.

"Mind if I come in?"

"I do."

Bradford smirked in that way he had. "Do you know Larry Gant and Kurt Meyers?"

Shit. Fucking idiots got themselves caught. "I work with 'em."

"Seems that they went after the Durbins."

"I don't know nothin' about that."

Marla made to close the door, but then Bradford said, "I don't suppose you know anything about that message that Gant sent you, either." Bradford's smile widened. "Or the picture."

Marla stiffened. She opened her mouth. She closed it.

"You have the right to remain silent, Ms. Brennan." Bradford pulled handcuffs from his pocket. "Anything you say can and will be used against you in a court of law."

Carli

*

Three weeks to the day after Gail brought Maya back, Carli drove down Route 47 toward the river, even though she knew that she shouldn't. She should be scrounging the racks at Goodwill for old clothes to wear to her new job, or at Walmart buying diapers, or over at Kelly's cousin's house, checking out the old couch he was trying to get rid of. Or sleeping. She hadn't slept more than two hours in a row for the last three weeks. But Paige had asked her to meet for coffee, and she couldn't stand up Paige after all she had done. Paige suggested Liberty Street Cafe again, but the weather was just too nice to be trapped inside with soybean farmers.

Carli received more help than she had expected over the past three weeks—and not just from Paige. The Second Chance Center helped her find a one-bedroom apartment in Minooka with drafty windows, carpets that smelled faintly of cat urine, and a small family of mice that seemed happy that the cat was gone. Randy and his truck helped her scavenge a TV, a kitchen table, and a bed from friends of people that she knew. She still needed a couch, but there were no Mountain Dew cans on the windowsills, and she'd rather smell the cat than cigarettes. Paige helped her get a job at KinderCare. She'd start on Wednesday if the background check came through by then. It didn't pay much, but she'd get to spend the day with Maya, and Maya could stay there at a discount while Carli worked at Giamonti's. If she started on Wednesday, her first check would arrive in a week and a half. And if she kept eating ramen from the food pantry, she'd have enough to pay down her credit cards to make room for gas and diapers and formula.

The parking lot perched high above the riverbank, because the river sometimes flooded. The playground nestled halfway to the water and didn't amount to much, just a set of swings, a merry-go-round, and an old metal jungle gym. A wooden picnic table huddled under an oak that promised shade when the leaves came in fully. Paige sat at the table looking out at the river.

Carli grabbed her backpack from the passenger seat and climbed out of the car. She unstrapped Maya and hoisted her onto her hip. She was getting heavier—a substantial, satisfying heavy. She stepped over the curb and walked down the grassy slope. As she neared the playground, the warm wind carried the stink of river mud up the hill to meet her.

Paige turned when Carli neared the picnic table. "Hey, there."
"Hey."

Paige got up and wrapped Carli and Maya in a long hug. Paige had hugged her at Liberty Street, too, and it caught her off guard. She wasn't used to hugs, and it made her feel stiff and scratchy. This time she allowed herself to sink into it a bit, and she felt Paige's warmth. When she was finally released, Carli settled onto the bench. She tugged a blanket from the backpack and wrapped Maya.

"You look like you haven't slept for a week," Paige said.

"Thanks," Carli said. "It feels more like a year."

"It'll get a little better at three months, when she starts to sleep through the night. Unless she doesn't." Paige poured coffee from a thermos into two black mugs. "She looks beautiful, though. She looks like you."

Carli didn't know how to handle compliments any more than hugs, so she said nothing. Instead, she took a gulp of the lukewarm coffee.

"How're you holding up?"

"It's hard," Carli admitted. "Harder than I expected." She could tell Paige that she was so exhausted that she sometimes closed her eyes, just for a moment, while driving, or that she went to the food pantry early, because she didn't want anyone to see her there. Or she could describe that greasy feeling in her gut when Maya cried for hours for no apparent reason, or the stack of bills on that battered kitchen table and her terror that she wouldn't be able to keep their heads above water. But something about the slope of Paige's eyebrows told her that she knew about all of it, or at least her own version of it, and that she didn't need to tell her. Instead, Carli looked down at Maya—at her nose and at the gray eyes that were starting to peek through the slits. "But it's good, too. Better than I expected."

Paige sipped from her own mug. "Anybody helping you?"

"My friend Kelly watched her for a couple hours when I went for my interview." It had taken Carli two hours to work up the nerve to call Kelly. It felt strange to ask her to watch Maya, and she was surprised when Kelly said yes right away. It also felt strange to call Kelly a friend again, but she didn't have another word for it. "And Wendy, my sister, watched her for an hour while I slept, but I think that her boyfriend made her do it."

"Whatever it takes. It's a start. Have you talked to your mom?"

Wendy told Carli that Marla was at home with an ankle brace-let, waiting for her next court date, which was just as well. It would keep her from showing up unannounced at Carli's apart-ment. Marla hadn't called Carli, and Carli hadn't called her. She was still digesting everything that had happened, trying to make sense of it. "Not yet," she said. Maya squirmed and crackled. Carli bounced her in the way that seemed to help her settle. She looked back up at Paige. "How're Gail and Jon?"

Paige studied her mug. "I talked to Gail a couple of days ago. I think that she's doing all right, considering everything. Jon—not so much. I told Gail what you said, but I'm not sure they're ready."

When they met at Liberty Street, Carli told Paige that Jon and Gail could come see Maya if they wanted to.

"You can't be feeling guilty about all that, though."

"I don't," Carli said. "I tried to feel guilty about it. It seems like I should feel guilty." She looked down at Maya. "But then I hold her, or even just smell her, and I can't manage it."

"Good," Paige said. "Is there anything else I can do? Anything else you need?"

She needed friends and more time in the day and money for her psych class in the fall and enough coffee to kill a bear and something to eat besides ramen for lunch and leftover pizza for dinner. She needed a couch and an extra set of plates and clothes for Maya as she grew and more diapers and formula and wipes. She needed one of those Diaper Genies, so that she wouldn't have to run down the back stairs to the dumpster every time Maya pooped. But Paige had already given her so much that she'd be ashamed to ask for more. And when she looked down at Maya, her daughter's lips squirmed in a way that Carli took for a smile, even though she knew that it couldn't be one yet. She knew that she didn't really *need* any of that.

"Thank you," she said without looking up from Maya. "But I have everything I need right here." And beneath all the exhaustion and anxiety and terror, she felt large and powerful and full when she said it.

Gail

*

Gail opened the door to Jon's office. He sat in his desk chair playing guitar. His leg, casted to the hip, was propped up on another chair. The scars on his forehead and around his mouth sill glared red. The song sounded like Jackson Browne, but Jon was toying with the melody, twisting it into something of his own, so it was hard for Gail to tell. She waited until his hands fell still.

"I'm going to bed," she said. "I've got an early account call in Glenview tomorrow."

Jon nodded. "I'll finish up soon."

"Good night," she said, and closed the door.

The guitar began to speak again. He was weaning himself off the hydrocodone, so he was able to concentrate a bit. His headaches had finally settled just the week before, allowing him to tolerate his own music. Gail knew that he might not stop playing for a while, but that was OK. The guitar always nudged Gail toward sleep rather than away from it. And it sounded so much better than the silence. After she had finally made him understand what she had done, the silence between them had roared.

Two months earlier, when she arrived back in Grand Forks, Gail and her dad went straight to the hospital. The policeman sitting outside Jon's door wouldn't allow her to see him. Instead, she found herself in jail for a night, until her dad was able to arrange bail. When she finally saw Jon, he didn't say much because of the morphine and the concussion. As they weaned him toward hydrocodone, and his short-term memory flickered back, he asked the obvious question, and she told him what she had done. She tried to explain why. She told him that she was sorry. They cried. That first day of talking, every time he surfaced from the haze, he'd ask again where Maya was, she would tell him again, and again they would grieve. It was terrible, that cycle of grief, but with each pass, Gail found that she was able to explain it to him more clearly, and each time, it made more sense to her, if not to him. They went through those horrible motions all day long, until finally, that evening when he woke, instead of asking where Maya was, he stared at her with a steely-eyed anger and growled, "Maya's gone."

Then he said a lot of things that couldn't be unsaid, things that Gail worked hard to blame on the pain and the drugs and the concussion and the grief. And then he fell silent. When he was well enough, and after they posted his bail, she drove him home. Those eleven hours of silence filled the longest day of Gail's life.

They slowly learned to talk again, beginning with the necessities like *What should we do about dinner?* and *Do you need another pillow for your leg?* and *What did the doctor say?* and *The lawyer called again.* The lawyer gave them plenty to talk about. He was working hard to get the kidnapping charges dropped, but the reckless endangerment and grand theft auto charges weren't going to go away. He told them that the man who rolled from the station wagon when Jon stole it had a broken collarbone. He said that they were lucky it wasn't worse. They talked about their next court dates and about how they would manage the jail time when it came to that.

Eventually, they started talking about Maya, but at first Jon was only able to use pronouns—her and she and hers. At some point he said her name again, and a few days later they both talked about how viscerally they still missed her, and they both cried for a long time. While they cried, though, he lay on the couch, and Gail curled into a chair. They didn't touch each other. Jon wouldn't look at her. It was more like they cried at the same time than together.

They did not talk about what Gail had done to the room that used to be the nursery, although it was impossible to ignore the banging and the sanding and the moving of the ladder those weekends that her dad put it right. They didn't talk about the paint color. Gail quickly picked a neutral beige, because it didn't matter what color you painted a room that used to be a nursery. They didn't talk about what would happen after the legal mess was squared away, after Jon healed, when he no longer depended upon her for just about everything. Gail didn't tell him that she went to visit Carli and Maya, because she wasn't sure how to tell him, and she was pretty sure that he wasn't ready to hear it. And she didn't tell him that she was pregnant.

She knew only too well what pregnant felt like. And the calendar pointed directly to that afternoon just after Maya came home, when Gail woke Jon from his nap. After Gail became certain, she thought a lot about that old knife that came into the shop that first summer. The tip was ruined—a butcher probably used it to pry open a drawer or some other such foolishness. One of the grinders tossed it into the scrap bin, but something about that knife caught her grandfather's eye. Maybe it was the ancient ivory handle, or the inlaid rivets through the full tang, or the perfect slope of the grind. Gail watched as he picked it up and hefted the weight of it. He tested the edge with his thumb, studied the handle, and then set it aside. Gail asked him what he was going to do with it. He picked the knife back up and studied it for a long time before he answered. He said that he'd shorten the blade to create a new tip. That would change everything, and he would likely regrind it from convex to hollow. The balance would be lost, and to restore it, he'd take apart the handle and thin down the tang. It might work, it might not, but if it worked, it would result in an entirely different knife. "That sounds like a lot of work," Gail said. Her grandfather considered the knife again before he spoke. He rubbed his thumb across the handle. "Before they ruined it," he said, "this was a wonderful knife."

Gail realized she was pregnant the week after her dad started fixing the room that used to be the nursery, but before he painted it. She stuck with the beige, though, because she refused to start thinking of it as a nursery. She started taking the vitamins that she still had stacked in the medicine cabinet, and she stopped drinking wine and coffee. But she refused to go to the doctor, because she knew what he would say anyway. And she didn't make any lists, because right now they didn't need anything. If she had learned nothing else, she had learned that right now was all that she could count on.

When Jon was finally well enough to play the guitar again, it felt like a blessing. Two nights ago, he played James Taylor while Gail lay in bed drifting toward sleep. That sounded to Gail a little bit like forgiveness, and she had wept into her pillow.

By the time Gail finished brushing her teeth, the guitar had fallen silent. After she turned off her bedside light and curled under the comforter on her edge of the bed, Jon's crutches squeaked their way down the hall. Gail heard him lean the crutches against the wall and felt the mattress shift as he lowered himself onto his edge of the bed. She heard his sharp intake of breath when he hoisted his casted leg onto the bed, and the long sigh as he settled against his pillow. Gail had tried to help him in the beginning, but he had made it clear that he didn't want her help.

While Jon's breathing slowed, Gail counted weeks. She'd start showing soon. If she made it that far, she'd have to tell Jon, and she knew that would change the course of everything. But she didn't know if it would salve the wound or rip the scab off anew. She thought he had fallen asleep when he spoke.

"Do you think Carli would let us come see Maya?"

Gail's eyes clicked open. She swallowed. "Yes," she finally managed. "I think that she would."

Jon said nothing for several minutes. "Can you call her and ask?"

"I will," Gail said. She smiled into the dark. "First thing tomorrow."

The sheets rustled, and Jon twisted his cast under the covers. At first Gail thought he was getting out of bed to return to his office, to play more guitar or to code. Instead, he moved across the center of the bed. He leaned into her, wrapped his arms around her, and squeezed tightly. It was the first time they had touched since Jon figured out how to climb off the couch by himself, and it startled Gail to realize how much she had missed it. She thought again of that old, broken knife. She found his hand, and she laced her fingers through his. She pulled it to her mouth and kissed his knuckles.

"I love you," she whispered.

"Me, too," he murmured into her hair.

About the Author

*

R.J. Hoffmann was born and raised in St. Louis and received an MFA in fiction from Columbia College Chicago. Hoffmann is the winner of the Madison Review's 2018 Chris O'Malley Prize in Fiction, a finalist for the Missouri Review's 2019 Jeffrey E. Smith Editors' Prize, and a nominee for the Pushcart Prize. He lives in Elmhurst, Illinois, with his wife and two children.